One of America's pioneer educ[ators], [so]ciologists, David Samuel Snedd[en, 1868–]1951), came to the profession from a California cattle range, a raw-boned cowboy who had not seen the inside of a classroom until he was fourteen. His own life story was one of upward social mobility. An outspoken, controversial, and important person in American education, Snedden distinguished himself by his ability to delineate boldly and articulate forcefully an ever-present possibility in curriculum planning — education for social efficiency.

In this professional biography of David Snedden, Mr. Drost has covered Snedden's development from childhood on the family ranch, through his years as a grammar school te[acher] ... [kn]owledge is

DAVID SNEDDEN
And Education for Social Efficiency

Walter H. Drost

DAVID SNEDDEN

AND EDUCATION

FOR SOCIAL

EFFICIENCY

THE UNIVERSITY OF WISCONSIN PRESS
Madison, Milwaukee, and London, 1967

CARRIE RICH MEMORIAL LIBRARY
CAMPBELL COLLEGE
BUIES CREEK, N. C.

Published by
The University of Wisconsin Press
U.S.A.: Box 1379, Madison, Wisconsin 53701
U.K.: 26–28 Hallam Street, London, W. 1

Copyright © 1967 by the
Regents of the University of Wisconsin
All rights reserved

Printed in the United States of America by
North Central Publishing Co., St. Paul, Minnesota

Library of Congress Catalog Card Number 67-25945

TO EDWARD A. KRUG

75105

Acknowledgments

As in any endeavor of this kind, the writer is heavily in debt to a great many people for locating and making available unpublished materials. I wish to acknowledge with my sincere gratitude permission to quote from the unpublished materials of David and Genevra Snedden granted by his four daughters, Mrs. Hope Carlsmith of Summit, N.J., Mrs. Ruth Shoup of New York City, Mrs. Paul Sears of Portola Valley, California, and Mrs. Janet Finch of Palo Alto, California. I owe a special debt of gratitude to Mrs. Finch for much kindly encouragement, numerous letters, occasional corrections of fact, and assistance in some of the details that go with publication. She generously made available for publication the several pictures of her parents found elsewhere in this volume. I am indebted to her for use of her mother's autobiographical typescript, "The Early Married Life of David and Genevra Snedden"; a detailed family "picture genealogy"; her father's privately printed autobiography, *Recollections of Over Half a Century Spent in Educational Work*; and her mother's *Mountain Cattle and Frontier People, Stories of the Snedden Family, 1867–1947*. I also wish to express my appreciation for the privilege of looking through Professor Snedden's last two manuscripts, "American Educations, 1950–1975; Some Sociological Anticipations" and "Toward Educational Science," granted by Mrs. Sears in whose care he had left them.

Miss Florence Seelman of New York generously provided several extensive and informative letters of reminiscence concerning her late brother-in-law Clarence D. Kingsley and the picture of Mr. Kingsley used in the book. Mr. Frank A. Ross of Madison, Wisconsin, graciously granted permission to quote from the papers of his late father in the State Historical Society of Wisconsin. Mrs. Lula Gabriel gave her kind permission to quote from the letter of her father, Richard M. Shackel-

vii

ford, to County Clerk Whicher in the San Luis Obispo County Clerk's Office. Permission to quote from the Ernest Carroll Moore Diary was generously given by Gilbert S. Moore of Los Angeles. Institutional permission to quote from the Moore Diary and from the David Eugene Smith Papers was granted by the Special Collections Departments of the Library of the University of California at Los Angeles and the Butler Library of Columbia University, respectively. Father Philip Conneally, S.J., of Los Angeles, shared with me his own continuing study of the history of St. Vincent's College and gave permission to quote from one of his papers. I am most grateful to all of these good people.

A great many people have freely given of their own time to uncover sources of information significant to the study. In addition to those already cited I wish to express my gratitude to Howard D. Williams, Colgate University Archivist, for a copy of Mrs. Kingsley's letter to Raymond E. Brooks of the Colgate Alumni Association; Mrs. Virginia Clubert of Paso Robles, California, for sharing information from her own studies of the local history of the area; Miss Helen Thorp, Assistant to the President, and Kenneth H. Beesley, Assistant Provost and Registrar of Teachers College, Columbia University, for material relevant to Snedden's and Kingsley's careers; Ernest Seelman of New York City for copies of local newspapers in his possession which carried extensive obituaries of Mr. Kingsley; Mrs. Lillian L. Stewart, Deputy Clerk for the Board of Supervisors of San Luis Obispo County who located petitions submitted in support of Snedden's appointment to the County Board of Education; Mrs. Alma Greene and Mrs. Frankie Lambert of the Ventura and the San Luis Obispo County Schools Offices, respectively, for locating dust-covered volumes of archival material in their offices; George Flamson, until 1961 superintendent of the Paso Robles schools, for assistance in locating the early school records; and Harvey Hall, Registrar of Stanford University, for providing a detailed description of Snedden's undergraduate courses.

For gracious and generous ministration of their professional skills I am indebted to Emily Olson of the Cubberley Library; Ruth Scibird of the Stanford Collection at Stanford University; Patricia J. Clark of the San Luis Obispo City Library; Marguerite Christensen of the Memorial Library of the University of Wisconsin; Josephine Harper of the State Historical Society of Wisconsin; Robert W. Hill of the New York Public Library; Herbert F. Ricard of the Ventura County Free Library; Mrs. Lois Higman of the Palo Alto Public Library; Joseph

Howerton and Jerome Finster of the Labor and Transportation Branch, Social and Economic Records Division, National Archives; James V. Mink of the University of California at Los Angeles; Hilmer Sieving of the University of Chicago; Kenneth A. Lohf of the Butler Library, Columbia University; Virginia R. Gray of Duke University; John Dobson of the University of Tennessee; and John H. Moriarty of Purdue University.

The privilege of visiting with contemporaries of David Snedden and Clarence Kingsley has been a source of particular pleasure in the course of this investigaton. For sharing with me a wealth of memories and the warmth of their hospitality I am under deep obligation to Thomas H. Briggs, Jesse B. Sears, Henry Neumann, Israel Thurman, and to the late William H. Kilpatrick.

To Edward A. Krug, my advisor in the doctoral program at the University of Wisconsin, I wish to express my sincere gratitude not only for his patient guidance, many leads, and for often providing just the right word, but also for the encouragement and the companionship of research which has made the study a thoroughly stimulating and rewarding experience. I also wish to acknowledge the insight and intellectual stimulation in the history of education gained in seminar and course work under Merle Borrowman in the department of educational policy studies at the University of Wisconsin.

W. H. D.

Valparaiso University
March, 1967

Contents

DAVID SNEDDEN
And Education for Social Efficiency

Introduction

David Snedden was one of America's pioneer educational sociologists and in that capacity served on the faculty of Teachers College for two decades. Before that he had been a prominent schoolman in California, a professor of education at Stanford University, and Massachusetts' first commissioner of education. He came to the profession initially from the California cattle range, a raw-boned cowboy who, in his own schooling, had not seen the inside of a classroom until he was fourteen years old. His life story is one of upward social mobility, appealing in itself. His significance in American education may be found in his ability to delineate most boldly and to articulate most forcefully an ever-present possibility in curriculum making, education for social efficiency.

Social efficiency is the position in education that calls for the direct teaching of knowledge, attitudes, and skills, intended to shape the individual to predetermined social characteristics. It presumes to improve society by making its members more vocationally useful and socially responsible. Those who "view with alarm" and blame the schools for not remedying the ills of society frequently look to it as the means to reform. It is a deceptively simple panacea because of its direct approach, and not infrequently its most vocal advocates are found in the ranks of the concerned lay public.

Applied to the curriculum, social efficiency usually leads to demands for reorganization of the studies, sometimes for a whole new synthesis of new and more "practical" subjects. Snedden called upon the traditional subjects to "pass in review" to determine their possible contribution to "the more specific and satisfactory aims of education." [1] Among the hundreds of courses he proposed were Business Letter Writing, Friendly Letter Writing, The Wonders of Synthetic Chemistry,

3

Man's Warfare With Insects, Ten Readable Dramas, and Practical Mathematics.[2]

At different times, variants of this position have appeared under other names. Social efficiency was the outstanding characteristic of the proposals for life adjustment education in the late forties and early fifties. In another form, emphasizing the selection and teaching with great care the minimum essentials of the organized studies, it appeared in the Essentialist Platform of William Bagley in 1938. Bagley himself had used the term "social efficiency" as far back as 1905.[3] At an even earlier date it was implicit in Herbartian Frank McMurry's "towers of strength," explained as a little knowledge thoroughly understood which would shape the thoughts that control conduct. The Herbartian reorganization of subject matter around a single center of interest may also have proved useful in stimulating the imagination of the educator for social efficiency. Regardless of the sect, all who take this position tend to reject the notion of pursuing a study simply for the pleasure of learning.

Snedden went a step further than many in the social efficiency tradition by proposing that a concerted effort be made to determine the probable destination of each individual in society and to prescribe a curriculum especially suited to promote his ultimate efficiency. This set Snedden apart from others like Franklin Bobbitt and W. W. Charters who were also in the social efficiency camp. Bobbitt's multitude of minute and specifically defined aims looked on the surface very much like what Snedden proposed. However, Bobbitt did not differentiate for people of varied destinations.

In 1915 when Mark Keppel wrote that efficiency was the greatest word in the English language, the efficiency movement in America was at its apex.[4] But there were numerous varieties. When David Snedden first used the word in 1900, he was already using it in a sense different from his contemporary Frederick Taylor. Though social efficiency and business efficiency shared a common ideal, to make people more useful, they sometimes took a collision course. In Massachusetts, Snedden's special normal school program for training a socially efficient rural school teacher was condemned by efficiency experts as economically inefficient. They measured the program in terms of cost per unit of instruction, while Snedden thought in terms of changed individuals. For his part he condemned "factory methods" that were attempting to reduce the cost of education by applying concepts of "quantity production and standardization of parts" to the schools. He said this system was only productive of "herd-like" uniformity which ran counter to the differentiation upon which his social efficiency rested.

It would seem that circumstances of life conspired to enable Snedden to make his mark in his chosen field. His professional career was contemporary with the age of reform in American education. His first principalship came in 1892, the year the Committee of Ten organized. In 1895, the year William T. Harris engaged the Herbartians in the "Great Debate" at Cleveland, Snedden entered Stanford University. His first important statement on the purposes of education came in 1900, only a year after the NEA Committee on College Entrance Requirements reported favorably upon a school program based on constants and electives. It was a time when the work of the school was under more than the usual scrutiny.

Snedden had been born into an intensely practical environment on the American frontier, in a cabin on the cattle range of Kern County, California. Here work was both a way of life and the very means of sustaining life. His childhood and youth were spent doing the work of a ranch hand — herding cattle, mending fences, and setting out feed. It was the kind of hard physical work from which he took great personal satisfaction. He would always hold useful work in highest regard as the end product of the educational process. Indeed, throughout his professional life he always referred to himself as engaged in "educational work," and the word "work" is given a prominent place in much of his writing.

Snedden's own education was along traditional lines. From a one-room California schoolhouse, he entered St. Vincent's College in Los Angeles, whose program was based upon a six-year classical course, four years of preparatory work and two years on the collegiate level. With hard work and good ability he completed the program in three years. However, his most significant educational experience seems to have resulted from a program of self-education embarked upon a few years later as a young schoolman in Santa Paula, California. There he devoted most of his free time to reading and study of the complete works of Herbert Spencer. This experience appears to have forever alienated him from the classical tradition.

When he felt a need for two more years of undergraduate work and the customary four-year bachelor's degree, he turned to Stanford University where he heard the doctrine of social control set forth by Professor Edward A. Ross of the department of political economy.

Though Snedden was nominally a student in the department of education, it was Ross who left the deepest impression upon him and gave him the perspective with which to explore Spencer's query, "What knowledge is most worth?" Later he pursued the doctorate at Columbia University under the direction of Edward T. Devine, the nation's foremost social worker. From him Snedden gained a greater insight into social ills, and the subject of his dissertation, the juvenile reform school, seemed to provide him with the ideal prototype of education for social efficiency.

As commissioner of education in Massachusetts, Snedden chose Charles Prosser, a former student, as his deputy commissioner for vocational education. Together they popularized a system of vocational schools of specific function. Prosser will also be remembered as the author, in 1945, of the now famous Prosser Resolution for life adjustment education.

Snedden also brought Clarence Kingsley to Massachusetts as his high school agent. A teacher of mathematics from the Brooklyn Manual Training High School, Kingsley was already active in the NEA and was soon to become chairman of the Commission on the Reorganization of Secondary Education, the body that produced the Cardinal Principles Report of 1918. Snedden's more extreme form of social efficiency is especially apparent when compared with the much milder variety found in the seven aims of the Cardinal Principles Report.

David Snedden fit well the popular image of the western personality. He was congenial, affable, and not one to easily take offense. The educational scene of his day was one in which opposing views were openly and often heatedly debated. He seemed to thrive in this climate of give and take and there is nothing to suggest that he ever considered criticism of his ideas a personal affront, even when on occasion the criticism was directed in personal terms. His usual reply, with an air of tolerance, was a kindly offer to explain again, more fully, his original position. A man of unusual intellect, Snedden read widely, seemingly omnivorously, and retained most of it. His friends recall that he could speak with a degree of authority on almost any subject though he was intense, almost singleminded, in pursuit of his sociological interests. Though he heartily enjoyed participating in serious discussion and welcomed frequent opportunities to speak before various groups, by his own admission he did not engage easily in idle conversation. As he drew near to retirement he seemed to regret that he never developed a hobby or consuming recreational interest. The ranch, the scenes of his child-hood, meant much to him and after retirement he returned there when-ever opportunity afforded.

In his earlier years Snedden sometimes experienced feelings of inse-curity, but usually overcame them with the ability to thrive on hard work and a splendid frontier optimism. It is possible that his tendency in later years to project his ideas as a forecast of what must surely come, first by 1925, then 1960, then 1980, rose from an optimism born of similar motivation. He seems to have taken his role to be that of stimu-lating the imagination of others along the lines he laid down. From 1900 forward he did not substantially alter his position although he became increasingly more creative in presenting his case.

Chapter I

EARLY DAYS IN CALIFORNIA

David Snedden was named for his paternal grandfather, a schoolmaster from Perth, Scotland, who came to Schuylkill County, Pennsylvania, about 1830. Initially he tested his luck as a prospector, then found employment as a miner, and finally opened a grocery store at Shenandoah. He had become prosperous when his son Samuel, David's father, was lured away to California by the gold rush. From 1850, for the next decade and a half, Samuel prospected for gold from the Fraser River in British Columbia south into Mexico. Like so many others he never made a big strike.

In 1867 Samuel married Irish-born Anna O'Keefe who had come to California with two sisters in the early sixties. He met her at the home of her sister Hanna, who had become Mrs. Gorman and with her husband maintained a general store and post office known as Gorman's Station on the stage route between Los Angeles and Bakersfield. When he married, Samuel turned to stock raising as a more dependable source of livelihood, first on the open range in the Kelso Valley of Kern County, later in the mountain meadows of Ventura County. David Samuel Snedden, born November 19, 1868, was the first of Samuel and Anna's five children.

The first home David Snedden knew was a cabin on Kelso Creek in the shadow of the Sierra Nevada. Since their herd was small, the Sneddens raised and sold potatoes to local miners to augment their income. At the age of seven, David was already riding herd and helping harvest the annual crop of alfalfa and meadow hay. Throughout his childhood and youth these activities were a part of his work, along with what assistance he could provide in constructing barns and cabins, irrigating the alfalfa crop, gathering wood from the mountains, clearing brush, digging ditches, and constructing fences. From the vantage point of eighty years of life, David Snedden looked back upon those days as part of a fortunate boyhood, one that provided excellent opportunities "for bodily health and growth," and typically, "for rich experience with work. . . ." [1]

Anna O'Keefe Snedden — in addition to the manifold duties of house-wife and mother, which included manufacture of clothing and repair of shoes for the whole family — was also for David, his brother, and three sisters their first teacher. The available books in the small cabin on Kelso Creek included *The Vicar of Wakefield, Pilgrim's Progress,* and some McGuffey readers, all of which David recalled reading at age eight. Unclaimed copies of San Francisco's popular *Pacific Rural Press* were generously provided the family by the storekeeper-postmaster at nearby Weldon, California. When at age fourteen David Snedden first saw the inside of a schoolroom, he was placed in the uppermost grade on the basis of those skills in reading, arithmetic, spelling, handwriting, and grammar he had brought from home.

The drought of 1877 cost David's father half of his herd. Overgrazing persisted in Kern County, and in the spring of 1879, Samuel Snedden moved his family and cattle to the Lockwood Valley of Ventura County. Located at five-thousand feet in the Coast Range, the valley provided abundant meadows and a more generous supply of water, but also a rather severe climate with heavy winter snows. The fresh-flowing streams supplied trout and watercress for the table, and the children gathered wild honey and piñon nuts. Although frosty nights, even in July and August, restricted vegetable gardening to carrots, onions, and radishes, freshly killed game added variety to their menu. The winter blizzards presented new problems for the protection of the herd. At these times David and his brother Bertram would take to skis to look after the animals. Twice each year Samuel Snedden made a trip to Bakersfield for supplies. In wet weather his two-horse team could not get the loaded wagon over Tejon Pass. On these occasions, he unloaded part of his cargo of beans, flour, bacon, coffee, and supplies of cloth and wire to be carried to the crest on his own back. A Los Angeles newspaper, received by mail, served as a more continuing tie with the outside world.

In 1884, at the instigation of Anna Snedden, the Alamo School District was created to serve the valley. Another family had moved into the area, and in keeping with the usual arrangements of the day, Ventura County School Superintendent C. T. Meredith agreed to provide a teacher if the local people would provide a schoolhouse. To comply with his part of the bargain, neighbor Cuddy hired a local woodsman to construct a school building and Samuel Snedden agreed to haul the necessary logs from Mount Pinos, some five miles away. David and a boy from the Cuddy family were delegated to assist in construction of the building. A local miner, with no children of his own, was sufficiently interested in the project to construct the necessary school furniture from redwood purchased in Bakersfield. The school opened in September, 1884.

The first teacher to come to the Alamo School, William F. Aram, had five years of teaching experience, had formerly been a miner, and had originally practised law in San Jose. His method of teaching was to assign large sections from the textbooks for memorization and to hear recitation of each pupil in turn. His major interest while serving the Alamo District was the invention of an improved type of waterwheel and to its development he devoted extended recess periods daily. Though he did not seem motivated to the teaching profession, the name William Aram continued on the rolls of Ventura County teachers well into the next decade.

When Superintendent Meredith made his annual inspection of the Alamo School, he recorded in his Journal of Official Visits, under the date of July 1, 1885, that the reading of the lower-grade children was "rather poor" and Mr. Aram's methods only "fair." The superintendent considered discipline "good" and rated both order and attention "number one." For that day at least, he evaluated the teacher's zeal as "earnest." The upper-grade reading, which would have included David, and language were both marked "good," while arithmetic was rated as "excellent." The superintendent conceded that handwriting was not as good as it should have been, but he placed the blame on the lack of a blackboard.[2]

David Snedden spent three years in this little one-room school. He was placed provisionally in the eighth grade the first year and remained to get what schooling he could in the two ensuing years. The school library of sixty volumes bought from the county library fund and school subscriptions to the *St. Nicholas Magazine* and *Century Magazine* provided him with new and interesting reading.

The school year was divided into two terms of fifteen weeks each. After David's first year with Mr. Aram, each term brought a new teacher. Two of them, a Miss Mosher and a Mr. Vance, made special efforts to encourage young Snedden to point himself to a college education. He remembered each as a "rare person."

Miss Mosher came to the log schoolhouse in the first term of the second school year. During David's first talk with her, he was thrilled to hear he would study algebra, English history, and high school English during the next term, even though these studies were properly beyond the scope of the Alamo School. Following Miss Mosher came Mr. Vance, a beginning teacher. Snedden remembered him as a scholarly man who provided continued intellectual stimulation in the study of algebra, geometry, rhetoric, English, classics, physical geography, and history. Consequently he gained the equivalent of two years of preparatory schooling while attending a district school.

David's father was land-poor during most of his lifetime. Expansion of his herds and protection of his water sources as new people moved into the valley necessitated a continuing program of land purchase. Little ready cash was available for anything else, including higher education. David Snedden's opportunity to go to college, the opportunity he considered the turning point in his life, came through Aunt Katherine Wilson of Los Angeles.

Mrs. Katherine Wilson was Anna Snedden's oldest sister. She had married Peter "Bull" Wilson, a Los Angeles blacksmith and drayman of some local reputation. With the expansion of Los Angeles from village to small city, Wilson expanded his cartage and hauling business and invested the profits shrewdly in local real estate. His most attractive property was the quarter block at First and Spring streets, the site of his original blackmith shop, which by 1885 was in the very heart of the city's business district. After his death, Mrs. Wilson devoted her full time to real estate management and grew wealthy as Los Angeles flourished. Like her sister Anna, Katherine was a devout Catholic. When the local St. Vincent's College completed a program of relocation and expansion in the spring of 1887, she saw it as an educational opportunity for her two nephews in the Lockwood Valley. She offered to pay all necessary expenses — board, room, and tuition — amounting to two hundred and fifty dollars each for the year; and Samuel Snedden agreed to get along without the assistance of his two sons so that both boys might receive the benefits of a college education.

Thus it was that in the spring of 1887 David Snedden and his brother Bertram went by stage to Lancaster and from there by train to Los Angeles — still for many, the "Old Pueblo" — and St. Vincent's College. The Santa Fe Railroad had recently completed its line from Chicago to Los Angeles and was offering a one-way fare of twelve dollars to new immigrants bound for Southern California. Los Angeles was experiencing its second great population boom and emerging as a new city. If Snedden saw any of the old, he was little aware of it. Rather, he saw the growing numbers of new people and what he thought was a recently established college.

In reality, St. Vincent's College was the oldest and largest institution of higher learning in southern California. It had come into existence rather informally sometime during the mid-fifties.[3] In 1869, it was chartered by the state of California and was the first college in the Los Angeles area privileged to confer the baccalaureate degree. From 1868 to 1887 it occupied a two-story brick building on Sixth Street between Olive and Broadway. There, boys ten years of age and older were admitted to a six-year classical program similar to that offered in the German gymnasium.

In January of 1884 the Society of St. Vincent de Paul sent the dynamic Father Aloysius J. Meyer as president. Father Meyer was a dedicated schoolman. He had been president of St. John's College of Brooklyn, New York, and in order to continue in the work he loved, had refused to become bishop of Galveston, Texas. Under his leadership and with the help of an expanding urban population, increased enrollments made relocation of the college a necessity. Again St. Vincent's moved to the outer edge of the urban area, to Washington Street and Grand Avenue. It was in this stage of its development, under new leadership and with a new campus, when David Snedden arrived.

Snedden spent three years at St. Vincent's, graduating in June of 1890 with a gold medal for "General Excellence" and as the second person in the history of the school to be awarded the A.B. degree.[4] The school program was organized into six forms, like European schools, though divided into four academy and two college years in accord with American practice. On the strength of his preparation in the Alamo District School, David was assigned to college classes in mathematics, rhetoric, ancient history, physics, and Latin. Although the school had a thriving commercial department which attracted the larger proportion of students, there is nothing to suggest he elected any of the business courses.

During his second year at St. Vincent's, Snedden was one of two students to elect Greek and trigonometry. During this year also, he attracted the notice of Father Martin Dyer, a professor of philosophy and classics remembered by some sudents as a solid teacher possessed of an admirable sense of humor. Father Dyer gave young Snedden much extra attention, which assured his early graduation, and attempted to inspire him to seek a career in the legal profession, possibly in the political arena. Forensics was an important extra-curricular activity at the college, and St. Vincent graduates were noted throughout southern California for their ability on the lecture platform. David excelled in this area and was awarded a second gold medal for "Composition and Speaking English" at commencement in June, 1890. The honor seemed a precursor of his prolific literary production and heavy lecture schedule two decades later. A two-volume set of Blackstone's legal commentaries, the graduation gift of Father Dyer, proved less significant to the course of his future career.

David lived at the home of Aunt Katherine Wilson in preference to the dormitory during his last two years at St. Vincent's. There, on academic holidays, he had the opportunity to become better acquainted with his cousin, Agnes Wilson, an undergraduate student at the University of California. It was she who first introduced him to the works of Huxley, Darwin, and Spencer, books he enjoyed reading and discussing with her, and ones unlikely to come into his hand under the tutelage of the Vincentian Fathers. She held the teaching profession in high regard, wanted to become a teacher herself, and conveyed some of these ideas also to her impressionable rural cousin. Snedden seems to have appropriated more ideas and ambitions from her than from Father Dyer.

Upon graduation from St. Vincent's at the age of twenty-two, Snedden intended to study for the bar, though, as he recalled later, he was never especially attracted to it. In order to earn money to finance his legal education, he took a school in the Fairview District of rural Ventura County. The school of about a dozen children, distributed over the first six grades, was conducted in an abandoned homesteader's cabin. Snedden recalled that his pupils were "always interested and well behaved."

When he presented himself at the county seat to take the examination for certification, he had his first look at his colleagues in the profession. He was impressed by the number of "mature eastern men and women" there for the same purpose.

The next year Snedden taught the district school at Fillmore in Ventura County's Santa Clara River Valley. Only four years old, Fillmore had been organized in 1887 when the Southern Pacific's coast line was constructed through the valley, and by 1891 about two hundred people "took their mail" at the Fillmore Post Office. Surrounded by oil derricks and rapidly becoming an important shipping center for fruit and garden produce, the settlement could boast a Presbyterian church, a lumber yard, several stores, a blacksmith shop, two hotels, and a schoolhouse. The school, organized only the year before, already had a reputation for being "tough," but the tall, range-hardened, young Snedden had no trouble with his forty to fifty charges. He managed the large number of pupils by assigning instruction of the beginners to a fifteen-year-old girl.

On Tuesday, December 8, 1891, Snedden was one of six applicants to appear for the annual Ventura County Teachers Examination, probably to qualify for a certificate of higher grade. The examination, prepared and conducted by the County Board of Education, covered mental and written arithmetic, algebra, geometry, United States history, geography, English, grammar, entomology, spelling, composition, physics, physiology, government, drawing, bookkeeping, music, methods, and school law. It required five days, from eight in the morning to five or six in the evening. A minimum grade of 80 per cent was required for certification. David Snedden was far at the head of the group with 88 per cent, a score good enough to earn the high school teacher's certificate.[5]

After the close of his own school on May 7, 1892, Snedden substituted for the sixth- and seventh-grade teacher in nearby Santa Paula for the remainder of the term there. At the end of the school year, he was appointed eighth-grade teacher and principal of the Santa Paula Grammar School for the following year. That year, 1892, he received the Master of Arts degree from St. Vincent's College. The record does not show when he matriculated for this degree, though it may have been during periods between school terms or even by correspondence study.[6]

When Snedden went to Santa Paula, the city was experiencing its second period of growth. Founded in 1872 as a land development of Blanchard and Bradley, flour millers and citrus growers, its growth was first stimulated in 1875 by discovery of oil in the vicinity. The second phase began in 1887 when the Southern Pacific built through the valley to connect Saugus Junction with Ventura on the coast. Wallace Hardison and Lyman Stewart, late of Titusville, Pennsylvania, had organized the Hardison and Stewart Oil Company the year before. In 1888 this company built an oil refinery at Santa Paula and in 1890 absorbed three other companies to form the Union Oil Company of California. Thus, the general offices of the foremost challenger to the Standard Oil Company's domination of the California market were located in Santa Paula.[7]

Santa Paula was also important for its agricultural production. Its newspaper, the *Chronicle*, described the city as "in the heart of the lemon country" and boasted that the vast Limoneira ranch, owned and operated by the Teague interests, employed "a small army of men."[8]

As principal, Snedden was in charge of six teachers and a school of good reputation dating back to 1882. Both of the important families in the community were represented among the pupils in his classroom; there were two Hardison children and one from the Teague family. The first year he had thirty-two pupils in his combined class of grades seven and eight, and the next year he had thirty-eight; the seventh grade was always twice as large as the eighth. The students' ages ranged from fourteen to eighteen years.[9]

The County Board of Education annually prepared and administered the county grammar school examinations required for promotion into the seventh and eighth grades and for a grammar school diploma. Twelve subjects were evaluated: arithmetic, spelling, grammar, American history, physiology, geography, bookkeeping, government, drawing, music, writing, and reading. The passing grade was 75 per cent, and the diplomas of graduation permitted entry in the nearest high school.

While Snedden was at Santa Paula, Superintendent Black proposed a system of county school accreditation to force local conformity to the county course of study. Under this plan, adopted by unanimous vote of the county board, the superintendent was given power to accredit those schools where the course of study was faithfully adhered to and each subject given its "proportion of attention." In accredited schools, students entered grades seven and eight by teacher promotion instead of the usual county examination. David Snedden's school was among the first accredited by the county superintendent.

Snedden's first eighth-grade class of eleven pupils was an outstanding success by the standards of the day. Ten pupils remained in June for the county examination, and nine of them graduated with scores ranging from 75 to 83.9 per cent. Snedden promoted sixteen of the twenty-one seventh graders, three with "conditions" in arithmetic and one in spelling. The ages of the seventh-grade students ranged from fourteen to seventeen years; four of the six seventeen-year-olds were among those not promoted.

The next year only seven of the fourteen eighth-grade students graduated and two left school. Again the older students did poorly. All of the seventeen-year-old pupils and one of the three eighteen-year-olds in the class were among the non-graduates. Snedden promoted seventeen of the nineteen seventh-graders remaining at the end of the year, three with conditions in arithmetic. Five students left before the end of the term. All of his pupils were fourteen years of age or older, the age group of special concern to Snedden in later years. For this group he would come to demand practical, meaningful, vocational education, preparation in real work through the production of marketable products in a school program covering most of the working hours of the day.

Robert Clarke and George Farrand were pupils in Snedden's seventh- and eighth-grade classroom in 1893–94. The following year, when the principalship of the Santa Paula Union High School was added to Snedden's duties,[10] they continued under his charge as high school students. Clarke learned enough bookkeeping in a single year at the high school to take a position as bookkeeper in the Los Angeles office of the Union Oil Company the following autumn. He returned a short time later to Santa Paula and in 1899 opened a law office in partnership with his friend George Farrand. The Santa Paula *Chronicle*, on November 24, 1899, described them as "up and coming" lawyers already admitted to the bar of the state supreme court. This was only four years after they left Snedden's classroom, and neither one was a high school graduate. In reminiscence of his school days, Clarke described Snedden as a teacher whom former students remembered with gratitude, a teacher who "permitted reasonable freedom of action among the pupils in moving about the schoolroom for the purpose of consulting the dictionary and reference books and even removing them to their respective desks."[11]

The Santa Paula High School was one of two high schools in Ventura County when Snedden was its principal. It served nine school districts in a community whose urban population alone was six times as large as he had found at Fillmore. Miss Emma Younglove, whom Snedden remembered as "a mature high school teacher from the East," instructed the sixty high school students in Latin, German, and English.[12] In addition to his duties as teacher and principal in the grammar school, Snedden also taught the high school classes in mathematics, the natural sciences, and history. A part-time teacher was hired for classes in bookkeeping.

Early in his career at Santa Paula, Snedden became an active member of the Ventura County Board of Education. On November 19, 1892, the County Board of Supervisors appointed him to the unexpired term of board member Dennison, who had recently resigned. The six members of the board were usually selected from among the more prominent public-school teachers of the county, with the county superintendent serving as secretary ex officio. Board membership was a paid position; appointment was for three years with two members appointed each year. In addition to its examination and certification functions, the Board of Education supervised the annual teachers institute, selected books for the school library list, and biennially revised the county course of study for the common schools. Snedden, Superintendent Black, and Principal Hickman of Ventura High School were appointed a committee of three to make the necessary revision in 1893.

Snedden recalled Black as a "driving scholarly man," and work with the committee on the course of study came to occupy most of his Saturdays from January to May of 1893. On February 25 and again on March 25, the committee asked for an extension of time to complete its work. Finally, after a furious three-day session late in June, with Snedden unexplainably absent, the committee adopted a new course of study and ordered five hundred copies printed.

In California, as throughout the country, the annual county teachers institute was conducted for four main purposes: to increase the teachers' general knowledge, to provide supplementary professional training, to provide professional inspiration, and to offer a vehicle of "special communion" within the profession. Attendance was required under California law, and most teachers complied.[13]

Snedden had attended his first teachers institute in October of 1890, during his first few months in the Fairview District, and found it a stimulating experience. One of the institute instructors, John Dickinson — a former clergyman and a professor of science at the University of Southern California and Throop Institute — "idealized the teaching profession" to him. In later life Snedden believed Dickinson had confirmed for him his choice of a life-long career.

Professor Dickinson returned in 1891, when Snedden was teaching in the Fillmore District, with lectures on "Literature Teaching in Our Schools," "Science Teaching in Schools," and "Physical Conditions of Success in Teaching." In a more negative vein, State Superintendent Anderson presented "Criticisms on the High Schools" and delineated the "Principle Causes of Teacher Failure" under ten possible categories. Samuel T. Black, school superintendent of Ventura County, dutifully urged the teachers to follow the prescribed course of study and to do something about beautifying their school grounds.[14]

The following year, as principal of the Santa Paula Grammar School, Snedden was appointed to the institute's Committee on Resolutions. He heard Charles Keyes, president of Throop University, speak on such varied topics as "The Australian Ballot," "Fundamentals of Arithmetic," and "Memory and Imagination and Their Rational Cultivation." Throop University, predecessor to the California Institute of Technology, was still a year away from becoming California's pioneer manual training school.[15]

The 1893 teachers institute provided Snedden with a variety of opportunities which seemed to anticipate his later professional career as commissioner of education in Massachusetts and as professor of educational sociology at Columbia. He was appointed to a committee considering the Ventura County Schools' exhibit at the World's Fair, probably the 1894 fair in San Francisco. He also served as one of a panel of six discussing a paper on "Scientific Temperance Instruction" and delivered a paper, "Elementary Geometry in the Higher Grammar Grades," in which he forcefully advocated teaching the metric system in connection with geometry. At the annual banquet he joined Principal Nicholson and President Keyes in offering the toasts of the evening. His toast was entitled "The Teacher that Never Grows Old."

At this institute Charles Keyes was reported to have delivered an eloquent lecture entitled "The New Education" in which he "traced educational work from the days of textbook bondage to the manual training schools" of the day. He said the aim of the "new education" was that "the hand and eye and heart be taught to realize the value of labor well done and so to make nobler men and women." The following day Keyes elaborated on the course of study adopted by the technical high school of Throop University. This may have been Snedden's first encounter with the burgeoning manual training movement, and it is likely that Keyes' message of the "new education" and the Throop program had its effect on the young grammar school principal. Keyes claimed to offer a more meaningful program of studies to hold the potential school leaver. He assumed that the established subjects were uninteresting and driving from the schools those who could find nothing in them of practical value. This was a position Snedden had not yet taken, but one he was to expound in years to come.

Keyes offered manual training for purposes of mental training; Snedden came to reject this objective in favor of the specific job training of the industrial education movement and what he came to call "real vocational education." However, Snedden came to this position only gradually over a period of years, and his encounter with Keyes left its impression upon him. At the California Teachers Association meeting a month later, one of the members pressed Keyes to show how two hours a day could be found for manual training in an already crowded high school program. He replied that at Throop University a little more than half the day was devoted to the regular studies and after that the students had an option to remain for manual training or to go home. He reported fewer than twenty-five of the two hundred students chose to be excused.[16] Snedden found this division of the day a useful solution in his own presentations before teachers institutes a decade later.

At Santa Paula, David Snedden roomed in the home of Dr. A. L. Kelsey, a young physician of four years practice and a source of intellectual stimulation to him. Mr. Vance also stayed there, and with this former teacher from the Alamo School, Snedden renewed the acquaintance with Herbert Spencer begun earlier in the company of his cousin Agnes. Together they undertook to systematically read and discuss the complete works of Spencer. In later years Snedden was moved to write: "More than those of any other philosopher or sociologist Spencer's volumes laid the groundwork for David's subsequent thinking."

Spencer's query "What knowledge is most worth?" proved especially intriguing to Snedden from this time forward. In "Essay I" of *Education*, Spencer observed that "with the mind, as with the body, the ornamental precedes the useful." He argued that nine out of ten boys who studied Latin and Greek made no practical use of it in the shop, office, or in estate management, and were "very little aided by this knowledge . . . [which] took so many years to acquire." Spencer did not dismiss the classics, or any other body of knowledge, as useless, but rather held that different kinds of knowledge had different relative worth. He urged that the "comparative worths of different kinds of knowledge" be studied to develop a program of education for "complete living." He suggested that the "leading kinds of activities which constitute human life" be analyzed and classified in order of importance. He offered five categories: "those activities which directly minister to self-preservation; those activities which, by securing the necessities of life, indirectly minister to self-preservation; those activities which have as their end the rearing and discipline of offspring; those activities which are involved in the maintenance of proper social and political relations; and those miscellaneous activities which make up the leisure part of life devoted to the gratification of the tastes and feelings." [17]

Snedden would return frequently to Spencer in later years for the solution of problems of curriculum organization. He would look to him again after absorbing the social control theories of Edward A. Ross, his professor of economics at Stanford. Gradually he would take as his own Spencer's bias for practical ends to education and would call repeatedly for the analysis of human activity as the basis for curriculum development. While Spencer's estrangement with the classics was only comparative, Snedden's would be complete.

The 1894–95 school year, David Snedden's last year in Santa Paula, was perhaps his most trying, though one in which he achieved a position of professional and community leadership. The previous June, during the important period of the county teachers examinations, he had served as secretary pro tem of the Ventura County Board of Education in the absence of Superintendent Black. The Ventura *Free Press* of July 20, 1894, reported his appointment as principal of the Santa Paula Union High School. He addressed the annual Ventura County Teachers Institute in November on "Some Reasons Why Children Leave School." The address clearly gives evidence of his concern for this problem, and though he offered no precise solution, he touched upon teacher responsibility and the "influence of the teaching materials." The second semester was occupied with the details of high school accreditation by the state university.

Upon acceptance of the position of high school principal, Snedden found that his trustees were ambitious for accreditation by the University of California. In addition to the obvious prestige of such recognition, graduates of an accredited school would be admitted to the University without having to take entrance examinations. Snedden felt such inspection would find him competent in mathematics and history, but he was less confident about his preparation in the sciences. Accordingly, during the summer of 1894 he took work in chemistry at Stanford University. University of California personnel visited the Santa Paula Union High School from January to May of 1895, and the *Free Press* announced on May 24 that the school had been accredited in English, mathematics, civil government, Latin, Greek and Roman history, medieval and modern history, physics, and chemistry.

At the end of the term Snedden brought Professor Wilbur W. Thoburn from Stanford to deliver the feature address. Thoburn, who taught ethics, spoke on "The New Citizen." The *Free Press* observed his "easy delivery" and "witty comparisons" were well received, and Snedden, who had paid the necessary expenses out of his own pocket, felt amply repaid. Perhaps significantly, one of the two candidates for graduation chose as his presentation "The Modern Municipality," a topic drawn from the political economy ferment of the late nineties.

The social activities of the young bachelor principal of the Santa Paula Union High School centered around intellectual interests — reading and discussing Spencer with Mr. Vance, discussions with Dr. Kelsey, and membership in the Political Economy Club. The club met on Tuesday evenings, twice each month, at the homes of various members during the spring of 1895. David Snedden was elected president. The topics for discussion in April were "Property under Socialism" and "Some Modern Objections to Socialism." From an apologetic note in the local newspaper it seems that Santa Paula misunderstood the purposes of the club. On June 14, 1895, the *Free Press* observed that the Political Economy Club had been "taken for a socialistic order of deep dye." The paper said that this was a mistaken notion as not a member knew what socialism meant when first taking up the study. The editor went on to assure the townfolk that ignorance of the subject alone impelled the club to study socialism. Furthermore, he said that "in all meetings the doors and windows are open, lights burn brightly, and no midnight mysteries shroud the assemblages from public inspection."

Only a week before, on June 7, 1895, the Ventura *Free Press* had reported Snedden's resignation from the club presidency, giving as his reason that he intended to leave town after the close of the school term as he did every summer. Mr. Vance was elected president, but on June 26 he adjourned the club for the summer, supposedly because so many of the members were away on camping trips.

Mid-July found David Snedden in Ventura serving on the County Board of Education. On July 13, 1895, he was elected to the presidency of the board for the 1895–96 school year, but when the board met again the following week he was absent. On July 19, the *Free Press* abruptly announced that Emma Younglove had been offered the principalship of the Santa Paula High School, but made no mention of Snedden. On August 10, he resigned from the Board of Education, and the following September he enrolled as an undergraduate student of education at Stanford University.

What caused this sudden change of plans? Years later, in his *Recollections of Over Half a Century in Educational Work*, Snedden attributed it to the formation in Santa Paula of a chapter of the American Protective Association. He believed they looked upon him with suspicion because of his two degrees from St. Vincent's College, and to save members of the school board from embarrassment he resigned at the end of the school year. However it may be recalled that as late as July 13 Snedden had accepted an obligation requiring his presence in the county throughout the coming school year. Perhaps the recent local misunderstanding of the Political Economy Club had also proved a source of embarrassment to him and influenced his decision to resign.

Another possible reason for Snedden's sudden departure from Santa Paula may be found in the school itself. From a professional standpoint his final school year had been a highly successful one, but enrollment had dropped to forty students by May of 1895.[18] When he first came to Santa Paula, average attendance had been sixty students; a year after he left, the school was reported as flourishing with an enrollment of seventy.[19] Perhaps the rigors imposed by accreditation standards and pressures transferred from the faculty to the student body worked to reduce enrollment and develop feelings of dissatisfaction within the community.

During part of the summer of 1895 Snedden supervised the drying and processing of four hundred tons of apricots at rural Fillmore to build up his cash reserve before heading north to enroll at Stanford in September. He hired, supplied, and paid nearly a hundred spreaders and cutters. Some years before, during his last summer at home in the Lockwood Valley, David, assisted by his three sisters, had produced all the adobe brick needed to construct a five-room house, the new family

homestead. The work of these two summers, added to his earlier experience on the range, sent Snedden off to Stanford with a broad background of practical accomplishment.

During these first five years in the profession, he had taken the extensive county teachers examinations twice and, as a member of the County
Board of Education, had prepared and corrected those of other teachers.
He had twice revised the county course of study. He had been a capable
teacher as evidenced by the high proportion of his students successful
in the county grammar-school examinations. By personal experience he
had seen the attrition of pupils from the seventh and eighth grades, as
many as one-fourth of his seventh grade and one-half of his eighth grade
failing promotion in 1892 and 1893, respectively. The school program,
the certification examination, and the grammar school examinations
were all organized around traditional subjects; yet pupils like Robert
Clark might leave after a single year of high school or less to assume
positions of responsibility in the burgeoning new industries of the
region, with little need to draw upon the subject matter of the course
of study. When Snedden himself needed to qualify as a chemistry
teacher, his master's degree in liberal studies was useless; but a single
summer of work in this field provided the necessary preparation. All
about him he thought he could see much to support Spencer's contention that in education "the ornamental precedes the useful" when, above
all, education should be of practical utility. Up to this time his concern
produced little more than a paper before the county teachers institute
touching upon the problem in a most general way.

In their institute deliberations, the Ventura County teachers looked
to child study and the manual training movement for the solution to the
problem of holding the pupil in school and providing him with a worthwhile program. S. D. Dresslar of the Los Angeles Normal School warned
the institute in 1894 the "first requisite for the successful study of the
child is the existence of sympathetic relations between teacher and
pupil" and said scientific facts should occupy a place secondary to personal observation. Superintendent Black said he "listened with delight"
to those who "skillfully directed the thought of our teachers away from
books and methods and led them into that broader and ever interesting
field, the study of the child." He compared the child to a steam engine
and the teacher to an engineer. The superintendent incorporated both
movements into his own suggested program for the schools: "We must
not look to the development of brainpower to the exclusion of the emo-

tional side of child nature. The two go together if we desire the highest type of character. And these are almost useless [unless] enveloped by sound physical conditions. Add to these the well-trained eye and dexterous hand and the result will be a citizenship capable of solving every problem in governmental policy that may present itself. Such a citizenship will produce a nation of brave and patriotic men, noble and virtuous women, and it will have within itself the power to reproduce a still more advanced type."

Snedden was ready to accept, at least tentatively, the tenets of the manual training movement, as he interpreted them in relation to his own experience with physical work. His approach to the larger problem of what should be taught in the schools was bound up with Spencer's query, "What knowledge is most worth?" He would spend the rest of his professional career developing and refining his own answer to this question. At Stanford, Snedden was to find, in Earl Barnes, a child study specialist then as widely publicized as G. Stanley Hall; following his own current interest in political economy, he would turn instead to the sociology of Edward A. Ross for the resources with which to fashion his theories of education.

Chapter II

SMALL TOWN SUPERINTENDENT

Leland Stanford Junior University in 1895 was only four years old. David Starr Jordan, its forty-four-year-old president, had carefully assembled a faculty of men personally known to him as aggressive young scholars. Some of these men had attended classes with him at Cornell; others he had come to know while president of Indiana University. His personal secretary and registrar, Orrin L. Elliott, had been recommended by Cornell president Andrew F. White, even as White had earlier directed Senator and Mrs. Stanford to Jordan's door. John Casper Banner, chosen for the chair in geology, had been a fellow member of the "Struggle for Existence," a student boarding club during Jordan's undergraduate years at Cornell. Edward Howard Griggs in ethics earned both his A.B. and A.M. degrees at Indiana, and Earl Barnes his A.B. there under the presidency of Dr. Jordan. Edward A. Ross, as a young Johns Hopkins Ph.D., had been attracted to Indiana by Jordan as the latter was preparing to leave Bloomington and had followed him to Stanford.

Once established in California, Jordan urged his faculty to accept as many speaking engagements as possible in order to publicize the University and attract capable students. It is not surprising then that the combination of youth and public service enabled Stanford from the beginning to enjoy prestige equal to that of the state university.[1] Almost from the outset county boards of education recognized the Stanford degree for purposes of teaching certification on a par with that of the University of California.[2] The professors of both institutions shared the burden of staffing the annual county teachers institutes throughout the state and profited equally from the fees paid for their services.

25

The Stanford atmosphere was permeated with the vigor, enthusiasm, and optimism of youth. Faculty and students hiked, camped, and picnicked together on weekends and during breaks in the academic calendar. In the words of Ross, the Stanford faculty, much to its own satisfaction, "didn't put on the dog."[3]

Early in his career as president of Indiana University Jordan had written, "Any pre-arranged course of study is an affront to the mind of the real student."[4] At Indiana only the program of the first year — English, mathematics, science, and a foreign language — was prescribed for the students. Beginning in the Sophomore year, the student's program was entirely elective under the guidance of his major professor. At Stanford, with the active encouragement of his faculty, Jordan carried the principle of elective freedom almost to the extreme; only English — The Art of Writing — was required. The Stanford student selected one third of his program, the major and minor requirement, under the guidance and possible direction of his major professor; beyond this, any subject for which the student could show himself qualified was open to him.[5] The student's program was indeed individualized and his own, except as his major professor may have wished to place restrictions upon the means to fulfillment of the major and minor requirements.

From the very beginning Senator Stanford opposed any charge for tuition. This policy remained in effect even during the days of financial distress growing out of the estate litigation after his death in 1894. When David Snedden enrolled in the fall of 1895, quality education by a youthful, aggressive faculty in an atmosphere providing a maximum of elective freedom could be had for the price of room and board; total expenses, were estimated at $225 to $300 for the school year.

Snedden found Stanford a small cluster of single-storied, sandstone buildings which today constitute the "inner quad." The buildings were of a pleasingly simple Spanish architecture, in the California style, set against a summer backdrop of golden hills spotted with the vivid green of live oak. The combination must have made the Stanford nickname, The Farm, seem most appropriate. Barracks, huts, and lean-tos, left by the construction crews — collectively known as The Camp — provided room and board at a minimum cost to students of limited financial means. Under private and rather informal management, it stood in sharp contrast to Encina and Robles halls, the regular Stanford dormitories, where room and board, "both of the best," could be had for $4.50 per week. Relatively affluent from his five years of teaching and a summer harvesting apricots, Snedden was able to enjoy the comparative luxury of Encina Hall.

He received two years' credit for his work at St. Vincent's and was enrolled as a member of the Junior class. His major extracurricular interest was the Alpha Literary Society, and his fellow students saw him as one who attained high standing with apparent ease.[6] David chose education as his major subject and, in consequence, Earl Barnes became his major professor and advisor.

Barnes had been a professor of history at Indiana when President Jordan took him along to Stanford as head of the department of history and art of education. Under Barnes this department came to offer courses primarily in history and child study. In 1894, Margaret Schallenberger, a recent graduate of the San Jose Normal School who shared Barnes' enthusiasm for child study, was added to the department. When Snedden enrolled as a student the following year, Barnes was already being compared with G. Stanley Hall as a leader in the child study movement[7] and his department was deeply committed to its point of view.

Snedden's program of studies, under Barnes' supervision, included seven courses in education, six in economics, and four in English.[8] Two courses in German and one in French, the latter specifically for reading knowledge, suggest he may have been planning a program of graduate study even then. He took only one course in the department of history, The French Revolution, with Burt Estes Howard, and he found it an attractive study, though he would one day declare himself an avowed foe of this discipline. No science or mathematics courses appear on his record.

In the years ahead Snedden seemed to hold science in high esteem as a process of thought and as a means to improve society. He repeatedly called for the "scientific" analysis of life activities as a necessary substitute for aspirations based on "faiths." It would seem his use of the term "science" was only casually related to the natural sciences for which he apparently had no special interest. That he did not elect work in mathematics represents a similar ambiguity, since he was known as an excellent mathematics teacher following his graduation from Stanford.[9] Yet, at Stanford he did not continue the work in mathematics. In fact he seems to have avoided taking a sequence of courses in any of the traditionally organized subjects.

His English courses were divided equally between rhetoric — including the required composition course — and literature. He seemed to enjoy his survey of English literature and his course in English and American poets with William Henry Hudson.

The English department at Stanford was especially strong. It had the largest number of students of any department in the University, and a surprisingly large proportion of them were looking forward to careers in writing and lecturing. Snedden too, for a short time, may have found himself attracted to this calling. The January, 1896, issue of *The Sequoia*, the student literary publication, carried what may have been his fledgling effort as a short-story writer. The story, "A Pioneer," was told in western vernacular and depicted the financial woes of a squatter. The setting was the Kelso Valley, familiar to his boyhood, and the pioneer was a Pennsylvanian, even as his own forebears. Here the similarities ended. The squatter in Snedden's story lost house and land because he was ignorant of the proper procedures for filing a claim. With rancor, then with resignation, he obeyed the law of right of property, despite the injustice done him. It was an odd theme from the son of a rancher, from one whose family prosperity was based upon ever increasing its land holdings and protecting them from squatters. The story was really more in keeping with some of the reform views popular in Stanford's department of political economy under Ross and Powers.

Of the seven courses in his major subject, education, only two, The Psychology of Childhood, and Aesthetic Qualities of Childhood, could be identified with the departmental emphasis upon child study. Snedden elected three courses — History of Civilization in Europe, Study of Educational Classics, and The Intellectual Development of America — from the departmental offerings in Barnes' second area of special interest, the history of education. To these he added European School Systems and Methods of Teaching Courses in Secondary Schools. In his professional career Snedden rejected both history and child study as means of approach to the problems of education; rather, he found his source of continuing inspiration in the six courses elected in the department of economics, especially those from Stanford's young social economist, Edward A. Ross.

Ross was a pioneer in the emerging field of sociology. His students remembered him as an amusing, friendly, exciting teacher with a talent for phrase-making. He provided Snedden with the doctrine of social control, and its dogma was useful to Snedden's own emerging theories of educational aims.

In the autumn of 1894, at the onset of his second year as a member of the Stanford faculty, Ross set down for his own scholarly contemplation a list of thirty-three means by which society controls its members. He identified this moment of inspiration as the "germ" of his social control idea.[10] During the two years Snedden took courses with Ross, this theory of social control was in the process of development, first in Ross's mind, then expounded before his classes, finally set down in a series of thirteen articles for the *American Journal of Sociology*, and subsequently published in book form.[11]

Ross described social control as "that ascendancy over the aims and acts of the individual which is exercised on behalf of the group," [12] and called it "a study of all the agencies by which men are held to their duties toward others." [13] In consequence he found "the moulding of the individual's feelings and desires to suit the needs of the group . . . the profoundest alteration of associated life" and to be regarded as "the most difficult work of society." Social control could be exercised through all sorts of "instruments" — religious, governmental, and political organizations, folklore, traditions, and even works of art.[14]

Ross was ahead of his time when he observed, "The efficiency of the social system, into which the individual . . . is born, is tested by its power to shape him. . . ." A decade later, Snedden and others of the social efficiency movement in curriculum development would come to see the efficiency of the school as measured in terms of its ability to shape the individual. Ross said, "The system of control, like the educational system, is charged not with revising the structure or functions of society, but with shaping individuals." [15] When Snedden later applied the theories of social control to school problems, he would "individualize" school experience by placing the individual into a pre-defined "case group" to be shaped according to the demands of society. Ross believed he was providing the "light" of sociology as a substitute for that of theology to the clergymen of America; [16] instead, educators in number — perhaps in part because of David Snedden — came to accept Ross's "new light."

The Stanford commencement of 1897 was a plain ceremony, lacking caps and gowns and academic pageantry. With typical western directness, President Jordan distributed the diplomas from a stage in the old wooden gymnasium.[17] After graduation Snedden went to Paso Robles as principal of the high school and supervising principal of the grammar school. His responsibilities were those of a superintendent, principal, and classroom teacher, as they had been at Santa Paula.

Richard M. Shackelford was the president of the Paso Robles Board of Education, and it was he who approached Dr. Jordan in search of a man with Snedden's qualifications. Shackelford was a businessman. He was the manager of the Southern Pacific Milling Company and the Salinas Valley Lumber Company, both Southern Pacific affiliates. He had become almost as prominent in educational circles as any professional educator in California during the quarter-century he had served as a school trustee in various communities of the state.

Shackelford was a man of strong personality. On the policy-making level, he actively opposed the practice of teacher certification by county boards of education. Instead, he proposed limiting the certification function to universities and normal schools as a means of building a stronger teaching force.[18] During the three years at Paso Robles, working under Shackelford, Snedden staffed his school almost exclusively with Stanford graduates.

The responsibilities of his office as a school trustee were a matter of serious concern to Shackelford. He regularly attended the county teachers institute with the teaching staff. He supported the state teachers organization and attended its conventions, often with his entire staff. His hopes for improved school administration lay in the possible organization of separate institutes for school trustees, and short of this, he urged separate sessions for trustees at teachers institutes.[19] In a very real sense, Shackelford represented the seminal demand for a professionally trained educational administration. In the years ahead, after Snedden joined the Stanford faculty and toured the state as an institute instructor, he offered just such special sessions for trustees. Perhaps from working closely with Shackelford Snedden first acquired the interest in educational administration that was to make him one of the pioneers in this field also.

Snedden found Paso Robles a lively, growing city, fifteen years old and in strong contention with San Luis Obispo, the county seat, for local prominence. Its main attraction was a lavish, newly constructed hotel, built to exploit the waters of the local hot springs and resembling the famous Del Monte on Monterey Bay. On holidays, people from the surrounding area gravitated to Paso Robles, to the hotel, to the hot springs, and to the county fair grounds, also located there. Paso Robles received them with parades and programs. Shackelford was its civic leader, in charge of the county fair and active in organizing the Fourth of July celebration, but his main interest was the schools.

Snedden's appointment as principal of the Paso Robles High School included the understanding that he would also serve as the grammar school principal without additional salary.[20] This arrangement was possible because the Paso Robles schools were housed in a single, new, three-story building. The high school occupied part of the second floor and used the assembly hall on the third floor. The Board of Control of the high school and the Board of Trustees of the grammar school were the same three men: Shackelford was chairman of both boards. Meetings of the two boards were held simultaneously, and David Snedden as assistant secretary — a duty that went with the principalship — kept the minutes and financial accounts of each board in separate books. The teaching staff of nine, in addition to Snedden, included one other high school teacher, who was assigned to teach English, German, and Latin. The high school also claimed part of the eighth-grade teacher's day for instruction in science. This division of teaching duties left instruction in mathematics and history to Snedden and presumably part of the day in the eighth-grade classroom.

The Paso Robles High School graduated its first class in 1896, the year before Snedden came. When an alumni association was formed in 1898, the first three graduating classes provided a total of seventeen prospective charter members.[21] School activities in a small city like Paso Robles, however, were matters of considerable community interest.

The Debate Society at the high school endeavored to provide entertainment and education for the entire community. From the beginning the society invited the general public to attend its meetings and even to join in active membership. The *Record* gave the club a column, evidently with the intention of stimulating interest in the bi-weekly meetings; however, the programs in themselves, each creatively different in format, were calculated to provide a source of continuing interest. Sometimes the membership was organized as the House of Commons or the state senate to debate a piece of legislation; at other times they would stage a trial of impeachment. Only occasionally was there formal debate with a stated proposition. The topics chosen for discussion ran the gamut of the controversial issues at the turn of the century. On various weeks the Debate Society directed its attention to the proposed Nicaraguan canal, statehood for Hawaii, expansion of the British Navy, free trade with Puerto Rico, and an impeachment of Secretary of State

John Hay.[22] Snedden was recognized locally as the "main stand" for the Debate Society.

At the end of his first year at Paso Robles, Snedden married Genevra Sisson, whom he had met while at Stanford. Like Snedden, she was a student in education; but unlike him, she shared the enthusiasm for child study that prevailed in the department. Her father, Harold W. Sisson, was a teacher in rural San Luis Obispo County and had been a respected member of the teaching profession since coming to California as a young man. At Stanford, Genevra was an assistant in education and taught a primary class of faculty children.

In teaching her class, Genevra's organization of subject matter followed the Herbartian center of interest, to which all class activities were related and to which the child study movement contributed insights of readiness and appropriateness of content and activity. During the school year of 1896–97, the year David and Genevra became engaged, she used the study of local history as the center of interest. The children soon focused their attention on the study of Indians because observation had shown, to Genevra's satisfaction, that children had "a sense of kinship with the wild Indian" rather than with the "sedate Franciscan monk." She assumed an understanding of primitive conditions would be more meaningful to a child than the study of the complex civilization in which he found himself.[23]

Genevra could find nothing suitable for children in the literature and decided to write some appropriate stories herself. She tried to make them historically accurate in detail, though fictional in plot. Finally she put the whole series, depicting various phases of Indian life, into book form.[24] The stories were written from an Indian point of view, that of an Indian boy, Docas, supposedly about the same age as her pupils. She reasoned that in so doing she would put the stories within the child's range of understanding. Child study investigations had shown conclusively, for Genevra, that children are interested primarily in action, in the use to which things are put, rather than in description of form, color, or static condition, and this was the basis for her choice of story material.

Sharing as they did a common professional bond, it is probable David and Genevra discussed the child study approach as the manuscript developed during the year of their courtship at Stanford. Snedden may have accepted Genevra's contention that the value of history was to be found in the cultivation of a feeling for the times and that wide reading, especially of the historical novel, would develop this kind of understanding of a period and its people. At least this was the position he took a few years later in papers before various county teachers institutes. His interest in Miss Sisson, however, did not lead to a more tolerant appreciation of child study.

David Snedden and Genevra Sisson were married during the summer of 1898, after his first year at Paso Robles. Genevra's father died only the month before. He had been a Quaker, and they found the Quaker marriage ceremony appealing for its simplicity and spontaneity. Professor W. W. Thoburn of the Stanford faculty officiated.[25] A Quaker himself and occasional preacher in the Stanford chapel, Thoburn will be recalled as the featured speaker at the last commencement exercise in Santa Paula under Principal Snedden; they were friends of some standing. On their honeymoon David took his bride to the Snedden ranch in Ventura County for a camping trip. Genevra was mightily impressed when the scholarly young schoolman felled a stag at two hundred yards from horseback with but a single shot.

Returning to Paso Robles, they rented a five-room cottage situated behind the school building, its back yard extending to the mountains. The galley proofs of Genevra's book, *Docas*, were returned in time for the spring vacation, and the Sneddens corrected them in the pleasant surroundings of the mountain wilderness behind their cottage. Before the end of the school year their first daughter was born. By now Snedden was planning for a year of full-time graduate study, and they managed to save one-third of their income for this purpose.

During his three years at Paso Robles, Snedden had much to do with the county teachers institute. In his first year there he found himself host to the annual affair, as it was held in Paso Robles rather than at the county seat. State Superintendent of Public Instruction Samuel T. Black, formerly superintendent in Ventura County, urged the teachers to prepare for the institutes of that year by familiarizing themselves with the reports of the NEA Committee of Ten, of Twelve, and of Fifteen.[26] Accordingly, a "working" institute was planned with the course of study the major concern. The visiting speakers were among the most prominent in California: Thomas Bailey and Elmer E. Brown from the University of California, Stanford's Margaret Schallenberger, and State Superintendent Black himself.

The bulk of the institute's work was conducted in sectional meetings divided according to subject organization. With so eminent a corps of speakers, Snedden's part in the program was no more than that of a sectional chairman. Arrangements for the institute had been placed in the hands of the Paso Robles Board of School Trustees, and their agent Snedden was presumably also busy with the details of administration. He instituted an improved system for taking daily attendance and eliminated the time-consuming roll call. As chairman of the committee appointed to prepare the official report of the institute for the California Council of Education, he became the official voice of the conclave. In this responsibility he was assisted by S. D. Merk, editor and publisher of the local Paso Robles *Record*, the politically liberal newspaper in the community. When the whole affair culminated with a grand ball at the luxurious Paso Robles Hot Springs Hotel, the San Luis Obispo *Tribune* said Paso Robles' hospitality had been "in the royal style."

Professor Schallenberger brought the gospel of child study to the program. She urged the teachers to study and classify their pupils, to put the quiet ones in one row and the opposite kind in another. She admonished them to grade their pupils according to character and disposition just as they graded them in the achievement of their studies. Isaac Wright, a local schoolman, presented a paper on "Algebra in the Grammar School." Snedden responded to his remarks, and the *Tribune* stated a profitable debate ensued. When W. O. Smith of San Luis Obispo failed to appear with his paper on nature study, Principal Snedden was reported to have very ably filled the spot with a demonstration of classroom experiments in chemistry and physics, perhaps as he had used them in Santa Paula. The teachers heard a rural colleague make an impassioned plea that bookkeeping be required of all students as necessary preparation for life.

When Snedden's committee presented the official report of the institute's deliberations, it urged that algebra and concrete geometry be correlated with arithmetic in the eighth grade rather than taught as separate subjects. The report acquiesced to the pleas of the rural teacher that bookkeeping be taught "to enable the pupils to keep a simple set of books and write the ordinary business forms." In the study of history, the institute may have followed the recommendation of William T. Harris' subcommittee on the correlation of studies as found in the report of the NEA Committee of Fifteen in 1895. It proposed that subject should be incidental to reading, language work, and geography in the early grades, but taught systematically in the last two grammar school years. The conclusions reached by the institute were probably an accurate reflection of the position informed teachers of the day were taking on the major issues of the curriculum.

The second year, the San Luis Obispo County Teachers Institute, presented a more varied program, one less concerned with the fundamentals of the course of study. A paper entitled "A Practical Lesson in Minerals," always a popular subject in California, attempted to familiarize the teachers with the geology of their county. One of the Paso Robles teachers, Miss Bertha Chapman, offered practical suggestions for teaching about insects, demonstrated with appropriate charts. W. O. Smith, who had failed to appear the previous year, conducted a round table on "Science and Nature Study." In contradiction to Miss Chapman, he recommended that "scientific nature study should only be conducted by skillful teachers who know how to correlate, without the formal study of the subject."

In sharp contrast to what appeared to be a scientific theme for the institute, Principal Snedden conducted a roundtable on English, with his teachers as participants. Each of the papers presented at the session sought to identify that type of literature most likely to excite the interest of children at a particular grade level. Genevra's book was soon to come off the press, and her husband, it would seem, was in accord with the viewpoint on children's literature that had inspired it. The conclusions reached in the papers were that literature should be taught apart from the reading lesson and should employ devices to arouse pupil interest; interest itself was "the keynote of directed reading for individual needs of the pupil."

The most spectacular of the three institutes in which Snedden participated while at Paso Robles was that of 1900. It was one he helped to plan as a member of the County Board of Education. The featured speakers included: Thomas J. Kirk, the new state superintendent of public instruction; Joaquin Miller, "The Poet of the Sierras"; Harr Wagner, publisher of the *Western Journal of Education*; and R. M. Shackelford.

County Superintendent Mrs. A. C. Spafford Woods became ill, and it fell to David Snedden, as first vice president of the institute, to preside at several of the sessions. The institute met at San Luis Obispo's Maennerchor Hall amid a festive profusion of ferns, flags, palms, and flowers. Snedden opened the session with a discussion on "Professional Inspiration" and in the evening he presented Joaquin Miller to an overflow crowd. Miller, a popular speaker throughout California, appeared on this unseasonably warm evening in his "Klondike traveling suit" of furs and boots to add a touch of realism to his lecture, "Our Alaskan Possessions." Always a colorful figure, his poetry and anecdotes on this occasion were acclaimed in the local press as the high point of the program.

In the course of its serious work, the 1893 Report of the Committee of Ten of the NEA was warmed over again for discussion. The teachers challenged its recommendations as too ambitious, particularly its proposal to place algebra, modern language, and concrete geometry into the grammar grades. State Superintendent Kirk counseled that these subjects be left to the high school years. A local teacher, Miss Grieb, said the report only reflected the selfishness of its authors, "college men and men interested in high school work." "The grammar school," she argued, "must provide the bare necessities of mental life to that large majority of pupils who cannot have the advantages of the high school." She was particularly obdurate in rejecting the introduction of new content to the grammar school course, especially algebra and the modern languages. By way of contrast, in its discussions two years before, the institute had found the Report of the Committee of Ten more acceptable. The feeling in 1900 seemed critical of its broad program and to favor mastery by all students of a limited number of subjects. Opinion in support of this position had not entirely coalesced, and Snedden was among those who remained apart from it. He read the paper of Miss McConnell, also one of his teachers, on "Aides in Teaching State History," and for his own part underscored the necessity for broad supplementary reading. Earlier in the session, books by Mrs. Harr Wagner and Mrs. David Snedden had been recommended to the teachers.

Miss Charlotte Teal, still another of the Paso Robles teachers, presented a paper on untruthfulness in children; it was supposedly based upon the scientific investigations of G. Stanley Hall. Snedden, as presiding officer at this session, used the occasion to note with regret that he could find only a few useful insights in the child study movement. He then proceeded to give evidence of some of his recent study by making a sociological diagnosis of untruthfulness as being an hereditary bequest from primeval times when it was sometimes necessary for self-preservation. "In modern times," he said, "the benefits to be bestowed by society are greater than those an individual could gain by lying," and the lie was no longer of any value. He urged children be taught to tell the truth because it is wise to do so.

In the final address of the institute, the Reverend William Betts of San Luis Obispo's Methodist church told the teachers theirs was a "divine calling" comparable to that of the clergyman. They left in the knowledge that it was "a privilege to be a trainer of the youth of the country."

Snedden also exercised local leadership as a member of the County Board of Education, to which he was appointed at the end of his second year at Paso Robles.[27] Married and firmly committed to teaching as a life career, he welcomed his appointment at this time. He was eager for a year of full-time graduate study, and the additional income, about two hundred dollars, would be a useful addition to his savings. He may have felt, too, that greater familiarity with the educational problems of the county would help him refine some of his ideas about the purpose of education.

When the Board of Education organized for the year's work in July, 1899, Snedden was named to the committee on the annual revision of the approved library list, to the committee on diplomas and certification, and to the committee on the course of study.[28] The major share of the responsibility for the most significant work of the board was delegated to him.

The previous year the Board of Education had adopted a nine-year course for the grammar schools. Under this arrangement pupils of the eighth grade merely received a certificate of promotion into the ninth grade instead of a diploma of graduation. Where the ninth grade was taught in the high school, as in the Paso Robles schools, promotion from the eighth grade meant automatic admission into the high school. Examinations for the grammar school diploma were given at the end of the ninth grade. Pupils in high schools were eligible to take them if they wished. The intention behind the plan was to encourage an additional year of education by delaying the point of normal termination of the common school. The effect, all too often, was to have the ninth year serve as a substitute for a high school education.

Snedden initially accepted the nine-year organization and offered a motion that all ninth-grade examinations, unlike those of grades six through eight, be conducted by members of the board at designated test centers. The resolution passed unanimously, and the examinations were given at five places in the county, including Paso Robles, the following June. That same month Snedden submitted another resolution, also passed unanimously, restoring the eighth-grade graduation and, in effect, killing the nine-year terminal elementary program.

San Luis Obispo County gave its teacher certification examinations twice each year, in December and June. Standards were rigorous; 85 per cent accuracy was required for even the primary certification. Grammar and high-school certificates were granted upon examination in additional and more difficult content. Of ten applicants for the June examination, only four passed and two dropped out.

No doubt the board was capitalizing on Snedden's previous experience in Ventura County when it placed the examinations in his hands. The questions posed, in the main, called for detailed factual knowledge and a minimum of interpretation. The candidates were asked: "Name the leaders in Congress from Washington's time to the present. Name the principal mountain ranges of the West. Name the coast counties of California which touch the Pacific Ocean beginning at the north. What effect has a dot placed before a musical note? Make a drawing in perspective of a vertical cylinder. Spell, Vladivostok, fetichism, icicled, saponaceous, cotyledon, orchid, obligato." [29] On the basis of this examination it seems that a competent teacher was expected to have much factual information and some capability in the skills of the elementary grades. This was in sharp contradiction to the image of the educational process presented in E. E. White's *Elements of Pedagogy*, the text prescribed for the San Luis Obispo teacher candidate.

White stated that the one comprehensive end of education was "to prepare man to fulfill the purposes of human existence; i.e., to live completely." According to his view, education had to be more than mere training. Its comprehensive ends could not be met "by training man to be an artisan, a merchant, a soldier, or even a citizen as such." The "purposes of a complete life" involved "the perfection of man's nature" and touched "all the relations of man *as man.*" White was a disciplinarian. "Knowledge," he said, "should be so taught that the act of acquiring it shall be of greater value than the knowledge itself." [30] In contrast to this position, Snedden valued knowledge for its probable usefulness, even as he now required his ten examinees to know five of White's seven principles of teaching, his method of teaching reading to the beginner, and his definitions of "instruction," "teaching," and "training." [31] He would also come to reject White's broad purposes of education in favor of narrowly defined and sociologically determined aims.

Because of his widely recognized ability to select good teachers, Shackelford, the man who brought David Snedden to Paso Robles, had been one of the featured speakers at the 1900 institute. In selecting a good teacher he looked especially for knowledge of subject matter and the ability to get along with pupils. He felt teachers should have professional training and that good faithful workers should be retained in the district if at all possible. He noted that even though California had a surplus of five thousand teachers and county certification procedures brought another thousand into the profession each year a good teacher was difficult to find.

During the three years Snedden was at Paso Robles, Shackelford seems to have done all in his power to support the eager young principal. Faced with an impending decline in enrollment, the Board of Trustees voted all of the teachers a substantial cut in salary, but kept Snedden at the same salary by the subterfuge of making payment for his otherwise gratuitous supervision of the grammar grades in an amount equal to his announced cut. When the annual Paso Robles school census was reported the following May, enrollment was found to have dropped by fifty-seven, or in excess of 10 per cent. The Paso Robles *Leader* said this was not so serious a loss as anticipated; nonetheless, it represented a decline in state aid of almost four hundred dollars. Ruefully, the newspaper observed, "but we still retain the same number of teachers." Clearly the time was right for Snedden to make his move.

While Snedden was at Paso Robles he did little to become a part of the community's social life. An Improvement Club was organized by Shackelford and other local businessmen to improve the appearance of streets, parks, and public buildings; its long-range goals were the attraction of new industry and community ownership of utilities. Although social improvement usually interested Snedden, his name was noticably absent from accounts of the club's activities, even from the list of speakers in its spring lecture series.[32]

Snedden's name was also absent from accounts of purely social functions in the community, including gatherings at which the majority of his staff was present. Except for those evenings when the Sneddens entertained the high school students and the young principal proved himself "as apt at entertaining as . . . at mathematics," or when Shackelford paid them one of frequent visits, David turned his attention to the study of sociology in anticipation of a graduate year at Columbia.

One room in the Snedden's cottage was devoted to David's books and papers. At the end of two years he had two bookcases filled with books, one to ceiling height. Snedden's school work and administrative duties were for the most part routine activities. The minute books of the high school board of control and the grammar school trustees give evidence of little business other than purchase of supplies. Even his weekly trip to the county seat to carry on the work of the County Board of Education was perfunctory in nature. During these years Snedden found intellectual stimulation in Lester F. Ward's two-volume *Dynamic Sociology*, which he had started to read initially under Ross while at Stanford, and in Franklin Giddings more recently published *Principles of Sociology*. From them he drew inferences useful to his developing interest in educational purposes and objectives.

Ward considered the development of intellect in the educational process as subordinate to the acquisition of knowledge,[33] and doubtless Snedden found this view compatible with his own. To buttress his position, Ward used Spencer's contention that man's intellect could never generate all of the knowledge he would need and therefore most of what he used came to him second-hand. Ward said, "Those who possess most knowledge upon an average possess most intelligence. . . . It follows that, as a rule, the inequality of condition among members of society is due to inequality of intelligence or, what is the same thing, to the unequal distribution of the extant knowledge of the world." Education, as Ward chose to define it here, was "a system of extending to all the members of society such of the extant knowledge of the world as may be deemed most important."[34] It would appear that it was this last part of Ward's message Snedden chose to accept in focusing his own attention on the problem of defining which knowledge might be "deemed most important." However, he rejected Ward's optimistic view that knowledge would mitigate inequality of condition among men and substituted a hoped-for equality within various classes. Giddings probably provided Snedden with the inspiration to make this modification.

Franklin Giddings also drew upon Spencer's theories of social evolution in concluding that "society, like the material world, . . . undergoes integration and differentiation. It passes from the homogeneity and indefiniteness of non-organization to the heterogeneity and definiteness of organization. The process of selection is based upon the differences growing out of the unequal conditions of both heredity and nurture to which man is born. Inequality — physical, mental, and moral — is an inevitable characteristic of the social population." Giddings concluded from this: "A population is therefore always differentiated into classes." He identified three types of class groupings: vitality classes, based upon birth and death rate; personality classes, based upon intellectual ability; and social classes, "created partly by the combinations of inheritance and partly also by the educational influence of association. . . ." These influences, he believed, continued "to act on the unequally endowed personal elements of the population." [35]

Ward appears to have reinforced Snedden's faith in the value of knowledge but not, as he had argued, for free and equal distribution to all. Instead Snedden accepted the natural inequality of men as delineated by Giddings with his several kinds of "classes" and proposed to differentiate society into "case groups," based upon a combination of hereditary and environmental factors. Snedden hoped to mitigate the inequality through educations suited to the particular destination of each group.

Ross had found Albert Shaw's *Review of Reviews* useful and interesting in his own contemplation of sociological problems; [36] Snedden probably first became acquainted with the *Review* as a student of Ross. The April, 1900, number carried an especially significant article about Hampton Institute by editor Shaw himself. The article obviously caught Snedden's eye, and a few years later he made frequent use of it while lecturing at various teachers institutes in California.

Shaw said Hampton Institute had as its purpose "the right kind of instruction" for the children of the colored people, who, having emerged from slavery "needed to be taught and trained in good conduct, the rudiments of book knowledge, and the plain tasks that go with farming, the ordinary handicrafts, and the duties of home and family." Shaw promised that teaching at the Institute "never for one minute loses sight of the general conditions under which these children have been born and the range of social and industrial possibilities that the future has in store for them." Hampton was concerned with "all phases of that most practical of questions — namely, how plain boys and girls and men and women under conditions now existing in our country can make their lives useful and successful."

Washing, sewing, gardening, and a wide range of vocational skills made up the bulk of the school program. In practice, purpose, and assumption, Shaw's description of Hampton Institute offered a good example of education for the rank and file not unlike that which Snedden would come to define. In this article too, Shaw asserted, "by all odds the finest, soundest, and most effective educational methods in use in the United States are to be found in certain schools for Negroes and Indians, and in others for young criminals in reformatory prisons." [37] Snedden accepted this assertion and included it in his doctoral dissertation six years later. He also found in the article suitable grist for the first major address of his career in May, 1900.

Early in March, Snedden was invited to Stanford's commencement ceremony the following May to address its recently organized chapter of Phi Beta Kappa and to be one of the select few of the earlier graduates to receive a key.

Snedden found the topic for his address in a problem posed by Denver School Superintendent Aaron Gove before the NEA the previous July. He had attended this meeting at Los Angeles, his first NEA convention, and was probably in the audience when Gove delivered the paper "Usurpation of the Home by the School."

Gove charged the public school with "encroachment" upon the American home and saw it as part of the growing paternalism evident in other aspects of the "social and political economy." However, he said this situation had developed because the character of the home had changed. More and more the home was relegating its function of providing spiritual and intellectual training to the schoolmaster. Gove said the main function of the home was coming to be merely the acquisition of wealth. Under these circumstances the state was being forced to assume new duties in the training of the child "for its own self-protection." He rejected the apparent trend to continued extension of the school day and the introduction of new content as a burden upon existing school staffs. Instead he suggested a second corps of teachers be employed to provide for all of the new responsibilities being relinquished by the home. Under his plan the present teaching staff would provide the "intellectual drill," and the second staff would provide "field work," described as "instruction in the forest, on the playground, in the public gardens and amid collections of animals." It would also be the responsibility of this new educational service to conduct home visitations and provide some tutoring.[38]

Although Snedden accepted the conditions of the problem as out-

lined by the Denver superintendent — that the educational responsibilities of the home and church were falling to the school — his solution
was the product of his own informal study of sociology during the past
three years. He called his address "Education for the Rank and File." [39]

In this paper Snedden drew upon Spencer in observing that society, as
nature itself, is governed by natural laws, and upon Ross in noting that
the institutions of society find "their justification in their ultimate influence on general society." He generalized that of all the institutions of
society "the school affected the social evolution as no other." His concern
for the moment was the effect of the school upon what he called "the
rank and file" of society, "those who do duty in the ranks . . . who will
follow, not lead." He was quite satisfied to leave the preparation for
leadership in the hands of the university; but for the "rank and file,"
public education must provide "not only training for culture's sake,
but that utilitarian training which looks to individual efficiency in
the world of work."

Even at this early date Snedden saw as the ultimate aim of education
the attainment of the "greatest degree of efficiency." Thus efficiency
should be a product of the curriculum. Training in the trades and business, he assured the graduates, was a legitimate function of public
education. Training for life, in the sense of securing broad efficiency,
"individual as well as social," was a public charge, and the public
school system would provide the necessary framework to carry it out.
He believed the need for this broad efficiency, aggravated by the decline
of the apprentice system, had caused the emergence of the manual training movement and brought about the establishment of the public technical institute.

He found social control a necessary tool for achieving efficiency. It
would prevent the "immense wastage involved when society leaves to
accident or uncertainty of individual choice" the necessary skills of
industrial education. He urged vacation schools, as a means of social
control, to prevent the "positive work of the schools" from being nulli-
fied by the "unwholesome influences of vice idleness." For Snedden, the
school was the prime institution of social control.

Ross recognized the home and the church as important instruments
of social control, though he agreed with Reverend Milton Fairchild of
Albany that the church needed to be reorganized to emphasize its
educational function.[40] Snedden found the church losing position in
the religious and moral education of youth and concluded it was "in-

evitable that the school should increasingly assume responsibility for many of the duties which have heretofore rested upon the church and the home." He identified the school as the "residuary legatee" of those functions relinquished by the home and church.

Snedden saw the educational arena as a scene of struggle between two fundamentally opposed ideals, the "old education" and the "new." The old education, he said, was "prescriptive and logical" and ignored the order of the child's development. It made the classical languages the basis of secondary education and obliged girls to master mathematics and physical science. Snedden accepted these subjects as necessary preparation for higher education, but questioned their value as preparation for life for the majority of students who would not go on to high school or college. He charged the "old education" — not poverty, or the attraction of employment — was the reason children were leaving school.

American society, said Snedden, was again facing new and untried conditions. The frontier had developed efficiency, a habit of independent action, and a keen sense of cooperation in its people; but his generation had been the last to enjoy its benefits. Now that the frontier was gone, the schools must be reformed to achieve these same three aims. This, as he saw it, was the task of the "new education." It would be illogically organized, based primarily on individual instincts and capacities, and question authority. His "new education" might also teach the classics, but as the "domes of the educational structure," not the foundation.

Snedden concluded, "training of the rank and file of society for effectiveness . . . is tending to the same individualism" which he said prevailed in the American Army. For the citizen in the ranks, obedience was no longer blind, he said, but rather it grew out of comprehension of the situation. By attaching less importance to "traditional knowledge" and more to "environing conditions," the new education would furnish a base for this kind of civic responsibility. He took comfort in the trend toward the elective principle as he saw it being put to work in the schools. He saluted Dr. Jordan for having struck "many a hard blow at the traditional pedestals of learning, the sacred tripos of Greek, Latin, and mathematics. . . ." Snedden did not favor free election — "hit or miss," as he put it — but rather, "an intelligent adaptation of work to capacity and interest with a view to permanent results." The responsibility for correct choice, he concluded, belonged "with those upon whom devolves the responsibility for the child's future."

As Snedden would use the principle of election it would become an instrument of social control. Proceeding from the assumption that the home had relinquished much of its responsibility to the school, he saw an "elective" program as an opportunity for the school to prescribe a regimen calculated to fit the child to his place in society. "Education today," said Snedden, "must from the first lead toward the realities of present life. . . ." When the child was properly "fitted," he would possess "such an intelligent understanding of authority as [to] make the exercise of arbitrary authority unnecessary." In his master's essay the following spring, "Flexibility in the Course of Study," he would expand upon this interpretation of the elective principle.

After the lecture, President Jordan told David he wanted him to join the faculty of the Stanford department of education the following year, in the fall of 1901, when he returned from Columbia with his master's degree.

David and Genevra returned to Paso Robles for the graduation exercises there. David gave the featured address, "Why We Educate." While no record remains of what he said on that occasion, the title provides ample latitude for repetition of the Stanford address.

On June 5 he tendered his resignation as a member of the San Luis Obispo County Board of Education. His seventeen-month-old daughter was left in the care of his two sisters at the Snedden ranch, and David and Genevra started on their trip east, by tourist sleeper. For them, the journey to New York took on some of the aspects of a grand tour. Along the way they stopped to see Salt Lake City, Denver, and Omaha. In Chicago they met sociologist George Vincent and visited Hull House in his company. The University of Chicago was a source of surprise to them; no older than Stanford, it seemed much larger. The verdure of the landscape east of the Mississippi in September was also a source of amazement, especially when contrasted with the golden hills of California. What seemed like vast unoccupied marshes and woodlands were no less surprising to them, the more so after having read the many articles in the *Review of Reviews* about the crowded urban conditions of the East. They spent a few days in Washington and were impressed by the nation's capital; then on to New York.

Chapter III

THE FORMATIVE YEARS

The Sneddens found New York City less impressive than the San Francisco of their day. Louis Sullivan's Chicago in this era was the birthplace of the "skyscraper," and as of September, 1900, even the twenty-story Flatiron Building had not yet intruded itself upon the New York skyline. The city's appeal to them centered about Teachers College and to some extent the Metropolitan and the excellent Astor and Tilden libraries. They were most cordially received at Columbia where Dean James Russell made it his practice to personally interview each of the new graduate students and to receive him at tea in his home. Perhaps impressed by David's letters of recommendation from President Jordan and R. M. Shackelford, Russell offered him a fifteen-hundred-dollar scholarship which had unexpectedly become available. With this sum, equal to the amount they had saved, David and Genevra could look forward to a year relatively free of financial worry.

They found a two-room, third-floor apartment on Amsterdam Avenue with a pleasant view of Morningside Park, and David plunged into his graduate work with enthusiasm. He sought out Franklin Giddings and found his two semesters of General Sociology from the vigorous, young, red-headed Irishman fascinating. He also had two semesters of work with Edward L. Thorndike, then in his first year at Columbia. Snedden was Dean Russell's student during the second semester in Practicum, after a semester of Critic Work and Practice Teaching under Frank McMurry and Samuel T. Dutton. Dutton had just come from a highly successful superintendency at Brookline, Massachusetts, and this was his first year at Teachers College. Snedden also took Dutton's course in School Administration, a seminar under his direction, and chose him as advisor in the master's program.[1]

The schools of Brookline had achieved national prominence under Dutton because of his programs of community service and school-home cooperation. In a book admittedly treating "a portion only of the field covered by the author in his course at Columbia University," Dutton identified recognition of the social function of the school as the "new education;" he called it the "new idea." By his interpretation the school was the "fountain of inspiration" to all the community, "to the adult who toils and sacrifices that his child may remain in school" as well as to the child during his school life.[2]

According to one interpretation, education for social efficiency, the reform movement with which David Snedden came to be identified, drew its inspiration both from those who sought a social service objective in education and from those who would use education for purposes of social control.[3] When he arrived at Columbia, Snedden was already acquainted with the doctrine of social control from his classes with Edward A. Ross at Stanford. At Columbia with Dutton, Snedden was to become better acquainted with the social service motive in education.

Samuel Train Dutton sprang from the oldest of New England stock. His maternal ancestors had come to the Massachusetts Bay Colony in 1635. His father, Jeremiah Dutton, was exemplary of the best in the Puritan tradition of stewardship, the ideal of plowing back into society or into the soil more than one takes from it. In this spirit, he steadily improved the rocky, glaciated acres of his Hillsboro, New Hampshire, farm until his fields and orchards became a silent testimonial to his dedicated labors.[4] With a similar spirit of dedication his son worked for community improvement through education.

Dutton was educated in academies at Francestown and New London, New Hampshire, and took his A.B. degree at Yale in 1873. After graduation he put aside his intention to enter the Congregational ministry — he thought temporarily — to accept a position as high school principal and school supervisor at South Norwalk, Connecticut. There he introduced a program of home and school cooperation to educate parents to support the schools. As city superintendent of schools at New Haven, Connecticut, a few years later, he broadened this program by bringing in famous speakers to a community lecture series, by starting kindergartens, and by working to establish a manual training high school.

Within a few years the public schools of New Haven were no longer subject to unfavorable comparison with private schools, as they had been formerly, but rather were accepted as of equal quality.

In 1890 Dutton took the superintendency of Brookline, Massachusetts, and achieved there his ultimate success. As had been the case at New Haven, the public schools of Brookline were considered inferior to the private schools, and probably were, when Dutton arrived. Part of metropolitan Boston, Brookline had a sharply defined social class structure which worked against community cohesiveness. Dutton organized the Brookline Education Society as his vehicle for bringing home and school together and for gaining community backing for the schools. Within a few years it had a membership of six hundred dedicated people, "the richest and the poorest together," organized into nine working committees. Through their efforts, the children were given opportunities to hear good music, to enjoy objects of art placed in the classroom, and to hear noted speakers brought into the community.[5]

For Dutton, the school was only one of many factors contributing to education in the community, though it held a central place. He also described the church as "a mighty educational factor," particularly as the institutional church had come to use "various educational forces to supplement preaching." The home, too, contributed "a fundamental element to education." The public library was also important as "a reservoir of knowledge and inspiration to the entire community." For Dutton, education could no longer be regarded as a matter belonging exclusively to the school; rather, all factors — church, home, library, art museum, newspaper — should cooperate with the prime factor, the school.[6]

Dutton said that man's chief function was as a social being and that education was for social ends, its ultimate aim being social service.[7] The school existed to create a better society, and its mission was closely related to other forms of social work. He observed that on occasion the schools had used to advantage those methods "found most successful in dealing with the vicious, the defective and the neglected classes." He told school people, "the methods, the aims, humanitarian spirit of the social reformer are essential to the life of every good school."[8] At the New York State Conference of Charities and Corrections in 1905, he told the social workers that schools and churches alike had been instructed and inspired by the settlement movement.[9]

During the fall of 1898, Dutton wrote *Social Phases of Education in the School and Home* in which he set forth his social service point of view. It came off the press in April, 1899, and the first week in May, Dean James Russell of Teachers College paid the Brookline schools a surprise visit. Impressed by what he saw there, he offered Dutton the position as superintendent of the Horace Mann Schools with a professorship in school administration. Dutton accepted. Columbia had a new Horace Mann building under construction at 120th and Broadway, which was Dutton's major concern during his first eighteen months at Teachers College. Snedden probably saw little of him, though he certainly drew upon the lectures and publications of his advisor in the preparation of his master's essay.

Snedden laid the foundation of the essay on the broad base of Dutton's *Social Phases of Education*. He also made ample use of two of Dutton's published addresses, his remarks before the New England Association of Colleges and Preparatory Schools in 1897, and a paper of a year earlier entitled "The Relation of Education to Vocation." [10] Presumably, he also drew upon some of the content that appeared in Dutton's next book, *School Management*, which he gained from course lectures.

In the Preface to *Social Phases of Education*, Dutton stated his point of view as "social rather than scholastic." It was from this viewpoint that he responded to an address by Clark University professor William H. Burnham at the 1897 meeting of the New England Association. He protested that college admission requirements, enforced by external examination, defeated the social purpose of the school, made it "unsocial" and "individualistic." [11] His was not the usual anti-classical position, however. Dutton made it clear he had no sympathy for demands that Latin be excluded from the high school. To the contrary, he found "nothing more fruitful to the young scholar" than Latin well taught. He merely wished to reduce the proportion of time devoted to both mathematics and the classics in order to leave more room for the new subjects — manual training, history, homemaking, and the sciences — which he considered equally valuable. [12]

Dutton took a similar broad view in his article, "The Relation of Education to Vocation." He treated the same problem Dewey identified in *School and Society* three years later, and Dutton's proposed solution was not unlike Dewey's. In essence both maintained that the machine age had produced a new social order to which the schools must adjust. In the machine age a vocation was no longer learned, as of old, in the home under the apprenticeship system. The new education must provide the habits of industry and responsibility and respect for dignity of labor previously acquired in the household. The school must provide new content, knowledge of economics, scientific habits of mind, and manual training, as the "connection link between the abstract and the concrete," to meet the new vocational demands. Dutton urged "enriching and broadening school life [with] the introduction of science, of literature, of art, music, and manual training." This kind of program would be "a long step toward . . . vocational success and happiness." His chief regret, one Dewey did not share with him, was that the grammar school graduate was unprepared to enter at once "upon pursuit of a handicraft." He saw a "pressing need of trade schools." [13]

In *School Management,* Dutton made it clear that he rejected "the new ideals of efficiency," the business efficiency espoused by followers of Frederick Taylor. He conceded that it might be interesting "to study the organization of a great commercial business," but not for purposes of applying the methods found there to the operation of the schools. The school was "not a factory and the schoolmaster not a foreman." His warning was severe: "The factory system applied to the school, while presenting an attractive exterior, is deadening as regards those finer products of feeling, taste, interest, and ambition which the school ought to nurture." [14] Presumably he communicated these attitudes to Snedden who never developed a great enthusiasm for this brand of efficiency. When Snedden later demanded vocational schools as factory-like as possible it was for another kind of efficiency, vocational efficiency, to shape an individual to a high level of vocational competence.

Snedden found the problem for his master's essay in the pressing demands of the new subjects on the school curriculum and in the imperatives of the social service ethic as annunciated by Dutton. His views, expressed under the title "Flexibility in the Course of Study," were really an expansion of his address of the previous spring, "Education for the Rank and File."

In the essay, which Snedden termed "a preliminary paper," he set out to evaluate the current status of the course of study, both elementary and secondary, and to suggest opportunities for its increased flexibility. [15] It proved to be an abortive effort. Only three of seven projected chapters, the part dealing with secondary education, were written. The typescript shows evidence of hasty preparation, possibly additional evidence of pressure to complete all degree requirements within the year he had allotted to himself.

In presenting his appraisal of secondary education at the turn of the century, Snedden drew upon his own past experience in California and the problems he encountered as a member of two different county boards of education. He chose to recall that while working on the course of study as a board member it had become apparent that the courses were "ill adapted to the children" and a source of dissatisfaction to the parents. In this essay may be found the beginning of his effort to identify aims of education based upon differentiation of destination. It was, in a sense, the concluding statement of his first ten years in education and the introductory statement to those problems about which he would build his future career.

At the outset Snedden paid his respects to the changed conditions brought about by the passing of the agrarian way of life, the obsolescence of the apprenticeship system, and the disappearance of the "old fashioned home." These changed conditions promised to place steadily heavier burdens on the school. He credited Dutton with the appraisal that complete education had to be more than "merely intellectual, but physical, social, and industrial as well."

What followed was a mixture of objective appraisal and hopeful prognosis. He observed that in the complex industrial society of the early twentieth century "the laboring classes" were no longer able to provide for their technical education. In consequence, this need could be met only with public support. With a marked degree of accuracy, he predicted the future would see a constant increase in public support for industrial education, a prediction he would help to fulfill a decade later in the office of commissioner of education for Massachusetts. In 1901, however, his understanding of technical education was probably still that acquired from Charles Keyes, the Throop Institute variety, making little distinction between manual training and vocational education. He called for "that kind of training which brings the worker up to the door of actual practice," but "not necessarily that which fits for specific occupations in all cases." This was a remarkable statement from a man who would make education designed especially for vocational competence his great cause in life.

Snedden still recognized the time-honored disciplinary purpose of education though he did not argue for it. Even while in California he had begun to claim as the ultimate value of each study the practical or social purpose served by its content; but his allegiance to this approach was not yet clearly defined. At this time he merely identified a shift in the relative importance of the various studies, many of which could no longer be considered indispensable because of their disciplinary value. Instead he put forward manual training, industrial arts, and the commercial subjects as possessing immediate practical utility and what he chose to call "educational value" by reason of their "recent development and organization."

In line with most commentators of the day, Snedden recognized the expansion of organized knowledge that had occurred in the scientific, historical, and industrial subjects. According to his optimistic view of the moment, he argued that their improved organization rendered them "no more difficult of presentation to the youthful mind than have been the subjects of the classical program." He had not yet come to reject the integrity of the subjects, old or new. But, though he accepted organized subject matter, he did not necessarily like it. Latin was already the object of his scorn. Noting its remarkable growth in popularity during the preceding ten years and unwilling to see any intrinsic merit in the subject, he attributed the increase to the introduction of college preparatory courses in the smaller high schools and to the improved methods of teaching the subject.

He had not yet developed his antipathy for history. The second chapter of the essay was an historical overview of the development of the secondary school course of study. Planned though never written, the fourth chapter was to provide the same perspective for his intended treatment of the elementary course of study. He even expressed the belief that the "laboratory" method applied to history had made it the most interesting of subjects. At this time, too, he felt it made a large contribution to the "preparation-for-life" function of the high school.

Snedden criticized the Report of the Committee of Ten for its failure to consider offerings in music and drawing subjects which promised to contribute to preparation for life. Other new subjects which Snedden felt might justifiably be considered included meteorology, "the new and more practical phase" of political economy, sociology, and Spanish.

The new subjects aggravated the problem of the overcrowded curriculum. Reactions to this dilemma had taken two opposite positions. One called for more intense work in fewer subjects, the solution of the San Luis Obispo Teachers Institute in 1900; the other provided a wide, but necessarily superficial, survey of all human learning. Any attempt to introduce some of the content earlier, notably Latin and algebra, was not likely to be found acceptable on the local level, as he himself could recall from Paso Robles.

At the moment his solution to this problem lay in the principle of election. Snedden proposed Latin and algebra be offered as electives in the grammar school, though not for the purpose of providing the terminal student with additional opportunity, as Eliot would have urged.[16] Rather, election would be used along with sectioning of classes according to pupil destination so the terminal student might avoid these subjects and instead find something which supposedly would have more appeal to him. This was his "flexibility," and he thought it most important in teaching literature, history, science, and the modern languages. It seemed inconceivable to him that any educator would arrange a course in the same way for those students "who would have no opportunity for further work along that line" as he would for those who intended to go on to high school.

Dutton believed there should be flexibility in the course of study too, but a type that proceeded from the teacher's initiative. The principle of election was little involved here. Instead, Dutton would have a single course, binding upon all, and the teacher would be accorded considerable freedom in "minor details" of its organization and execution. By "minor details" he referred to supplementary topics intended to provide the better student with a more intensive study of a subject.[17]

Snedden's solution, at least for the purpose of the essay, lay in uniformity with flexibility. Flexibility at the grammar school level encompassed the election of some subjects and the sectioning of others, in both instances based upon pupil destination. His last two chapters were to have been devoted, respectively, to the "desirableness" and the "feasibility" of "increased flexibility." Although these chapters were never written, his entire outline was included in the paper. It listed as the expected advantages of increased flexibility: individual development, interest and effectiveness in studies, maintenance of business and industrial courses, introduction of advanced work, and improved teaching. The disadvantages enumerated were waste of time and energy in unwise choices, earlier specialization, administrative difficulties, and social and moral effects — not otherwise elaborated upon.

The failure of the Committee of Ten to "assign educational values" was, in Snedden's eyes, one of the major deficiencies of its report and one that would have to be corrected in order to give direction to flexibility in the course of study. Though he lamented the lack of any standard of values, he reasoned that the committee was probably wise in its refusal to attempt to set such a standard because none of the social and economic laws upon which educational values must ultimately be based were yet sufficiently worked out.

On the secondary level Snedden proposed the principle of correlation be employed in order to provide a program not "solely with the end of higher education in view, nor yet . . . so remote . . . as to cause waste of time to the [college-bound] student." The major difficulty likely to be encountered by this approach was that "the advocates of the subjects under consideration" for correlation were never willing to have their own particular specialty "submerged in this way." As a man quite uncommitted to any subject or academic field Snedden could rise above such loyalties and promise that better trained teachers would tend to use correlated material.

In word and concept, "correlation" came from the vocabulary of the Herbartian movement, a vital force in American education from 1890 to 1910. Not unlike Snedden, the Herbartian found the end of education in knowledge drawn from content rather than in the training provided by the studies. In short, subject matter was useful for substantive rather than formal purposes. They had little respect for the line of traditional subject organization. Instead, the content of the various subjects was to be reorganized — correlated — around a center of interest. Interest was achieved by appealing to the child's apperception, taking that with which he was already familiar and proceeding from the known to the unknown.

The Herbartian solution to the perennial problem of the "congested curriculum" lay in the correlation of elements drawn from various subject areas around a single center of interest. "People are controlled . . . by the thoughts they have," reasoned Frank McMurry, and their thoughts are based upon their knowledge. Frank McMurry, who with his brother Charles and Charles DeGarmo was one of the leaders of the American Herbartian movement, drew the natural conclusion, "A little knowledge thoroughly understood is like a tower of strength." "The advocates of concentration" planned to build such towers "by massing ideas according to their closest relations."[18] It may be recalled that Snedden took Critic Work and Practice Teaching with McMurry.

Snedden never entirely espoused the Herbartian movement though he found the Herbartian vocabulary of "apperception," "interest," and "correlation" useful in his speeches during the next four years before various California county teachers institutes and in the *Western Journal of Education.* There is some evidence to suggest that his course in General Method was largely Herbartian method. He may have been alienated from a full commitment to its cause by the pseudo-sentimental arguments drawn from the child study movement and employed by its proponents. The disposition of the Herbartians to the reorganization of subject matter into different groupings from its traditional organization had a continuing appeal to him, though his purposes were different from theirs. While the Herbartians sought reorganization around a single center of interest, on the assumption that more meaningful content could be taught in this way, Snedden sought reorganization for purposes of social control.

With David's essay accepted and the master's degree won, the Snedden's could reflect upon their year in New York. They had enjoyed the cultural opportunities of the great city, including several visits to the Metropolitan. Her first book a success, Genevra had begun work on the second. This time she drew her theme from Norse history and during the first semester had devoted every morning to gathering material at the Astor and Tilden libraries. Their only son had been born during the year, arriving conveniently enough just after David had written the master's examinations. They named him Olaf in consequence of Genevra's current interest in Scandinavian lore.[19]

David and Genevra returned to California by way of Detroit to attend the NEA convention there in July, 1901. David attended the meetings faithfully, three sessions each day, just as might have been expected of him had this been a California county teachers institute. However, when G. Stanley Hall spoke before the newly organized Child Study Association of America, David remained in their room with the month-old Olaf so that Genevra might go to hear the great high priest of child study.

The department of education at Stanford when Snedden joined it in 1901 was quite different from that he had known as a student four years earlier. Ellwood Cubberley had replaced Earl Barnes in the fall of 1898. Cubberley thought of education primarily as a function of government,[20] and he directed his own scholarly pursuits to the history of education and the administration and supervision of school systems. Edwin D. Starbuck, a recent Ph.D. from Clark University, represented the child study movement on campus. Unlike Barnes, Starbuck made child study but one facet of a rather broad range of interests in the field of educational psychology. In a paper, "The Passing of Child Study," given before the child study section of the California Teachers Association, Starbuck described its growing "ill repute among serious, thoughtful people" and said the time was past when it attracted mainly enthusiasts and sentimentalists. He promised that the future of child study was in the hands of the psychologist and expert.[21]

Like many another Stanford professor, Cubberley came from Indiana. In fact, Jordan had personally recruited Cubberley as a student for Indiana University while on one of his speaking junkets through the state. At Indiana Cubberley majored in physics and in his senior year accompanied Jordan on his lecture tours. On these occasions he brought the technical insights of the physicist to the intricacies of stereopticon projection which Jordan used to illustrate his talks in every Indiana crossroads hamlet.

Cubberley had gained experience as a district school teacher, then as a college instructor in science; in 1893, at the age of twenty-five, he became president of Vincennes University. In 1896 Jordan arranged for him to come to California as the superintendent of schools for the city of San Diego, and two years later he joined the faculty at Stanford. Up to this time he had taken only two courses in education, elected in his senior year at Indiana. With Snedden coming to join the department in 1901, Cubberley had the opportunity to do more work in education and to get a master's degree of his own at Columbia.

Snedden regarded his four years at Stanford as the most strenuous of his career. His teaching load was heavy, and the volume of institute work increased each year, eventually bringing him an income almost equal to his regular salary. The first year, in Cubberley's absence, Snedden also had to shoulder the burdens of temporary department chairman and supervise the Teachers Bureau maintained by the department.[22] For better than half of these years he was an active participant in the affairs of the California Teachers Association and the California Council on Education, and during most of the time he was also an active member of the exclusive Scholia Club and the somewhat larger California Schoolmasters Club. It was a stimulating time to be in northern California; his colleagues there included Elmer E. Brown, Ernest Carroll Moore, Frederic Burk, C. C. Van Liew, and Henry Suzzallo.

In his first year at Stanford, Snedden taught Introduction to Education, Elementary School Problems, Secondary School Problems, and School Management to undergraduates; and on Saturdays he offered

Education and Society and Principles of General Methods primarily
for teachers from the field.

His first lecture, he felt, was a good one, comprehensive and lucid;
but it was so comprehensive that he feared he had left little more to be
said during the remainder of the course. Subsequently, however, he
found ways of expanding each topic he had touched initially into a
separate lecture and much of his apprehension was relieved. At Columbia, Frank McMurry had been "a past-master of class discussion" and
when Snedden resorted to this device to fill some of his class periods,
he discovered "he loved leading a spirited class discussion more than
almost anything else in the world." To relieve the tensions of these first
months, the young instructor turned to the Stanford woodworking shops
one hour each day. There he produced bookcases, window seats, tables,
and a steady stream of redwood furniture which the Sneddens found
useful throughout their lives together.

Of all the courses David Snedden handled at Stanford perhaps the
most significant was Education and Society. It had been introduced by
Edward A. Ross in 1895 and had been offered in the department of
political economy, though cross-listed with the education department
until 1900. The previous winter, while Snedden was at Columbia, Ross's
long-standing disagreement with Mrs. Stanford had flared again and
culminated in his dismissal from the university. When Snedden came
the following September, the course was shifted to the department of
education and remained in his charge until he left Stanford in 1905.[23]
The course description — "a study of the tendencies of society to consciously improve itself by means of education" covering "the function
of the school as related to the home and church" and "specific problems
in connection with social education, as relating to defective and criminal
classes, foreigners, negroes, etc." — stamps it as one of the pioneer
courses in educational sociology. Snedden's growing interest in the
social service and social control aims of education are easily discernible.
Several of his institute lectures during the next four years would broach
these problems of aim and objective and appear as the natural extension
of ideas expressed in his Stanford commencement address, his master's
essay, and presumably the course content of Education and Society.

When Ellwood Cubberley returned from New York in September,
1902, the Stanford department of education was reorganized. Hence-
forth the department would accept as majors in education only those
students who intended to follow a career of educational administration

or planned to become teachers of education in a college or normal school. All others, including those who aspired to become classroom teachers, could select education as a minor subject only. The Teachers Bureau, the placement agency Snedden had supervised in Cubberley's absence, was moved into the registrar's office.[24] Cubberley concentrated upon educational administration and the history of education; Edwin Starbuck taught the courses in educational psychology. The courses most closely identified with teacher education — the subjects of the minor sequence and the Saturday program — fell to Snedden.

Under the reorganization, Snedden's responsibilities included his Education and Society, a course entitled simply Secondary Education, two courses concerned with the elementary school, his General Method, and School Management, along with the supervision of practice teaching. The course in secondary education examined the "preparatory, culture, commercial, manual training, and industrial aspects" of the high school program in terms of the "purpose, value, and limitations" of the various subjects.

With passage, in November 1902, of an amendment to the state constitution permitting the legislature to appropriate funds specifically for support of the high schools, the function of this institution came up for discussion and review throughout the state. C. C. Van Liew, president of the normal school at Chico and one of the state's foremost Herbartian educators, charged the existing high school course lacked a "practical touch with the world" and was a "junk shop of traditional material" and "a mere feeder to the traditional culture courses in colleges."[25]

Frederic Burk, president of the San Francisco State Normal School and also an Herbartian, called the high school course of study "a bone of contention among several masters." He identified these masters as the university with its demand for control of the "preparatory feeders," the mechanic and the business man who wanted "trade schools in their lines," the pedagogue who rejected any type of special preparation in favor of education "for citizenship and general intelligence," and the traditionalist who insisted that the high school "continue along the line of the past." He believed the universities and the traditionalists held sway, supported by young men and women "fresh from the universities bearing with them college prejudices." On the disciplinary value of the studies, he said, "The pedagogue declares that this is traditional nonsense, that a power gained by exercise in one field cannot be transferred to another field." He used the favorite whipping boy, algebra, to demonstrate his point. "The kind of reasoning gained in algebra applies only to algebra," he said, "and unless algebra is for universal use, it can have no claim to universal treatment in the high school." President Burk called upon departments of education to make a "pedagogical impression upon their graduates different from popular tradition." He asked the questions David Snedden would ask over the period of the next thirty years: "What is the product of four years in Latin? What is the output of algebra? What is the value of the narrow and prescribed course in literature?"

Snedden found himself projected into the ferment of inquiry fresh from his year at Teachers College and its contacts with the social service viewpoints of Samuel T. Dutton and the Herbartian reorganization of studies of Frank McMurry. The locally important men in the profession, some with national reputations, were expressing discontent with the existing high school and pressing for answers. It was a climate that encouraged him to draw upon the doctrines of Ross, Dutton, and McMurry, as he knew them, to address these questions of purpose in education.

Three organizations provided a forum for many of these discussions — the California Schoolmasters Club, the newly organized High School Teachers Association of California, and the equally new California Scholia Club. Snedden belonged to all of them.

The California Schoolmasters Club was a select group of educators limited in number to 100, later 125, and always had a long waiting list. The club met in San Francisco three times each year.[26] David Snedden was an active member and, in 1902, chairman of its committee on the code of ethics. In 1902 also, the High School Teachers Association was organized under the auspices of the California Teachers Association. It was intent upon "threshing out" the questions of purpose in the high school course. Under the chairmanship of David Snedden, a Committee of Ten was directed to deal with the "pedagogical issues" involved.[27]

By far Snedden's most stimulating connection was his membership in the relatively small and exclusive California Scholia Club of San Francisco. The club was organized late in December of 1902 when Ernest Carroll Moore of the University of California invited some of the leading educators of northern California to a dinner meeting at a San Francisco restaurant. Twenty responded, David Snedden among them, and the club was born that evening.[28] Its stated purpose was "the cooperative study of educational problems in a scientific spirit." Subsequent meetings of the club were held monthly in the regal splendor of the Palace Hotel. The general topic for study during the first year was "Formal Discipline." Each paper under this general heading was announced two months in advance to give members sufficient time to prepare for "full and frank discussion." Membership was held to a select twenty-five so that all would have opportunity to express themselves.[29]

Ernest Carroll Moore delivered the keynote address of the series, an address he repeated before the California High School Teachers Association a month later, in January, 1903. Moore took the middle ground in the question of form versus content; his position was far short of the defeat Burk anticipated for the disciplinary goals in education. Moore divided all studies into two classes, "those which prepared for specific occupations and those which train the mind as a whole." He used the arguments familiar to those who declared themselves against something called "faculty discipline" when he said, "not *the* attention, or *the* senses, or *the* memory . . . constitute the objectives of all teaching." However, mere acquisition of content did not constitute education either; he contended there were "plenty of chemists chock full of formulae" who could recite theory and who knew the textbooks by heart, but who could not resolve fresh problems as they came up in the laboratory. He said education must develop "ways and habits of attending, observing, and remembering"; it must develop disciplines of "general usefulness" as opposed to "general disciplines." For Moore, the chief object of studies was "the imparting of social methods which can only be done successfully where these methods are well interwoven with the material upon which it is desired to operate by their use."[30]

Around the table at the Scholia Club Snedden also heard A. W. Scott, a San Francisco feed and grain dealer and perennial school trustee, place all subjects "on trial" and require them "to justify their place in the curriculum of the modern high school." Scott proceeded to place mathematics on trial and to justify its place both as a formal and a content subject. He set up the dualism of "general culture" and "immediate utility," both as necessary to the school curriculum. By his standard, "the value of any particular subject in the curriculum [would] depend on the degree and manner" in which it satisfied "the demands of social and industrial life."[31]

Scott assured the educators that arithmetic and objective geometry had a place in the elementary school because they described the material world. However, on the secondary level, mathematics functioned entirely as a formal subject and was not so universally acceptable. There were some students "capable of development in imagination, sympathy, and the social and ethical instincts," but who were "lacking in mathematical sense." For them Scott, like Snedden, urged flexibility with an element of social control. He was reluctant to accept a student's "self diagnosis" of a lack of ability for mathematics and declared, "I would compel him to demonstrate to me by at least one term's work under intelligent supervision that he was deficient in the mathematical sense." The student would then be excused from mathematics, at least "until he should become more mature." It is hard to escape the conclusion that Scott felt mathematics good to study, but thoroughly unpleasant.

Several of the papers were devoted to the disciplinary values of the individual subjects; Latin, algebra, arithmetic, English, and manual training were among those to come up for consideration. In general, the papers presented before the club did not present the extreme view of Burk.

In 1903–4, the theme of the Scholia Club was the investigation of the course of study of the elementary school. David Snedden read his paper, "Literature in the Grades," before the club on November 21, 1903. Snedden brought to the club's circle of discussion applications of Ross's doctrine of social control and Dutton's social service aim of the school. Snedden rejected the teaching of literature as an end in itself; instead, he said, "it must serve as a means to uplift the individual, to make him a better member of human society." In fact, it must "so mould him that he enrich the lives of others." He believed literature was second only to the personality of the exceptional teacher as an agency by which the school might "influence" the life of the child and should be part of the school program "from the opening day of school forward."[32]

Snedden said man's "ideal forming propensity" was instinctive, but the particular ideal chosen depended largely upon the environment and presumably on the exercise of a certain amount of social control. Therefore, in fitting the child to live an effective social life, the school must thwart his unsocial tendencies, diminish his instinct to fight, promote an appreciation of the value of persistent and honest labor, and stimulate the emotional tendencies which make for cooperation. He promised, "in proper hands . . . literature may become a powerful agency in stimulating the growth and guiding the expression of all that part of our nature which is called social."

Interest, he said, was really manipulated by the capable teacher and indispensable to good results. The ability to tell stories "brightly" and read "sympathetically and appreciatively" were important to the teacher in the formation of interest. Children were very amenable to suggestion, he thought, once the teacher had found their "apperceptive level" — in the parlance of Herbartian psychology.

He thought teachers tended to impose "the old classics" upon growing boys and girls who wanted content that expressed "current ideals and current symbolism," literature "not too remote from their own age." Interest in literature must be direct, drawn from the content, he maintained, if it is to achieve its purpose. The atmosphere should be one of "ease," not "work."

He used this talk frequently and with considerable success before various teachers institutes throughout California. In the weeks prior to his presentation before the Scholia Club he tried it out first at Hollister, then at Redding, and found the teachers very much interested. The following March this address was acclaimed "the feature of the day" at the San Diego County Teachers Institute; in September it provoked "an animated discussion" in the Trinity County Institute at Weaverville and was "highly appreciated" by teachers far to the north at Yreka City, according to reports in local newspapers.

David Snedden spoke before a great many teachers institutes during his years on the Stanford faculty. Invitations came to him from throughout the Golden State from Yreka City to San Diego. At first he spoke from a carefully prepared manuscript, reading large sections with some trepidation. One night at Colusa, either by design or by accident, the lights failed in the middle of one of his speeches. He carried on extemporaneously and received good audience reaction. In the future he spoke from notes or outline only. His topics covered the whole range of school problems: "Formal Work and Drill," "Some Suggestions on General Method," "Supervision of Rural Education," "The Significance of Contemporary Social Conditions on the Work of the Public Schools," "The Possible and the Impossible in Correlation," "Teaching Children the Great Lessons of Habit," "My Definition of a Teacher," "The Possibilities of the Teachers Reading Circle," "The Physical Side of Geography," and "The Reception and Application of New Ideas," to name but a few.

Snedden became a popular and sought-after institute lecturer. "Magnetic," "forceful," and "eloquent" were the adjectives used by the Weaverville *Weekly Trinity Journal* in September, 1905, to announce his appearance before the Trinity County Teachers Institute. "Professor Snedden will not only attract audiences but will hold their interest throughout," was the promise of the *Placer County Republican* the previous October. Having heard him the week before, the *Weekly Press* of Santa Barbara commented: "Professor Snedden spoke well; his address was interesting from start to finish."

Under the topic, "Arithmetic Possibilities of Scope and Method," he directed the teachers first to identify the aims to be achieved because, as he reasoned, content would largely be determined by aims, once they were defined. He believed there were two phases of arithmetic teaching, one concerned with developing an appreciation of "situations in life," the other having to do with "facility and accuracy," "painful practice," and "drill work." The content for study, he argued, "should be determined almost wholly by the aim of practical utility . . . to the large majority of pupils." This he defined as "the ability to apply the subject . . . readily and accurately, to those practical activities which come within the range of average life." In this way the subject would be made to contribute to the "practical efficiency" of the largest number.[33]

As he had for literature, David Snedden found a social control aim for history; that of "giving pupils right ways of feeling about historical situations and personages." The teacher's first concern was to establish pupil interest and the materials she chose to use need not be "strictly history." In fact, he said, "patriotic poems, stories, the personal admiration and dislikes of the teacher" were applicable and "frequently desirable." He was ready to substitute a topical organization for the traditional chronological development of the subject, so that fewer topics would be treated more "amply," "interestingly," and "richly." Snedden urged that the questions posed on the county examinations be such as to stimulate the right kind of history teaching and thereby serve as a means of control over the teacher.[34]

In his popular institute talk on "General Method," Snedden used the Herbartian doctrine of correlation to promote his own growing concern that teaching be related to specific outcomes and precisely defined purposes. He proposed correlation should be limited to the introduction of new material; once the child's interest had been aroused the subject needed to be isolated from outside details. Correlation, if continued, he warned, would defeat the aim of the school, as the pupil was likely to know neither of the studies correlated.[35]

Snedden accepted as true the criticism that the schools of 1903 were not turning out students possessed of the same accurate information as formerly. He put the blame on the course of study which expected teachers to cover too much material. The situation could be remedied if the student and teacher alike worked to "a definite aim" so the child's attention could be focused "on a specific thing, . . . one thing at a time." If, in addition, the subject content were "correlated" with actual life situations better teaching would result. "Only applied knowledge is vital to us," he said, and he assured the teachers, "we do not teach anything nowadays that is not to be applied to current life."

The entire system of state-subsidized teachers institutes was under review during the years Snedden was on the Stanford faculty. The state of California spent from $150,000 to $200,000 each year to maintain the institutes, and attendance was required of all public school teachers in the state. Editorially, the *Western Journal of Education* argued that the professionally trained teacher found little of interest in the program while the novice needed much more instruction than could be given during the usual three- to five-day institute.[36] Perhaps in consequence of this criticism, the superintendent of the San Francisco schools decided to make his a "working institute" organized into small group meetings. Snedden fitted comfortably into the new format; in fact, of the several "practical teachers" from the outside invited to work with the various groups, he alone was one of the familiar figures of the institute circuit.[37]

At Santa Clara, Snedden applied the principle of social control to a time-honored institution, the reading circle, in master-minding another institute innovation. He organized some three hundred teachers into several reading circles; one representative from each met with him from time to time during the year in a "master circle." The readings were to form the basis for discussion at the next annual meeting.[38]

His versatility notwithstanding, it was on the lecture platform Snedden shone. He was probably at his best when he appeared at the San Diego Teachers Institute during March of 1904. The meetings were heralded as the "most successful in years," with Superintendent Foshay of Los Angeles and Professor Snedden dubbed "the heroes of the occasion." Under the headline "Professor Snedden a Favorite," the San Diego *Sun* lauded Snedden's "earnestness," "frankness," and "his logic combined with many practical suggestions." There he met Leaton Irwin, a visiting school board member from Quincy, Illinois, and their meeting made this institute especially memorable to Snedden. Like many another zealous school trustee, Irwin had at one time been a school teacher himself before turning businessman.[39] He invited Snedden to give a week-long institute at Quincy, and this invitation made it possible for David to attend the NEA convention that year at St. Louis, held in conjunction with the Louisiana Purchase Exposition. In fact, he "did the fair" as Irwin's guest.

The institute at Quincy was a full week of work for Snedden, one to three lectures each day spread over a seven-day period beginning with a keynote address at the Methodist church on Sunday evening. The public was invited to all sessions, and the evening lectures were on general topics likely to be of interest to a non-professional audience. The afternoon sessions were conducted as roundtable discussions and focused upon a different grade level each day. Snedden handled all of the sessions all week by himself.[40] The Adams County teachers had concluded their school term, but contracts were not yet signed for the coming year; it was made clear to them that they were to be present at the institute unless otherwise engaged in summer normal work. At least two-thirds of them were in regular attendance.

Snedden came to Quincy touted as "a thinker," and an "extremely practical and constructive" educator, who would provide teachers with "an unusually valuable week." Quincy was not disappointed. The teachers expressed themselves as "delighted with his practical way of dealing with educational themes." In his opening address, "The Relation of the Public School to the Home and Church," Snedden prognosticated that the school would come to do more and more of what was formerly done in the home because the home had ceased being the influence for good it had once been, especially in the large cities. The program of the school would not be complete "until the whole boy and the whole girl are sent to school for instruction." His concern was especially for "the moral part of their natures" which, to his view, was still all but neglected. He drew upon some of the content of his Stanford address, "Education for the Rank and File," to contrast the authoritarian European classroom with the democratic American classroom where children "learn to think for themselves." This address got the week off to a good start for Snedden. Quincy found "the line laid down showed him to be a man of good modern school ideas" and described his address as "a wholesome, practical talk" from which all came away feeling "much benefited."

For the remainder of the week Snedden brought out and refurbished many of his most popular institute lectures. "Some Phases of the Problem of Education for Citizenship" and "The Practical Side of Nature Study Teaching" were his first and second evening lectures, while "Literature in the Grades" and "Conditions Necessary to Improve Geography and History Teaching" were selected for the morning audiences. He stated his conviction that the schools were making a fad of arithmetic and materially less of it would be required in the future. He also said that high school students should not be required to learn non-essentials when there were so many essential things to be learned. Among the many "practical ideas" with which Snedden delighted his Illinois audience was one that called for an ungraded room in each building "where the misfits of all rooms should be sent to the great relief of all the teachers." The "misfits" were not necessarily limited to incorrigibles, but also might include the brighter pupils who wished to advance to the grade ahead and slower pupils who had fallen behind through illness. His solution to the problem of scheduling new subjects into the school program, particularly manual training, was the same one Keyes had inaugurated at Throop Institute in Pasadena — enough intellectual material in the forenoon for the whole day and the afternoon "devoted to the manual arts and . . . building up the health of the child in various ways."

As the week wore on, Snedden merely gained greater hold on his audience. Thursday, the day he questioned the value of Latin and mathematics, his talks were "most enjoyed." The newspaper said, "using the most simple and direct language" Snedden "adapts himself to his audience." On Friday he became petulant. He criticized the Quincy salary structure for paying a higher salary to upper-grade teachers than to those teaching in the lower grades. He advised the teachers that where desks were uncomfortable, as were those at the high school, "parents should be made uncomfortable" and he observed that it was criminal "to require children and teachers to go up three flights of stairs." Always the advocate of good physical development, he advised, "children who cannot be induced to play should be turned over to the school physician." [41] As for the curriculum, he found "a good deal of rubbish in grade and high school programs"; the colleges were replacing Latin and Greek with other studies and the teachers could draw their own conclusions.

On Saturday evening Snedden concluded the series at the Luther Memorial Church with an address, "Advantageous Features in Various State School Systems," and on Sunday he and his host, Leaton Irwin, were off to the St. Louis Exposition.

The following fall Snedden included in his repertoire of lectures one entitled "Observations of the St. Louis Exposition." It was received by enthusiastic audiences at Auburn, at Weaverville, and at Yreka City. He had come away from the Exposition much impressed by the industrialization of Japan, Germany, and the United States — industrialization which he felt placed man in a position subordinate to the machine. He observed that America was clearly ahead of the rest of the world in agriculture because the American farmer had become a scientist. He also noted that manual training had been prominently displayed in the educational exhibits of all the states. Tying together these two observations, Snedden could see how important it was that "the education of the next generation be as much of the hands as of the head. . . ."[42]

California understood well the promises of the manual training movement. When San Luis Obispo was selected as the site for the newly created California Polytechnic Institute, the local teachers institute went on record to "hail with joy the fact that very soon the boys and girls of our state may be taught useful arts and trades without the necessity of being first committed to reform institutions." The teachers recommended that all the "engineering, brickmaking, and stone quarrying . . . incident to construction of the buildings and decoration of the grounds" be performed as far as practicable as part of the industrial education of the students.[43]

One of Snedden's most popular and most frequently used institute lectures was entitled "Recent Educational Experiments and Their Significance." This talk was based on Albert Shaw's article about Hampton Institute in the *Review of Reviews* of April, 1900. His emphasis was upon the "high degree of efficiency" attained by the individual educated under a program that combined vocational work with "cultural" work. Snedden made Dewey's laboratory school at Chicago an example of his belief that "the best cultural education comes in connection with a vocational line of work." "Dr. Dewey," he said, "believes that every child is deeply interested in some industrial line of work and all other interests should grow out of occupations." Therefore, by Dewey's example, the child's education should be built around "the subject or work of most interest to the child." "Education is to make men efficient," he said, and for Snedden this was "the fundamental idea of education" as early as 1903. Because the home could not give "the scientific knowledge . . . essential to this age of progress," it must become the special job of the school.[44]

Another of his institute lectures, "The Influence of Recent Economic Changes in our Educational Ideals and Standards," also related social efficiency aims to the program of the schools. This address, more so than any of the others, was repetitious of his Stanford commencement address of 1900. He saw the competitive system in industrial economics giving way to a more cooperative one. Relating school problems to business efficiency, he said, "the great secret of business success is to so calculate energy expended that it may yield greater returns." Applied to education he made the modification necessary to social efficiency by calling for an estimate of "the lasting value of each subject of study . . . [to] determine how much time and thought ought to be devoted to its development." If the teachers worked cooperatively at this task more "practical education" would accrue, and Snedden hoped more industrial schools would follow as a result.[45]

The *Educational Review* of December, 1903, carried a short article from Snedden's pen which seemed to represent his continuing concern for the kind of flexibility he had urged in his master's essay. The article, "The Six-Year High School," made a strong case for election by course after the sixth elementary year. The terminal course, in his plan, was to include some manual training or technical work in the last two years; the course for those who would continue on to high school was to incorporate mathematics, beyond arithmetic, and foreign languages as substitutes for several of the studies ordinarily pursued. His argument for a more practical terminal course was based on the claim that it would more adequately meet the "social needs" of the community. He maintained that differentiation, based on destination, in the elementary school would tend to lessen the heavy dropout rate from the high school. Students coming from the preparatory course of the elementary school would be more likely to accept the increased difficulty of the high school subjects.

With the beginning of the 1903–4 school year Snedden was promoted to the rank of assistant professor. The *Stanford Quad*, the student yearbook, that year caricatured him with a quotation from Chaucer: "Nowher so besy a man as he thar n'as. And yet he semed besier than he was." It is likely the student editor was not fully aware of the new assistant professor's many responsibilities. His salary, modestly increased to $1,350 for the academic year, was augmented that year with $500 in fees from institute work, and not the least of his responsibilities centered about the work of the California Teachers Association.

At the December meeting, the California Teachers Association appointed Snedden chairman of a Committee of Seven on School Revenues and Salaries and a member of the Committee on Preparation of Teachers. He prepared both reports. In the report on school revenues Snedden concluded the profession was unable to retain male teachers because the best salaries, $2,000 to $2,500 per year, offered little opportunity for a man to build a house, raise a family, and acquire some financial independence. In the report on the preparation of teachers, he charged departments of education were too concerned with the development of professional culture but not with "practical efficiency." [46]

During 1903 Snedden had also been appointed to the Committee on the State Reading Course. Although the chairman, Kate Ames, the Napa County superintendent, prepared the annual report of 1904, it was quite different from her 1903 report and bore certain distinct marks of David Snedden. The purpose of the reading course was now to set "the standard of efficiency"; she soberly confronted each of her fellow superintendents with "the fact that the efficiency of his staff [would] not rise above the standard set for it." The "standard" was the "check" imposed on daily work when it was criticized by reading.[47]

The California Teachers Association met in convention at San Jose in 1904. Snedden was almost the man of the hour. He was appointed to a committee on the supervision of rural schools and named chairman. He submitted his reports on the preparation of teachers and on the distribution of school revenues, and he participated in the presentation of committee reports on the reading circle and the teachers institutes. At this meeting, too, Snedden was named to the exclusive fifteen-member Council of Education to fill the remaining two years of the unexpired term of one A. E. Shumate. In a paper before the Manual Training and Drawing Teachers Association, in session concurrently with the state asociation, he said: "The best work of our age is that which is dominated by the tendency toward specialization. . . . The division of labor is the key to modern efficiency." [48]

Jacob Riis was the featured speaker at the convention. His message, "What Is It That Makes True Americans?", argued for manual training and cooking classes, boys' clubs, and athletics, as means of mitigating the influence of the slum. Riis was concerned about the "mountains of despair," "sin," "drunkenness," and "inefficiency" found there. His personal plea was for "schools, not jails."[49] Snedden may have found special inspiration in his words, particularly in the demand for schooling that would encompass more of the practical life objectives in education. Though he did not know it then, within the year he would be back at Columbia to pursue the doctorate, but not in teacher education, the field in which he had been working at Stanford, or in the prestige field of educational administration, his area of work for the next ten years. He was not even to resume investigation of the social phases of education with Samuel T. Dutton. Rather, Snedden would investigate the educational arrangements of the reform school under the direction of the greatest social worker of them all, the man to whom Riis himself looked for leadership, Edward T. Devine.

Until the early summer of 1905 and the return of Ellwood Cubberley from Columbia with his own Ph.D. degree, Snedden had no thought of continuing his academic pursuits. He had established himself in California where he was a popular and sought-after lecturer. His term on the California Council on Education would not expire until December, 1906, and he had been appointed by the State Board of Education to the Advisory Board of the *Western Journal of Education*. During the 1904–5 school year he and Genevra had built their first home, at Amherst Avenue and College Terrace, on a piece of property conveniently abutting the Stanford campus; and now, even before it was entirely finished, when they had just moved in, they were to leave it.

When Cubberley returned from Columbia, he took a pleasant but firm position concerning the professional preparation of his staff. He informed Snedden that a man lacking the doctorate "could not indefinitely be acceptable" on the faculty of Stanford's department of education.

David had the opportunity to move to another school. Isadore Dochweiler, who had preceded him as the first baccalaureate graduate of St. Vincent's College, urged him to join the faculty of the San Diego State Normal School. Another old friend and one-time school superintendent of Ventura County, Samuel T. Black, was president of the San Diego institution, and it was hinted that upon his retirement Snedden would replace him in that post. After giving some consideration to the offer, David decided to acquiesce to Cubberley's demand at the earliest possible date, though he personally had little interest in the higher degree. He requested leave for the 1905–6 school year and began making arrangements to return to Teachers College. The year just past had produced a good many outside lectureships in addition to a summer session appointment at nearby San Jose State Normal School and two teachers institutes early in September. He had money enough at least to begin the school year. He was confident that once at Columbia some type of financial assistance would be available to him.

David spent most of the summer cramming French and German in anticipation of the language requirements he would have to meet at Teachers College. The house, the fresh bloom of newness still about it, had to be rented to cover the monthly payments due the building and loan association. David and Genevra divided their savings equally between them, and Genevra took the children, three of them now, to Pacific Grove where living expenses were low and old clothes the order of the day. When their funds were depleted, it was agreed Genevra and the children should go to the Snedden ranch in the Lockwood Valley and wait there for David to return. Once again this profession based upon dedication and service brought the Sneddens moments of insecurity and an unexpected change in the regular routine of life. When he left California David Snedden fully expected to return to the house on College Terrace within the year and to take up his Stanford professorship, but this was not to be.

At Teachers College, David sought out Professor Dutton and was appointed his teaching assistant for the year. He was also asked to teach a course in educational administration, and the income from both positions helped finance his year of doctoral study.

Teachers College was generous, too, in its appraisal of Snedden's academic status. It granted him credit for several of the courses he had taught at Stanford and in so doing made it possible for him to compress the work of his doctoral program into a single year, though it was a year that afforded him few moments of leisure. There are seventeen semester courses on his transcript for that year: three semesters with John Dewey, including one semester of Social Life and School Curriculum and a full year of Psychological Ethics; two full-year courses with E. L. Thorndike, The Application of Psychological and Statistical Methods to Education and the advanced course in Genetic Psychology; a course with Edward T. Devine, The Application of Psychological and Statistical Methods to Education, given in the department of social economy; and a course with Franklin Giddings in Statistics. In the selection of his program it appears that Snedden intended to put to good use his recognized ability as a mathematician. Philosophy of Education with McVannel, Administration of Public Education with Dutton, and Foreign School Systems with Richard Charles Russell made up the remainder of the program.[50]

His association with Dutton remained cordial, both socially and professionally. During the year Snedden agreed to join him in the preparation of a text in educational administration to supplement his earlier book, *School Management*. However, for his doctoral program Snedden chose to work under Edward T. Devine.

Devine was from Iowa. He was a graduate of Albion Seminary and Cornell College at Mount Vernon and taught Greek, Latin, and German in the seminary at various times during his collegiate career. After graduation he gained considerable experience in public school work as a principal successively at Albion, Marshalltown, and Mount Vernon. He left Iowa in 1890, after taking the master's degree at Cornell College, in order to work under political economist Simon Patten at the University of Pennsylvania. He earned the Ph.D. degree there in 1893 and served for the next three years as secretary of the American Society for the Extension of University Teaching.

In 1896 Devine was appointed general secretary of the Charity Organization Society of New York. It was as the executive head of the society that he was appointed, also, the first director of the New York School of Philanthropy upon its establishment in 1904. The following year he took on still another teaching responsibility as the occupant of the Jacob H. Schiff Chair in Social Economy at Columbia University. Thus David Snedden was one of his first students at Columbia. Devine was editor of *Charities and the Commons* and probably the most informed person in America on all phases of the social work movement. Jacob Riis, Ida Tarbell, Jane Addams, and William H. Allen were among his intimates, colleagues, and co-workers.

David Snedden's dissertation, "Administration and Educational Work of American Juvenile Reform Schools," was prepared under Devine's supervision and ultimately submitted to the faculty of philosophy for the doctor's degree. It was a scholarly presentation and represented his major work of the year.

The roots of Snedden's interest in this facet of education are not altogether clear. Perhaps Albert Shaw's expressed faith that "by all odds the finest, soundest, and most effective educational methods in use in the United States are to be found in certain schools . . . for young criminals in reformatory prisons,"[51] gave Snedden the challenge to pursue this study. Or perhaps it was the prevailing opinion of his immediate colleagues, as expressed in the resolution of the San Luis Obispo teachers citing reform school education as preferable to the common school because it offered manual training. His interest may have been stimulated by Jacob Riis's talk at the convention of the California Teachers Association the previous December, although Snedden did not take Riis's view that the improvement of the total environment — all agencies of education — was necessary to mitigate the conditions of the slums. Instead, Snedden focused on but one educational agency — for him the primary agency to which the others would gradually relegate their own educational functions — the school.

Snedden took the position implied by Shaw and by the San Luis Obispo teachers that the reform schools offered a superior education and public school men might look to them with profit. As examples of the ultimate in social control and of an educational program disciplined to the standards of social efficiency, there is little doubt that this group of schools offered features compatible with Snedden's thinking.

Harr Wagner had editorialized in the February, 1905, issue of his *Western Journal of Education* that the public school was "the best expedient which preventive penology [had] yet devised to keep children out of reform school." Snedden probably reasoned that if the school were to serve this larger function the work of the reform school might well be a subject of study. He expressed the belief that "the work undertaken by these institutions . . . represented more fully the idea of state education than the work of any other part of the educational system." In these schools he found "the entire round of educational effort" represented, including those phases of education ordinarily carried on by the home, the church, and the shop. He presumed all public school people would soon become equally concerned about this larger view of education, as the home and church came to relinquish more of their responsibility. The public school, he thought, was at fault for having "failed largely to cooperate with and learn from juvenile reform schools."

For the pupil in the reform school the home had already broken down completely and the school had to provide the total educational effort. Faced as it was with the task of reshaping the "warped" character and mind, the reform school represented to Snedden an ideal of social control in the work of the schools. He considered the best program one in which the youthful offender received a minimum sentence of two years, the time necessary to earn seventy-three hundred of the school's "credits." Failure to live up to standards set by the institution resulted in loss of credit and accordingly extended the sentence. Here was a system that provided the ultimate of control, and Snedden was unrestrained in his praise of it. He gloried: "every hourly act, every faithfully executed task or lesson, contributes to this end (release) or withholds the child from it. The result is a system of control which, for persistence and effectiveness, has no equal in the majority of cases; and which seems to contribute most effectively to character-building."

The dissertation offered little that Snedden had not said before, usually to audiences of California teachers, but it provided him the opportunity to more precisely identify his position on control in education and to explore educational arrangements for classification of pupils based upon their supposed "needs." He viewed education, more than ever, as a kind of "treatment" rather than the transmission of the cultural heritage. With this view, industrial education and moral education assumed major importance in the treatment of the normal as well as the reform school pupil.

Snedden's concept of the total educational program was divided into four categories: physical education, moral education, vocational education, and school or literary education, the latter being the traditional fare of the schools and the category he gave the least attention. His dissertation devoted forty-eight pages to vocational education, thirty-six to moral education, and a sparse six pages to literary education.

He found the physical education of the reform school much broader in scope than that usually taught in the public schools of the day. The reform school pupil was acknowledged to be, in most cases, healthy but in need of "nurture and cleanliness." For this reason, gymnastic work had a small place in reform school physical education, which was more concerned with "regular physical work," "regular rest," and "instruction in hygiene and counteracting certain habits of vice."

Snedden viewed the moral education given in the reform school as especially interesting because "the entire responsibility devolves upon the school" and in a sense "character-forming and moral education are the chief work of the school." He had acknowledged "little is known of the methods and means of moral education," and perhaps in consequence, he took some interest in identifying those techniques employed in the reform schools. The practices they had worked out empirically suggested to Snedden useful techniques of social control; that these techniques had to be developed in this way did not bother him. He reasoned, "moral and industrial efficiency . . . is very complex and almost incapable of measurement." For Snedden, "efficiency" was at all times the goal of education, but he never permitted himself to become involved with efforts to measure the extent of efficiency achieved.

Literature was taught in the best of these schools in the way he had suggested before California audiences that it should be taught, for "moral development"; and he urged that librarians, as highly skilled as teachers of music and art, be sought to provide the right kind of material. Content alone was not enough if literature were to be useful for purposes of control; in addition the teacher must select material intellectually digestible to the child and likely to interest him.

In the reform schools the traditional school subjects occupied about four hours each day, leaving substantial time for industrial education. Snedden repeated his belief, expressed at Quincy two years earlier, that the public schools would also eventually find this system advantageous. The content of "literary education" in these schools was limited to the minimum essentials in reading, writing, spelling, and arithmetic with some "opportunity for self-expression" in music, printing, and letter-writing. He asserted that the value of the literary subjects unquestionably lay in their disagreeable nature and the self-discipline involved in their mastery contributed to the formation of character, to "fitting for independent adult life." He felt that these subjects "must be forced on all pupils alike under any circumstances. . . ." He also noted that children committed to the reform schools seemed to produce especially high-grade penmanship and he came to believe this was an identifying characteristic of the "class" found in these institutions, a class possessing special talent for mechanical and imitative work.

Snedden considered the system of classification used in juvenile reform schools to be their "most powerful instrument of moral education," and invariably productive of good results. It prevented contamination of the less hardened and less mature, adjusted discipline, freedom, and educational needs to groups of differing character, and became a "moral stimulus" in those schools where one cottage was designated an "honor cottage." He offered as the ideal form of classification one that separated children "according to the necessities of moral education, as in the case of physical disease, those most likely to be sources of contamination . . . at some distance." In applying this system to the organization of the public school Snedden thought the few ungraded rooms already established were steps in the right direction. He called for more sweeping systems of classification "according to dullness or aptness, . . . good or bad moral character, . . . [and] strong interest in school education." With the introduction of more industrial work into the schools he would introduce special forms of classification according to talent and interest, after the example of the reform schools.

Perhaps recalling his own use of the Stanford workshops, Snedden urged manual training in the reform school for its sedative and moralizing influence. At this time, too, he claimed it had a special usefulness as the basis for all trades, a position he would soon repudiate. According to this argument it provided "concrete experience" and had value even for those who were incapable of learning a real trade. He deduced that many of the boys committed to reform school seemed permanently destined to fill the ranks of unskilled labor. The problem of providing adequate industrial education for girls remained to be solved; few available jobs were appropriate to "this class of girl."

Snedden held out the hope of rendering unnecessary the work of the reform schools through adoption of their practices by the public school. The failure of the public school, as he put it, was that it neither made an effective appeal to its pupils nor sent them forth into society equipped for usefulness. He put forward industrial education as the means of correcting both of these failures and for the moment accepted manual training as "the beginnings of something of this direction."

In an article entitled "The Public School and Juvenile Delinquency" for the April, 1907, number of Nicholas Murray Butler's *Educational Review*, Snedden attempted to relate the work of the public school to the reform school. He believed the "two systems" needed to be brought together to provide "the treatment most appropriate to each class" and so that each institution could profit by the experience of the other. The public school, he thought, would benefit most from this contact, particularly as it appropriated from the reform school's store of experience with industrial and moral education.

Full enforcement of the compulsory attendance laws implied to Snedden "the location and control of all children of school age," and with the cooperation of the juvenile court they could serve to bridge the gap between the day school and the reform school. The court might well become the coordinating agency for the special schools or rooms which should be established "to provide for the children who do not fit the graded school system." He thought the present situation was wasteful, even harmful, because of the excessive division of function among the various unrelated agencies. His solution was centered in the public school.

From his doctoral dissertation, Snedden gained insights he would find useful in developing his own program of education for social efficiency. He believed the reform schools had already discovered that some children could become skilled workmen and others would forever remain in the ranks of the unskilled. They had discovered, too, that "the most potent means both of discipline and of education is work which is vocational in character," and by this reasoning he prognosticated "we shall go to the reform schools for their experience."

Classification was the second area of reform school experience Snedden believed public school people might appropriate to their advantage. According to him, the reform school had gone much more fundamentally into the program of grouping children for educational purposes. For Snedden "the group" was the unit of consideration and the individual who broke the "unity of the group," be he a "moral, mental, or physical misfit," claimed too much of the teacher's energy with little benefit to himself. He was especially concerned with that class of children whose parents were laborers and unable to exercise "adequate control over them." Snedden charged these were the children who were frequently truant and often suspended from the public schools, and for them classification promised a means toward "the most appropriate treatment." He concluded, "Society has a right to demand from parent and school an accounting for every child committed to their charge."

Snedden had his dissertation completed before the deadline date of April 1, 1906; but degree requirements demanded that it be submitted in published form, and after a year in New York he lacked the necessary funds. When he finally managed to secure money enough to cover his printing costs, he was faced with a printers' strike and the degree was not officially granted until 1907.

Chapter IV

PROFESSOR OF
EDUCATIONAL ADMINISTRATION

"I grind out some stuff each day but the time flies fearfully," wrote David Snedden in March of 1906 to his young wife in California. His dissertation was still his major concern, and he had resigned himself to spending the summer in New York, if necessary, to finish it. Nonetheless he was feeling keenly the loneliness born of the year-long separation from his family.

In this same month of March, Dean Russell and Professor Dutton asked Snedden to consider remaining at Teachers College as a member of the faculty. He would teach certain courses in educational administration for Dutton and assume the major burden of the course in European School Systems. The offer appealed to him, but throughout the month he remained apprehensive over his prospects of getting the job. He wrote his wife, "I have suspicions that the Dean has more than once had schemes for additions that have been turned down by trustees or superior bodies and I am not sure but that my case will go similarly, even if he is willing. . . . I do not know what is coming." During the year he had come under the spell of the city. Its "million of lights," viewed from his apartment window — "whole sides of apartment houses, streets extending far across Brooklyn and Queens, . . . moving elevated trains and steamers up the sound" — all fascinated him. The power of the city, under whose lights "flourish nearly everything of good and bad, enjoyment and suffering, that any city in the world can show," left its sobering and somewhat overwhelming impression upon the man who had come to it from sparsely settled California. He would be able to live in New York and draw stimulation from this great city.

During the spring semester, David Snedden and George Strayer were selected by Teachers College to join the tour of southern educational institutions sponsored annually by Robert Ogden, whose wealth flowed from the operation of Wanamakers' New York store. Ogden had a strong philanthropic interest in Hampton and Tuskegee institutes and in providing educational opportunities for the South in general. These interests had led to the establishment of the Southern Education Board, an endeavor that brought him into association with Albert Shaw, Walter Hines Page, Edwin Alderman, Philander P. Claxton, and others usually identified with the social service purpose in education. The annual tours, conducted by special train, began in 1902. The 1906 tour took Snedden to Cincinnati, where Charles W. Dabney's pioneer efforts in cooperative vocational education were gaining the attention of the nation, and to agricultural colleges in the South, both Negro and white. The trip afforded him the opportunity to become better acquainted with Edward T. Devine, under whom he was doing his dissertation, and to obtain data on juvenile reform schools for his study.

When his appointment to the Teachers College faculty was approved, it was as adjunct professor of education with a three-year contract at a salary escalating from $3000 to $3600 in the third year. Stanford had offered him $1850 as an assistant professor upon his return. His total income during his last full year at Stanford had been $3000, but $1400 of it had come from lecture fees. According to the terms of his Columbia contract there would be no lecturing; instead the time was to be devoted to developing his courses.

In accepting the appointment, David agreed to spend two summers in Europe, at University expense, to gain experience for the course in European School Systems. He taught the summer session of 1906 and left on August 15 to spend two months in England and Scotland. There he met Professor John Finley, a former student of Wilhelm Rein at Jena and the head of the department of education at the University of Manchester, and Patrick Geddes, Scotland's famous social worker and city planner.

While David was abroad, Genevra brought the family from the Snedden ranch in California to a fourth-floor, walk-up apartment at 120th Street and Morningside Avenue East which he had engaged for them before he sailed. She took full advantage of this opportunity to travel. After the usual wagon trip to the railroad at Bakersfield, she and the children went north to Vancouver, across Canada to Montreal, and from there to New York — most of the way by tourist sleeper. With characteristic apprehension for the future, David had wanted the family to locate in a boarding house, at least for the first year. He said he was not sure how well he would do in an eastern university. However, Genevra had faith in his ability and insisted upon more permanent quarters.

When he returned from Europe in October, David found the apartment comfortably though economically furnished, and as in all of their subsequent moves, he was able to enjoy his evening meal at his own table on his own linen and plate the first evening in his new home. Genevra had handled all of the details with her usual deft touch.

Before leaving for England, Snedden had been appointed to the editorial committee of *Kindergarten Magazine and Pedagogical Digest*. The October, 1906, number of the magazine carried an article of observations on school administration in England under the byline of its "staff correspondent" David Snedden. He wrote about England's 1902 legislative change which had abolished local school committees and placed the schools under the local political governing unit. He thought it a sociologically desirable feature of the plan that the school was no longer separate "from police, sanitation, and other public functions which minister to social welfare. . . ."

The previous issue of *Kindergarten Magazine*, that of September, 1906, carried Snedden's first professional contribution as an adjunct professor of educational administration. In "Present Day Problems of School Administration," he identified seven problems and concluded that in almost every case, the solution, the improvement of educational efficiency, would have to await the preparation of professionally trained school administrators. Last, perhaps for emphasis, he cited the administrative problem of providing for industrial education. He considered it "unquestionably the next great advance in American education" from the standpoint of curricular change. "Specious arguments about the traditional functions of public schools" were being used by some administrators, he thought, to delay the movement that was "sweeping" in upon them.

Snedden prepared the article only weeks after Massachusetts' Douglas Commission issued its report in April, 1906. Even as the September number of *Kindergarten Magazine* was going to press, legislation was in process to establish a separate system of industrial schools in that state.

In January, *Kindergarten Magazine* gave Snedden opportunity to address the problem of the terminal pupil in the elementary school. This was the pupil likely to drop out of school sometime between the ages of twelve and sixteen. Snedden believed it was during the last two years of elementary school as well as during the first two years of high school that education had least appeal for the pupil. He said the shortcomings of the schools during these years were numerous, but the primary need was for a differentiated program. Little of what was offered currently had any bearing on "vocational efficiency." The mathematics and foreign language of the traditional program, he said, were of "very doubtful utility" for the children who were soon to become wage earners. He contended parents and children alike expected the school to offer content which would be demonstrably practical to this large percentage of the school population which intended to spend, at most, two years in high school.[1]

Snedden charged that school people were not doing their share to make the school "obviously attractive and profitable." He urged school administrators to make a more accurate diagnosis of the vocational, social, and intellectual needs of the various classes of children from twelve to sixteen years of age. He suggested differentiation in the courses of study "along lines of interest, capacity and probable future career," a pedagogy appropriate to the age level, and cooperation between home and school so that the school official would come to understand "the economic situation of children as it bears on the line of studies they may most profitably pursue." In this way the school program could be made to relate to the student's probable future destination. The vocational education movement itself fit comfortably into Snedden's understanding of the school as an agency of social control with social efficiency as the all-inclusive aim for education.

Snedden had finished his dissertation during the month of March, 1906. He had found much satisfaction in the task and wrote Genevra, "I have a mood for writing and shall go on writing indefinitely I suppose." Triumphantly, the letter was signed "David Snedden, Ph.D."

Snedden's feelings about writing must have been welcome news to Samuel Dutton. After completing *School Management* in 1903, Dutton had projected a definitive work on school administration as a companion volume but had not yet carried out his plan. In promoting Snedden's appointment to the faculty of Teachers College, Dutton was gaining a colleague who enjoyed writing and shared many of Dutton's own views. The time seemed right to begin work on the book, and he invited Snedden to join him as co-author. Though they were to share the profits equally, David expected to do the larger share of the work and looked forward to it. He was "not crowded" now and thought he could devote two or three hours to writing each day. They planned the book during the spring of 1906, and a big book at that, some six hundred pages, two-thirds of which were written by Snedden. The major part of the work was done during 1907, and it was published by the Macmillan Company in 1908.

This book, *The Administration of Public Education in the United States*, enjoyed wide acceptance as a college text for the next twenty years. Some of the chapters are so closely related to Snedden's previous publication and to his doctoral dissertation that they can easily be recognized as his work. The final chapter, "School and Society," was the joint effort of both authors. It viewed the school as the integrating agency of the several different educational institutions within society. In this chapter the school emerges as the agency of social service it had become at Brookline under Dutton's own administration.

For his part, Snedden was particularly proud of the chapter entitled "The Administration of Vocational Education." Here he identified four chief aims of education — physical well-being, moral and social efficiency, personal culture, and vocational education.[2]

He believed the chief objection to vocational education for many people was its tendency "to monopolize all effort of the learner and to become frankly utilitarian." In reaction, educators were attempting to claim as long a period as possible for the purpose of "so-called liberal education." Snedden declared both tendencies were wrong "from the standpoint of the social economy." He cited Hampton and Tuskegee institutes as models for his type of "integral education." While the fundamental aim of these institutions was vocational, "at no point [were] other lines of development ignored." Physical training, "a variety of studies and practices fitting for civic life," and development of "personal culture" through the cultivation of aesthetic and intellectual interests were also emphasized.

Snedden castigated as "remote and unfunctioning" the study of Latin or ancient history for students in the mechanical arts. "Integral education" demanded that educators identify "for each class primarily pursuing vocational studies . . . the social and cultural pursuits which will most effectively function for them." It was his belief that cultural and social education should be related to the special kind of vocational education prescribed for the student.

At this early date Snedden was already urging a separate school for each type of calling. He promised that this arrangement would develop an individual possessed of "greater efficiency," though admittedly it would also emphasize class differences. Snedden conceded America already had too much misunderstanding and lack of sympathy between the various classes; but he was not yet prepared to resolve the dilemma whether or not efficiency should be sacrificed in order to keep the social classes in contact with each other. In subsequent publications he would rationalize the value of a separate system of vocational education in a democratic society and would come to see it as a positive good rather than an admitted evil. Perhaps this chapter had little permanent effect on the development of vocational education in America, but for Snedden it was indeed a presentation that anticipated all of his later work in this field and one he came to consider "prophetic."

In this first year on the faculty of Teachers College, Snedden found opportunity to criticize the teaching of two subjects in the curriculum of the common school, history and mathematics. Using the criteria laid down in his chapter on "Administration of Vocational Education," he brought his familiar arguments — the need to study local environment, to fit the content to the maturity of the child, and to relate history and geography — to his criticism of history as traditionally organized. What was new to his argument was the subordination of history to the "social education" of the child "to make the child a better socius — a more fit member of a complex and largely artificial society." Not only history, but also all of the traditional subjects of the elementary and secondary curriculum must "pass in review . . . with a view to determining not only their actual contributions to the valid aims of education, but also probable changes which should be made in method and content in order to realize the more specific and satisfactory aims of education."[3]

Snedden defined "social education" as "the effective control of native propensities and instincts" of the individual "so as to produce . . . the habits, appreciations, knowledges, and ideals" that would make him a worthwhile member of society. He assured his readers that, though still imperfectly understood, special procedures could produce "habits of social character" and said, "instruction of a particular kind will lead to

social appreciation and knowledge." Relating his new contempt for
subject organization to his position on differentiated education to meet
the "needs" of a particular class, he deduced, "the study of human history as an end in itself is for the elect few only." He continued, "for the
majority of children it must serve as instrumental to some kind of personal or social efficiency."

On the subject of making school studies functional, the adjunct
professor of less than a year did not consider it inappropriate to offer
detailed criticism of Columbia's distinguished mathematics educator
David Eugene Smith. At times Smith was accorded a position in University protocol second only to Dean Russell himself, but this made
little difference to Snedden who was usually affably and irrepressibly
direct. The mathematics educator proposed to relate algebra and geometry by teaching them in alternate time blocks to the same students. In
a letter to Smith, Snedden based his attack upon what he considered
to be a non-functional principle of correlating subjects. He accepted
the correlation of studies only with some reservation, limiting the
organizing center to something that would relate the subject to the
environment and make it "functional." He believed Latin represented
an example of bad correlation because it harassed the child with content from history, archeology, grammar, and English and Latin vocabulary. As presently organized, he found mathematics of no great
educational value — "utterly non-functional" — but conceded that by
giving the student a precise, definitely stated task to achieve, it had a
singular appeal for the learner. He said he was anxious to see mathematics "so developed as to become real and vital in connection with
the mental and social activities of the children who are learning it."[4]

Snedden suggested that isolation should be substituted for correlation and that in so doing educators would be applying the adage
"Divide and conquer." Isolation, as he interpreted it, would make possible direct application of mathematics to practical problems and
"remove the reproach of the non-functioning which now attaches to
the subject." Thus, though rejecting the principle of correlation of itself,
Snedden would use the freedom it afforded to move toward his own
reorganization of the traditional studies relating concrete aims to specific content. He closed his letter somewhat patronizingly, assuring
Smith his projected course was "along right lines."

David also found "class" lines drawn within the teaching profession.
He was sure any kind of course reorganization, to be successful, would

have to be accompanied by a well-prepared handbook, because high school teachers were unlikely to carry a principle to practice. It seemed to him the average teacher was most successful at "the kind of work that one finds in all industrial lines . . . carrying out plans which have been laid down in some detail by the relatively few people who have the native or acquired ability or the time to think and organize." Accordingly, in Massachusetts a few years hence, the teachers manual became his means of imposing course reorganization upon the teachers of that state.

David went back to Europe in the summer of 1907, and Genevra took the family to Lake Morey at Fairlee, Vermont. This second summer Snedden went to Germany as well as to England, traveling part of the time in the company of another young member of the Teachers College faculty, George Strayer. At Jena they attended the lectures of Wilhelm Rein, whom he described in one of his letters to Genevra as a "sort of sociologist." Rein claimed American educators Frank and Charles McMurry, Elmer E. Brown, G. Stanley Hall, and James Russell as his former students. Snedden sensed the famous German educator was imposing a subtle form of recruitment on them and told Genevra that Rein was "a great man as a propagandist." Thoroughly unimpressed, David averred that America was doing more really scientific work than they were at Jena. Moving on to a manual training congress at Stuttgart, he found "nothing in it"; the Germans were far behind, and the meetings impressed him only as being overly emotional.

Ever in search of sociological interpretations, Snedden gave much credit for Germany's apparent success as a rising industrial nation to the "country population" she had made into a city people. This was a population, he believed, naturally endowed with qualities of thrift and a capacity for hard work. The first generation would be all right; but he feared that the second generation, reared in an urban environment, would become "as 'hoodlumish' as the people of England."

In the course of his association with Edward T. Devine, his doctoral advisor, Snedden held a brief membership in the Charity Organization Society of New York and, on occasion, delivered a paper before the national organization. It is quite possible that through this association he first became acquainted with the controversial figure, William H. Allen.

When David Snedden first met him, William Harvey Allen was the general agent of the Association for Improving the Condition of the Poor, New York's pioneer welfare agency. The AICP was quartered in Devine's Charity Organization Society Building at 105 East Twenty-second Street, and this fact alone made it convenient for Allen to serve occasionally as a guest lecturer in Devine's school of philanthropy. For a brief time he was book review editor for Devine's magazine *Charities and the Commons.*

Allen had come to New York in 1903 with a doctor's degree in economics from the University of Pennsylvania where he had worked under Simon Patten, Devine's mentor. Under Allen, the AICP took an active interest in the health of school children and in the expenditure of school funds. Initially, Allen brought the AICP into school affairs to oppose budget cuts leading to the curtailment of vacation night schools, recreation centers, and popular lectures. From this he turned to concern for pupil accounting and became involved in a struggle for the control of child welfare work. In the course of these efforts he thoroughly alienated New York's able superintendent, William Maxwell.

Allen was no stranger to the classroom or to the problems of the school. For two years, early in his career, he had subdued an unruly upper-grade room of the district school at Wykoff, Minnesota. As editor, while at Pennsylvania, of the "Municipal Department" of the *Annals of the Academy of Political and Social Science*, he had publicized an attempt by Erie teachers to win increased salaries through increased property assessments. In New York he found new opportunity to make the problems of the school his own.[5]

Superintendent Maxwell had long been a force for the improvement of "hygienic conditions" in the New York schools. He was credited with the establishment of a staff of school nurses, the introduction of medical inspection of school children, and the supplying of eyeglasses to pupils in need of them. Allen, in turn, promoted the AICP as the agency to which school principals should turn for assistance when it became apparent that a pupil was in need of clothing, shoes, medical care, or better nutrition. The AICP maintained a telephone vigil which Allen said had been used by 115 of the city's principals to report cases of distress during the 1905–6 school year.[6]

Continued friction between the social workers and the superintendent over control of the work led to organization, by the AICP, of the New York Committee on the Physical Welfare of School Children in May of 1906. This committee was under the general chairmanship of C. C.

Burlingham, former president of the Board of Education and something of a figurehead for Allen. The stated purpose of the committee was to gather information and provide resources to the social workers in their struggle with the superintendent. The image Allen wished to create for the committee was that of a "clearinghouse" of accurate statistics about the real needs of the city's school children to support the allegations of social workers and hopefully to protect the workers from the charge of sensationalism.

The committee conducted its investigation in three sub-committees; their reports were prepared within a year. One group examined the homes of fourteen hundred families of children with physical defects. It concluded that the defects were due to home conditions and not confined to any single class or group in society. A second group investigated fifty of the city's school buildings. It concluded that the existing school environment aggravated the physical defects, and in some cases caused them. The two reports supported the position of the third, "A comparative Study of School Reporting," which was intended to show school statistics could be made more useful and more readily available to the social worker. The report was published in New York in 1908 by the Macmillan Company as a volume entitled *School Reports and School Efficiency*. Its authors, David Snedden and William Allen, constituted a committee of two. In publication, each chapter was carefully delineated as the work of either Snedden or Allen.

Edward Devine had found a place for Snedden on the program of the National Conference of Charities and Corrections in 1906. The membership of twelve hundred social workers convened in Philadelphia that year to consider the central theme of "social statistics" — their accumulation, interpretation, and use. Snedden's paper, "Social Statistics as Presented in the Reports of State Boards of Charities," was one of several on this general topic. He called upon the social workers for more scientific description of social phenomena and reminded them that "social bookkeeping" was an important phase of the work of social agencies and state boards. Their reports should be written with the general public in mind, kept compact for the consumption of busy people, and thereby make the most of their publicity potential. They should watch for measurable results growing out of their work and include these data in their reports.[7] To all of this, including the use of reports for publicity purposes, Allen could readily agree, particularly since his own initial orientation to social work was statistical.

In their broader assumption about the function of institutions in society, especially about the purposes and outcomes of schooling, Snedden and Allen potentially had much in common. If their interest in social statistics had not brought them together at this time, it is likely they would have found common cause in the belief that "efficiency" was the means to a better society.

Like Snedden, Allen had been active in trying to inject the discipline of efficiency into educational decision-making. In May, 1905, the New York City Board of Education met to consider the desirability of reducing the five-hour school day for pupils of the first grade. Over a period of the past ten years, overcrowding had made necessary a shortened school day and double shifts in certain schools of the city. Along with most social workers, Allen opposed any reduction in the school day. He argued that a full school day was necessary to keep children from the "vicious" influences of the street and to give the "foreigners" in the city "the longest possible contact with the refining, Americanizing, atmosphere of the school." As Allen viewed it, the five-hour school day was only a compromise, short of "a compulsory recreation center, a compulsory supervision by the city of tenement children for at least five hours daily." In the face of the immediate program, whether or not to reduce the school day to three-and-a-half hours, Allen demanded "facts" — facts about the results of the two systems, facts about scholarship, attendance, spirit, interest, truancy, crime, and health. When Superintendent Maxwell countered that educational results did not easily lend themselves to a "statistical test," Allen labeled this seeming "disdain for business methods" as "demoralizing." [8]

Snedden's chapters in *School Reports and School Efficiency* included "Purposes of Educational Statistics" and "The Beginnings of School Reports in American Cities." The latter was a comparative study of the school reports of various cities and suggested certain economies in school reporting. Allen contributed a short chapter reviewing the past efforts of the NEA for the improvement of school reports and a longer chapter of critique specific to Superintendent Maxwell's 1906 report to the New York City Board of Education.

Only one chapter, "Important Questions Not Answered in Existing Reports," bore the joint authorship of Snedden and Allen. Like the rest of the book, this chapter dealt mostly with pupil attendance and promotion statistics, school cost accounting, and health records. Only one question posed jointly by the two authors — "What evidence is there that school training has prepared children for industrial efficiency?" — foreshadowed an important area of inquiry for the efficiency movement in the years ahead. In the chapter "Suggested Improvement in School Reporting," Snedden briefly returned to this question by noting that beyond attendance records and records of promotion "the public possesses no means of ascertaining whether the work of the system is worthwhile or not."[9] Here Snedden worried about the student who complied with the compulsory education laws but nonetheless could see no value in his schooling. Not many years hence he would use this pupil stereotype to justify the need for an efficient curriculum, practical and specific in aim and content.

The book was well received in most quarters. United States Commissioner of Education Elmer E. Brown wrote Snedden that it was the sanest criticism of school statistics he had ever read.[10] The San Francisco *Chronicle* of April 19, 1908, applauded the "admirable methods of sociological investigation" outlined in the book, and the Cincinnati *Inquirer* of April 6 entered into the spirit of the report by declaring it identified those facts "school boards should demand of a superintendent in order to decide as to his fitness for his post; and what the taxpayers have a right to demand of boards of superintendents in order to judge whether the school system they are supporting is up-to-date and efficient. . . ." In *School Review* the following December, F. A. Manny of Western State Normal thought the tone of Allen's demands "somewhat destructive," but he commended Snedden as "a sane and able schoolman" who lent the work an "impression of constructive rather than merely negative criticism."

It seems evident that in the summer of 1908 Allen was anxious to launch an extensive study of school administration and wanted Snedden to join him in the project. Snedden declined, giving as his reason the desire to retain his ties at Columbia University. Though both men could find much agreement in what they considered the proper aims and purposes of schooling, Snedden found Allen personally "a nice fellow at a little distance." Informed of Manny's comments in *School Review*, he confided to Genevra, "part of the book deserves a bad review. . . . The better part will not suffer in the process."

When Simon Patten came to New York later in the summer, Snedden fancied Allen had given him a favorable introduction to the famous political economist. After a two-hour walk along Riverside Drive with Patten, who also had drawn upon Ross's doctrine of social control, he said he had had "a fine intellectual feast." Snedden seems to have been serious in his intention to "keep a little distance," for even though both he and Allen spent most of their lives in the same city they never again collaborated.

David felt a great urgency about his writing during the summer of 1908. He wrote Genevra, "As far as I can see ahead, though the years I'll have writing to do." With Genevra and the family off to Lake Winnepesaukee in New Hampshire for the summer, David remained in New York, teaching in the summer session and preparing two papers for the NEA convention at Cleveland. The year 1908 saw publication of three books bearing his name in addition to several articles and book reviews for Butler's *Educational Review*. Besides giving two papers, he also appeared twice as a discussant at other sessions of the convention and at this point seems to have hit full stride as one of the bright young men of Dean Russell's faculty.

John Remson Bishop, scholar of Sanscrit and classical philology with a doctorate from the University of Cincinnati, was among those at the Cleveland convention who called for a reorganization of the conventional program of studies. He told the NEA that if Latin and Greek were unable to show sufficient intimate relation to present life to give the subject immediate practical interest and value, they must go. He said, "If geometry and algebra cannot relate themselves intelligently to immediate natural interests, some other classification of mathematical facts must and will be found that will do so." At the moment Bishop was principal of Detroit's Eastern High School and actively engaged in editing a volume of Cicero's *Orations*. Addressing "the tyranny called college domination," he urged the secondary curriculum be left "to the skill and conscience of those whose business it is to fashion high school work to the needs of each community which the school serves."[11]

Snedden thought Bishop's an "excellent paper," one to which he could take no exception. As a discussant he sought merely to supplement it by broadening its scope. There were many kinds of education for adolescent youth — vocational, industrial, technical, manual training; all, he thought, were deserving of the title "secondary." The time was right, he said, for the American schoolmaster to assert himself, to "break loose from traditional lines," to "cut loose from college domination and all other dominations."

In his own papers before the convention, Snedden related the supposed "demand" for a six-year high school to the European practice of differentiation at age twelve or earlier. He considered the last two years of elementary school and the first two years of high school the "weakest point of American education" and urged differentiation for school leavers during this period. Significantly, these were the grades with which he had personally gained most of his teaching experience in his native California. He felt that during these years the traditional fare of the public school neither interested nor satisfied the needs of the student who often left school at sixteen, either for reasons of desire or economic necessity. Under his plan identical work for all would be provided only in English, history, and geography; over the remainder of the program students might choose from parallel courses in commercial subjects, agriculture, household arts, or industrial arts differentiated so as to serve the dominant types of local industry, as alternatives to the traditional academic course.[12]

Snedden assumed school leavers came from the "wage-earning classes" for the most part and said they made up a large part of the high school population.[13] If provided with a special differentiated program of studies, including vocational education, he hoped they might be induced to remain in school. They would then be available for what he called the most vital teaching, one or two hours of "the right kind of study" that would accomplish more in the way of cultural and civic training than the conventional school offerings. He envisioned the only problem as one of making "the most effective adjustment possible between it [vocational education] and that measure of liberal education which is possible for each considerable group of children." He cautioned that the small amount of liberal education people seemed able to appropriate should not be "sacrificed on the altar of demand for vocational education."[14]

Snedden was not completely satisfied with *The Administration of Public Education in the United States*, his book with Dutton. It had been a "quick" book; but, as he told Genevra, it was "as good as they could do for the present," even if they had had "three months to do it." The book he felt he must get underway, the one he believed to be his "chance for a fresh field," was going to be called "Educational Sociology," a term not yet connotative of a separate branch of study.[15] Although this book was often delayed and did not appear until 1920, his plan for it at this time suggests he had already defined his approach to the solution of educational problems. In the intervening years his utterances more and more bore the stamp of the educational sociologist rather than the professional school administrator.

Snedden came to look upon educational administration as the means of achieving his sociological purposes through manipulation of the total school program, and he was already a practicing educational sociologist. His public utterances during the fall of 1907 through the spring of 1909 made frequent reference to the "teachings of social economy" and by implication one would conclude he saw himself as a social economist. He was especially concerned about what he came to call "cultural education" for fear it would be overwhelmed by the growing enthusiasm for vocational education. In his writing and in speeches before audiences of interested teachers he set out a broad program for the reorganization of the curriculum of American secondary education. It was a program based upon his principle of "differentiation" of education for special groups, one that looked to the subordination of subject matter to cultural, social, physical, moral, and vocational education, all of which were subordinate to the larger aim of efficiency.

Snedden was asked to address the New York High School Teachers Association in March of 1909 as part of their year-long project of curriculum revision. In his paper he purposely chose to use the term "secondary education" because, as he put it, its meaning was broader than merely "high school." He proposed several different educational aims for the "rank and file of the people," but at this time he believed all forms of education should be subordinate to physical education, in the larger sense of the term. Instruction in this area should lead to more than merely athletic skill and should include hygiene and "the kind of knowledge which reacts on physical health."[16] He ranked vocational education as next in importance and "a pressing need." It was the responsibility of the school to fill this need because it was the only agency of the state capable of being compelled to provide the vocational education the home, shop, and farm were incapable of providing. His ideal program continued to be the "integral education" of Hampton Institute. A third field of education Snedden felt should receive more consideration was that which prepared boys and girls for social living and developed their moral character. Snedden included within its bounds somewhat vaguely defined units of civics, ethics, morals — anything through which the individual might be "directly and consciously" given the habits and ideals to fit him for social life. To achieve these ends the logical organization of subject matter would have to yield to a new "pedagogical" organization, a change Snedden termed "momentous."

He found much of the value of the individual subjects to be substantive in nature, useful for the facts they contained. In education for teachers, the vocation Snedden knew best, he felt that there existed a special content to be extracted from the fields of English literature, history of education, applied psychology, and foreign language which would make of the teacher a cultured gentleman and influential citizen accepted in his community. He reasoned literature, poetry, or music were not ends in themselves but simply sources of content calculated to produce the patriotic ideals and proper attitudes necessary to the profession. Pedagogy itself, he said, must be founded upon "the solid ground of fact" about children, society, and method; [17] any given organization of subject matter was subordinate to the utility of its components.

Cultural education, Snedden's fourth kind of education, included most of the secondary school subjects. With increased attention to physical, vocational, and social education, the time remaining to cultural education would of necessity be restricted. In his scheme, cultural education was education for leisure-time activities, and he counseled that the school should never "entirely ignore" this side of individual development, even though it was not aiming solely at producing cultural persons. He believed interest should dictate choice in cultural education and that the schools must come to offer a wider range of elective subjects to serve this purpose. In that way those who liked Greek, few though they might be, could follow their interest, and those who liked physics might follow theirs.[18]

Snedden suggested that some cultural subjects might also serve a vocational purpose, for instance, history, economics, and foreign languages as offered in a high school of commerce, and completely excluded only stenography from this dual function. Greek, branded a "dead" language, did not have a dual function in Snedden's scheme, though physics might when used as a prerequisite for certain vocational lines. He believed that studies in cultural and social education should be related to the vocational course chosen by the student. Only physical education would be offered to all without differentiation except as to sex.

"Vocational instruction means efficiency" and "efficiency means specialization," Snedden proclaimed in giving direction and purpose to his program. Presumably the key to his organization of the school program for efficiency was based upon the kind of flexibility that permitted all subjects of vocational, cultural, social, and physical education to prepare the individual for his particular station in life and vocational calling.

One of the more prominent members of the New York High School Teachers Association in 1908, Clarence Darwin Kingsley, would within the next ten years seek to reorganize secondary education to meet not four but seven functional aims, six of which — health, vocation, worthy use of leisure time, worthy home membership, citizenship, and ethical character — fit comfortably into Snedden's four categories. In his Cardinal Principles Report prepared in 1915 and published in 1918, Kingsley seems to have divided Snedden's social education into citizenship and ethical character and his cultural education into worthy use of leisure time and worthy home membership. Whether he was aware of it or not, Kingsley, like Snedden, was following Herbert Spencer's functional use of subject matter to serve aims based on life activities. It is possible Kingsley appropriated the inspiration for this approach from Snedden's paper before the high school teachers in 1908. Before the Cardinal Principles Report, attempts to reorganize the program of the schools — the Committee of Ten in 1893, the Committee on College Entrance Requirements of 1899, and Kingsley's own Committee on School and College Articulation of 1911 — merely tried to rearrange the existing pattern of subject organization. Life activities aims were new to the education scene in 1918, and Snedden's remarks in 1908 were very much in anticipation of them.

In his address before the New York high school teachers, Snedden also anticipated the comprehensive high school and at this time favored such an institution. The day of the uniform secondary school program was past, he said; Europe was already providing for the needs of different social classes with a variety of secondary schools, but he felt America was moving in the same direction by providing varied educational opportunities within the same school.

Snedden returned to England in the summer of 1909. While there, he addressed the West Riding County Teachers Summer School at Yorkshire and spelled out what he perceived as some of the "modern tendencies" in American education. He identified three major tendencies in the address: the first toward vocational education, the second toward "integral" education, and the third toward the development of a system of educational method. Of the first, he said that America had already accepted vocational education in theory and now only awaited the means, the staff, and the necessary legislation to put it into effect. Part of the appeal of vocational education rested in its having a base in "concrete reality." He said that shopwork, field work, and actual service were the methods of genuine experience most appropriate for "the rank and file of workers," not theory, even the little theory demanded for applied science and applied mathematics. Snedden claimed this program provided a protective shelter for "the less intellectual four-fifths of humanity" from what he called the "relatively unreal" bookishness with which education seemed burdened.[19]

He found justification for vocational education in the purported findings of "the student of social life — the social economist." These findings supposedly showed "the largest factor in the production of the vicious and the incompetent, the criminal and the pauper" to be "incapacity to produce effectively, to work productively." He concluded it was a marked shortcoming of American education that "the only effective school vocational training for the rank and file of workers has been given in schools especially for Negroes, Indians, and delinquents."

The second tendency Snedden identified for his English audience was the movement toward integral education, which he described as education that "takes cognizance of the physical, vocational, moral, and cultural development of the child." Here, too, he rested his argument on the demands of "modern social economy" and promised "physical and vocational efficiency." To achieve integral education, the responsibilities of the several institutions of society — the home, the church, the shop — must be taken over by that institution under the direct control of society itself, the school.

Lastly, he said, education in America was developing a system of method. The method currently in use on the primary level was generally acceptable because it was based upon aims growing out of the study of young children and was little concerned with subject matter; but for the twelve- to eighteen-year-old group Snedden again advocated the development of a "new pedagogy" to meet their needs. This pedagogy, like that for primary children must be based upon specific aims, which would then guide the selection of appropriate ways and means. Solution of the problem would have to await proper identification of that subject matter of "permanent worth" to the "varying classes of pupils." He compared education to medicine and the prescription of the proper academic fare to application of the healing arts and promised such prescription foreshadowed the beginning of "a science of education."

One evening early in November, 1909, David Snedden received an unusual telephone call at his New York apartment. The caller asked to visit him to talk over the school situation in Massachusetts. Snedden had to meet his seminar that evening and the appointment was set for a fairly late hour. With some apprehension concerning so unusual a request and out of caution, possibly stemming from his rural background, David dismissed his seminar early so as to be at home before his caller arrived. The mysterious visitor turned out to be Frederick Perry Fish, a famous corporation lawyer from Boston whose major achievement to date had been a series of corporate consolidations creating the American Telephone and Telegraph Company. Fish had recently been called upon to serve as chairman of the newly organized State Board of Education. He came to offer Snedden the position of commissioner of education for Massachusetts.

The Massachusetts position was looked upon by some as difficult at best. Legislation passed in 1908 created a new Board of Education representing a consolidation of the old board, which dated from the secretariat of Horace Mann, and the Commission on Industrial Education organized in 1906. Massachusetts' concern for industrial education was closely related to its growing concern over the migration of the textile industry to the South and West and to the decline of its agricultural production.

In 1905 Governor William I. Douglas had appointed a Commission on Industrial and Technical Education "to investigate the educational needs of the various industries in the Commonwealth" and to consider "what new forms of educational effort" might be advisable. After a series of hearings, the commission prepared a report that urged the creation of a separate board to supervise the establishment of a system of vocational schools throughout the state. They reported an awareness "of the growing feeling of inadequacy of the existing public school system to meet fully the need of modern industrial and social conditions." The nature of this inadequacy was understood to be based upon educational fare "too exclusively literary in . . . spirit, scope, and methods." In taking this position the commission claimed to align itself with "the broader minded students of education, men who look at their own work in the light of all its relations to society." These men, they said, proposed that the kind of program "used in the education of the feeble-minded, in the reformation of wayward and vicious children at reform and truant schools, and that . . . being used to elevate the colored race in the South" be employed "in preventing as well as curing juvenile delinquency, and in improving the social conditions of white as well as black children." Specifically, industrial education promised the poor "a means of securing earlier and greater efficiency as wage earners, more self-reliance and self-respect." [20] Snedden would find an agreeable climate for his ideas among the proponents of industrial education in Massachusetts.

The schoolmen of the state never really accepted the Commission on Industrial Education which had been created in 1906 following the report of the Douglas Commission. Governor Draper, personally sympathetic to its cause, had urged consolidation of the Commission on Industrial Education with the State Board of Education to form a new board with an appointed "commissioner" as its chief executive officer. This new Board of Education was created in 1909 by an act of the Massachusetts General Court obligating the Governer to appoint to its membership four members from the old Board of Education, one from the Commission on Industrial Education, and four new people. The commissioner was to have two deputies, one specifically to supervise the system of industrial education and the other to look after the interests of the common schools. In editor Winship's estimate, had the old board chosen to exert itself, its many friends throughout the state could have successfully prevented its dissolution; rather, it died through its own disinclination to oppose the consolidation.[21] It is probable that its membership included others who like Winship were proponents of the "new" practical education and this made its position on reorganization ambivalent at best.

Snedden may not have been the first person to whom Fish offered the commissionership. Earlier, possibly in October, he had talked twice to William H. Allen about the position and then he had tried to get Albert Ross Hill, the recently inaugurated president of the University of Missouri.

Either because he was interested or impelled by vanity, Allen talked the matter over with several of his acquaintances. Charles Coffin, chairman of the board of General Electric and a member of the board of trustees of the Bureau of Municipal Research, urged him to accept the position as a chance to improve his status by becoming a policy-maker, but Allen didn't see it that way. He was especially wary of the restrictions a board might place on his freedom of initiative. The Bureau of Municipal Research was gaining a national audience and while some of the trustees were growing restive, Allen, currently executive secretary, thrived on the publicity. He felt the bureau was a better vehicle through which to exercise his influence.

Allen also shared the dilemma of his decision with Jesse Burks of the Philadelphia Bureau of Municipal Research, and Burks in turn talked to Arthur Dean, chief of the division of vocational schools in the New York State Department of Education, about the job offer. Dean was born in Massachusetts, graduated from the Massachusetts Institute of Technology, and until 1908 had spent all but one year of his professional career in the Bay State. He knew first hand the tensions that brought about the consolidation of the Massachusetts educational structure under a single board and he expressed the belief the new commissioner would find his lot extremely trying.[22]

Fish appears to have gone from Allen to President Hill. Hill was a student of Kant; his doctor's degree had been taken in the department of philosophy at Cornell. He was a comparatively young man, a year Snedden's junior, and only in his second year as a university president. The previous summer he had delivered a paper before the national convention of the NEA entitled "Has the American College Failed to Fulfill Its Function?" At that time he concluded American higher education was fulfilling its purpose in the most practical terms.[23] It was he who was reported to have suggested David Snedden's name to Fish.

The position in Massachusetts was attractive to Snedden. He was in the last year of his three-year appointment at Teachers College. When Fish approached Russell about Snedden, the dean had given his blessing. Snedden himself believed at this time his best opportunities were in the field of educational administration and that the Massachusetts commissionership was the equal of any administrative position in the country. The salary, $6500 per year, though not the highest in educational circles, was a substantial increase over the $3600 he was currently receiving at Columbia. This increase in itself was a strong inducement. He had a large and growing family now, the fourth child having arrived in the summer of 1908.

Russell probably thought the move a strategic one for the college as well as one that would contribute to Snedden's development and future usefulness. It was a Teachers College boast that all of her graduates were placed, and many of them very well indeed. Russell took a personal interest in creating this reputation for success, and Snedden in Massachusetts put a Teachers College man in a position of importance in a section of the country where the college had previously placed few men.[24] Then too, Snedden's association with Allen in the publication of *School Reports and School Efficiency* had probably proven embarrassing to the dean in so far as one of Allen's chapters had rankled the New York School superintendent, William Maxwell, with whom Allen had been feuding for years. The chapter, highly critical of the New York City school report, appeared in the context of the book as an application of general principles set down by Snedden. Direct, sometimes vitrolic, Maxwell had pointedly asked Dean Russell why Teachers College kept a man like Snedden on the faculty. Russell had passed the remark along to David without further comment, but the implications for the College's continued good relations with the New York City schools were inescapable. From several points of view, the move to Massachusetts seemed a good one at this time.

Snedden's acceptance of the commisssionership was widely acclaimed in educational circles. Nicholas Murray Butler, in the December, 1909, number of his *Educational Review*, gloated that Snedden was the fourth member of the Columbia faculty to accept an important administrative post in education within a short period of time. The other three were the newly appointed presidents of Dartmouth, Carnegie Institute, and MIT. The *Stanford Alumnus* said the position was "one of the greatest honors" the field of education had to bestow. William H. Allen was very pleased with Snedden's appointment and provided Massachusetts with an extensive introduction to the new commissioner in a long article for the Boston *Herald*. He said Snedden had the ability to inspire confidence and that it was his habit to ask questions and to listen to others. He believed it likely the new commissioner would be guided by the same point of view he was putting forth in his evening class at Columbia. Allen gave Educational Sociology as the course title and said the class considered the part schoolmen might play in the solution of social problems. He described the course as relating child labor, prison reform, sanitation, education of delinquents and defectives, and other causes in the social service movement to the larger area of responsibility of the school. His mode of approach, according to Allen, was to "plan for children in groups and not merely for individuals." [25]

In his journal, Winship predicted Snedden would take some time to fit himself into the position and that immediate and sweeping changes should not be expected. He promised that ultimately Snedden would win his way and gain command of the situation. He came close to being correct.[26]

David Snedden,
June 27, 1890.

David Snedden as a graduate student at Columbia, 1906.

Genevra Sisson Snedden, 1926.

David Snedden at Teachers College, Columbia, 1932.

Clarence Kingsley, about 1912.

The Snedden family at their summer camp at Lake Winnipesaukee, N.H., 1917.

David Snedden on the Snedden ranch, 1935.

Chapter V

COMMISSIONER OF EDUCATION
IN MASSACHUSETTS

David Snedden took office immediately upon accepting the position of commissioner of education for the state of Massachusetts, on November 15, 1909. It was within four days of his forty-first birthday. His classes at Teachers College met on Mondays and Saturdays so it was possible for him to spend the major part of each week in Boston, commuting to New York on weekends until the end of the semester. After January 15, 1910, he spent almost all of his time there, absorbed in his new duties, and returned to his family in New York only at those odd moments when he could get away.

Genevra remained in New York with the family until April, 1910. They moved first to a large, rambling house at Rockport on the ocean. The NEA met in Boston that summer and the big house afforded ample space to entertain guests from New York and California.

In the fall they moved to Brookline, chosen because of the quality of its public schools. By Albert E. Winship's estimate, everything of which the educational world could boast in 1910 — industrial arts, domestic science, school gardening, physical training, playgrounds, swimming "apartments," school baths, "a homelike atmosphere in the schools" — all had been Brookline's for the past quarter of a century. There were two high schools in the community, classical and industrial arts. Snedden chose the classical high school for his children when the time came for their secondary education.

All of the Snedden children had the greater part of their primary

101

education in the home, and Genevra couldn't remember a time during the first twenty years of her married life when she was not actively engaged in teaching one or more of them. While they were in New York, only one of the children took full advantage of Columbia's excellent Horace Mann School. At age eight, without any previous formal training, Olaf had taken a great interest in reading. Genevra taught him writing and arithmetic, supplied him with books, and catered to his interests as they appeared, but, under the advice of the family physician, he had not yet begun to attend school full time. Olaf was supposed to be out of doors as much as possible and spent most of each day in Morningside Park, across the street from the Snedden apartment. During the final year in New York, he had gone to Horace Mann to join the third grade in its daily gym class and the geography lesson that followed.

In September, 1910, two of the children were enrolled at the neighborhood elementary school — Olaf in the fourth grade — and one child received Genevra's expert instruction at home. The following year Olaf was advanced to the sixth grade. Though they attended school intermittently, the children never fell behind and sometimes they skipped a grade.

The Snedden home was rich in educational opportunity and offered a good example of the kind of environment David believed the less fortunate would be provided through compulsory school attendance. Until homework intervened in the later years, evenings in the Brookline home were spent with Genevra reading the childhood classics to the older children. In keeping with David's interest in practical activities, he provided them with a workbench and a set of tools.

At Columbia, David taught most summer sessions and frequently served as a guest lecturer on western campuses between sessions; but when opportunity afforded, and on his annual vacation during the Massachusetts years, he joined his family in New Hampshire. At these times he sought out the most strenuous manual labor, often removing large boulders to level and improve the road to the campsite.[1] Useful work was always a source of pride to him; throughout his professional career, he referred to his chair at Teachers College and to the field of educational sociology as simply "David's work."

In the summer of 1913 Olaf was "boarded out" to a farm family at Elmwood, New Hampshire to learn "farm ways." The Sneddens paid for his board and an additional fee to cover his "instruction and supervision." His host was described as one of the most "enlightened and efficient" farm operators and had two sons who had graduated from an agricultural school. Usually a lover of the out-of-doors and the strenuous life, Olaf managed to talk his father into rescuing him from this ordeal a week ahead of schedule. Olaf's subsequent experience with manual labor and the outdoor life proved more satisfying to him. The summer of 1915, he constructed his own cabin at the Snedden's summer place in New Hampshire. The year the Snedden's returned to New York from Massachusetts he spent twelve months on the Snedden ranch in Ventura County, which he thoroughly enjoyed, and as a Stanford student he frequently made the trips across the country by motorcycle, sleeping out-of-doors at night, even as his father had once traveled about California on a bicycle.

In Massachusetts, Snedden took special pleasure from his membership in the Twentieth Century Club of Boston. Open to both men and women from a wide range of callings, it concerned itself with municipal, social, and civic problems and was considered locally influential. Matters of educational concern received considerable attention, but always in an atmosphere of idealism. One of David's colleagues from the California institute circuit, Ernest Carroll Moore, who had also migrated to New England, to Yale, appeared frequently as a speaker at the Saturday luncheon meetings. He remembered this large and thoroughly congenial group as "a club of causes, new causes and lost causes."[2] Although highly articulate about the value of practical affairs, Snedden nonetheless reveled in this environment of speculative theorizing.

After taking office, Snedden went about the appointment of his deputy commissioners only after considerable delay and presumably much thoughtful deliberation. William Orr was appointed deputy commissioner for general education during February of 1910 and took office March 1. By tacit agreement one of the two deputy commissioners had to be a Massachusetts man. Orr filled this requirement nicely; he came to the job from the principalship of the Springfield Classical High School. He had been at Springfield for over two decades and had won wide respect as head of the science department there for half of that period. In 1897 he had been placed in charge of the high school's newly established evening division; in 1900, when Dr. Frederick W. Atkinson was named commissioner of education for the Philippines, Orr became principal of the high school.[3]

Orr was probably the most likely candidate in the state for the position because of his reputation as a forward-looking educator. Even before the Board of Education had been reorganized, rumor had made him a candidate for some state post. He was ready to move, and it appears that he had been quietly looking about for something attractive during the previous year. When the news of his appointment broke, the congratulatory messages carried with them substantial endorsement of Snedden's leadership. The principal of Hopkins Academy at Hadley, Massachusetts, said he thought Orr would find it a great pleasure to work under a man of Snedden's stature, and Joseph Groce, proprietor of a Boston-based teachers bureau, believed he would find Snedden a splendid co-worker. Atkinson, now president of Brooklyn Polytechnic Institute, told Orr that Massachusetts needed the kind of work Snedden planned to do; but he also counseled that public opinion in Massachusetts was not yet ready for leadership of educational affairs on the state level. In his judgment, Snedden's position would be a difficult one.[4]

Snedden chose his deputy commissioner for industrial education from the circle of friends he had found at Teachers College. David and Genevra's first years at Columbia provided the same kind of informal social life they had enjoyed at Stanford but were never again to find after leaving Morningside Heights in 1910. Their circle of young, congenial faculty members and graduate students included the McMurrys, the Monroes, the Strayers, the Throndikes, the David Eugene Smiths, the Duttons, and one of the graduate students, Charles Prosser and his wife. The Sneddens and the Prossers became close friends, assisting each other in times of illness and exchanging baby clothes as their children grew out of them. When he decided to leave the University in 1910, his dissertation still to be completed, Prosser had seven job offers from which to choose, including professorships offered by two separate departments of Columbia; instead he accepted the appointment to Massachusetts from Snedden.

Charles Prosser was from Indiana, a graduate of DePauw University with a law degree from the University of Louisville. Acclaimed as "one of the noblest and best sons of the Hoosier State" by the Indianapolis-based *Educator-Journal*,[5] he had come to Teachers College in 1908 after five years as a teacher of science and English literature and eight years as city superintendent of schools in New Albany, Indiana. During his two years as a graduate student at Columbia, Prosser was the superintendent of the Children's Aid Society of New York.

The fact that Prosser, like Orr, had been a science teacher did not escape notice by New England schoolmen. Orr's appointment to the principalship of the Springfield Classical High School had at the time been a marked break with tradition, elevating as it did a man of scientific background to a position hitherto reserved to the classicist. Now, with Snedden as executive officer of the State Board of Education also recognized as being in the scientific tradition and both of the deputy commissioners identified with scientific subjects, popular feeling in the state recognized a "distinct departure" from the "old regime" with its strong loyalty to the classics.[6]

After appointing his two deputies, Snedden set about a division of the work in the department. He assigned to Orr the "schools of the less densely settled areas," transportation problems of the small high school, teacher institute work, and supervision of union superintendencies.[7] Prosser, with his legal degree, some business college background, and experience in social work and school administration, was really quite inexperienced in vocational education, the specialty for which he had been hired. However, Snedden gave him full responsibility to develop a comprehensive system of vocational schools within the scope of the broad educational policies established by the commissioner. The special schools Prosser was to establish were intended to serve the population Snedden liked to call "the children of the rank and file."

Snedden reserved the state normal schools for his personal supervision. This was the time-honored responsibility of the chief executive officer of the old State Board of Education. As the first occupant of a new office, he could easily have relegated this duty to a subordinate — perhaps to an agent for normal schools — had he wished to do so. However, the normal schools provided him with an opportunity to put into practice some of his ideas of subject reorganization for functional purposes. It is in his supervision of these schools, rather than in the system of vocational education, that one finds the impress of his creative efforts in Massachusetts. He developed both the system of vocational education and the educational programs of the normal schools along lines of organization first set down in his paper "The Six-Year High School" in 1903.

The experience of these years would develop in Snedden a greater concern for educational programs designed to meet specifically defined vocational goals, a concern logically growing out of his original interest in Herbert Spencer's query, "What knowledge is most worth?" To this end he would attempt to marshall the support of all subjects in the school program through their reorganization to meet the social, physical, cultural, and vocational needs of a truly efficient individual.

Each year in January, the State Board of Education published its annual report. Under the old board it was almost entirely a statistical summation of the year's work. Under Snedden's administration the body of the report took on some of the characteristics of a textbook of educational policy and theory. The *Seventy-Third Annual Report*, published in January, 1910, was still a perfunctory presentation in the pattern of the old reports; Snedden had been on the job only forty-five days, certainly having arrived after the book had gone to press. The *Seventy-Fourth Report*, that of January, 1911, was totally different and unmistakably his own. It called for more effective statistical reporting after the manner of *School Reports and School Efficiency* and urged "flexibility and differentiation" in the upper grades of the elementary school.

Upon entering his new position in Massachusetts, Snedden had made a personal survey of the state's educational system. His report endeavored to evaluate the state of education in the Commonwealth and to set out his plans and recommendations for the future. Always the sociologist in outlook, he based this presentation on the needs and the demands of "modern social economy." He said, "Social economy finds its origin in efforts to cure and prevent such evils and weaknesses in society as crime, vice, ill health, ignorance, poverty, and shiftlessness." The aims of social economy, for Snedden, were identical in many cases to those of popular education. It sought to promote the physical, vocational, civic, and cultural well-being of the child, as did Snedden's four kinds of education. He numbered public-supported education as one of the subordinate agencies of the social economy.[8] Viewed in this way, public education could properly be expanded to include kinds of service not previously recognized as legitimately part of the public school program, including preparation for vocations, health, citizenship training, and opportunities for play and recreation.

He dodged direct responsibility for this impending reorganization of education by claiming the schools were obligated to respond to demands for an expanded curriculum coming from outside of the ranks of professional educators. He alleged that new demands were being made by the general public for a more inclusive program encompassing vocations, civics, hygiene, music, and other topics previously taught in the home, church, and workshop. He cautioned that adding such new content to the school program would likely dilute the teaching of the traditional subjects — spelling, grammar, penmanship, composition, arithmetic, geography, and history — all of which required considerable time and effort. His solution to this dilemma called for "a more organic formulation of the work of the school." By keeping the supervision of the normal schools to himself, Snedden could make them examples of how the schools in general might be reorganized to meet the demands of objectives based upon life-activities. After his first year in Massachusetts, he was able to cite an experiment conducted by two of the normal schools in which hygiene was taught, not as a separate subject, but correlated with certain of the existing subjects and with local activities related to the domestic life of the farm and the community. He urged against special, fragmented courses, and favored reorganization around "a center of correlation" drawn from life.

Other parts of his program for the state called for minimum standards for each grade in reading, penmanship, and the "skills and knowledges" of arithmetic, history, and geography. He urged flexibility in the "interest and appreciations subjects," which he identified as nature study, literature, and manual training. Snedden also called for flexibility in providing alternate courses in the upper grades in the "difficult subjects" to rescue what he believed to be "large numbers of children" detained in the intermediate grades until they dropped out of school. Since he had some doubts about the ability of teachers to organize their own work, probably gained as a member of various California county school committees, he said the state would prepare a teachers manual to detail the reorganization in specific terms.

He realized the normal school was an agency of higher education for young women, quite apart from the vocational education it provided. Aware that the average graduate remained in the profession only four or five years, he believed the normal school could be made an agent of social efficiency whose graduates would receive excellent training for life in the community and the household.

Snedden saw the normal school student as a person of "distinct social limitations" and of "only average capacity for original work and abstract thinking." Too limited to master the wide range of cultural and technical studies the normal school imposed upon her, the student was reduced to a round of frantic cramming, totally lacking in the wholesome physical and social development necessary to the future teacher. His solution to the problem tended to support the establishment of the six-year high school, which he had advocated since 1903; if the six-year plan were adopted, the normal school student would be able to concentrate her time and energies on mastering the content of the primary and intermediate grades only, leaving to specialists the work of grades seven through twelve. He believed a limitation of this kind in the normal school program would make "a considerable step forward in procuring technical efficiency" for its graduates. To encourage social and personal development, Snedden proposed a "cottage form" of dormitory, a system he had seen used in various juvenile reform institutions and which he had already approved in his doctoral dissertation.

During the first year of his administration, Snedden introduced his concept of "flexibility" and "differentiation" into the upper-grade courses of the practice school of the Fitchburg State Normal School. The boys and girls were permitted to choose from among three courses, one providing ten hours per week of manual or household arts, another providing five hours of practical arts and five hours of commercial subjects, and a third permitting the substitution of five hours of foreign language for a like amount of practical arts. All took English, geography, history, music, and drawing as "common elements." The first two courses were intended for the "school leaver," while the third option was provided for those who intended to go on to high school and ultimately to college.

Programs to train teachers of agriculture, household arts, manual arts, and commercial subjects were instituted at the Hyannis, Framingham, North Adams, and Salem Normal Schools, respectively, while the normal school at Westfield, under Snedden's stimulus, was engaged in experimental work to "vitalize science." This latter experiment sought to reorganize the traditional subject matter of chemistry, physics, and biology so as to relate the content of these subjects to the affairs of everyday life, the composition of food stuffs, the preservation of health, and local industrial processes. Snedden also proposed an attempt be made to train elementary school teachers that subjects should not remain in isolation, but rather must be coordinated with the life activities of home, playground, and workshop — activities Snedden termed vital and important. He elaborated upon this viewpoint in 1931 in a small but highly significant volume, *American High Schools and Vocational Schools in 1960*, a book that anticipated some aspects of the life-adjustment movement in education by fifteen years.

In other of his recommendations at this time Snedden proposed fairly extensive changes in the reporting of school statistics so that they would conform to the standards he and Allen had set in *School Reports and School Efficiency*. He believed teacher institute work would be more profitably pursued if organized around a plan of supervised reading, not unlike the program of reading circles he had supervised for the Santa Clara County teachers in 1903. He recommended special ungraded rooms for misfits, as he had elaborated at Quincy in 1904, and enforcement of compulsory school attendance by an agent of the State Board of Education, as he had urged in the *Journal of Education* in 1907. There was little here that was new; he had been advocating most of it for the past ten years.

At the close of his first year in office, Commissioner Snedden spoke to the Massachusetts Teachers Association on "Combining Democracy and Efficiency in Public Education." His message was little more than a restatement of broad guidelines previously established in an article in 1910 for *Education* entitled "Centralized Versus Localized Administration of Public Education,"[9] but his position was far more significant now that he himself was a practicing administrative officer. He left to the lay board of education the privilege of final judgment on the policy laid down by professional specialists. He held it incumbent upon the board to demand of its specialists — in Massachusetts, the commissioner and his deputies — statements of well-defined policy; once these were agreed upon, the board should hold the specialists accountable "mainly for results." To carry out their function, the professional specialists must be given the security of long tenure — Snedden's term was for five years — and control over the subordinates and instruments necessary to execute policy.

Snedden was obviously describing for the schoolmen of Massachusetts the relationship of his new office to the State Board of Education and to the public. It was a relationship the board, under Frederick Fish, found comfortable and one with which Fish concurred.

In his report for the Board of Education, published in the *Seventy-Fifth Annual Report* for the 1910–11 school year, Chairman Fish expressed the entire satisfaction of the board with the two years of zealous and energetic service Snedden, Orr, and Prosser had given the state. The board was looking to its experts not only for execution of policy, "but also to a large extent for the initiation of these policies"; in the office of the commissioner it found both soundness of view and administrative capacity. It seems evident that the program of reform developed in Massachusetts properly belonged to Snedden and his deputies.

In the summer of 1910, Fish delivered a paper before the National Council of Education that could easily have been given by Snedden himself. He predicted the future would see a system of vocational schools, parallel with those of the ordinary type, that would appeal to the probable dropout and hold him another two years. He called for a revision of values so that the schools might provide training to meet "the practical needs of life." Fish also hoped for an early determination of the student's place in life; it would then be a simple matter to provide training specific to the special line of work the student was likely to pursue. Recognizing the enormity of the task of individualizing instruction, Fish fell back upon Snedden's favorite recourse, the identification of the individual with a group of similar destination.[10]

In the *Seventy-Fifth Annual Report*, Fish said that training "in character and efficiency" was the state's major responsibility in the education of its youth. He found the promise of this "superior" kind of training in the state's expanding program of vocational education and in the further development of the normal schools. The normal school graduates must be trained not only to be "effective teachers," but also "to promote to the utmost the physical, mental, and moral welfare of their pupils." These two concerns — the contribution of vocational education and the reorganization of the normal school — made up the body of Snedden's report.

During the course of this year, Snedden had organized a series of conferences with the normal school principals and all members of one department of instruction on each of several successive Saturdays. The Ford Building, where the offices of the State Board of Education were located, had a large parlor ideally suited for meetings of this kind. The Snedden's eldest daughter and the wife of one of the several normal school principals served refreshments each week. These conferences became the vehicle of communication between the commissioner and the normal school teachers through whom he hoped to work his program of reform.

The normal schools were receiving more requests for admission than they could possibly accept, and Snedden believed higher entrance requirements would permit them to eliminate certain of the academic studies from the course. By simplifying the program of studies and limiting teacher preparation to the work of the first six grades, the schools might give the students sufficient time to do their work more thoroughly as well as enough free time for social development. In these conferences Snedden showed considerable concern for the means through which students might be trained to "efficient womanhood," those means which would promote good health and physical development, responsible social values, and cultural and civic interests to help her serve her community more effectively as a teacher.[11] As a result of the conferences, the normal school teachers were also put to work on a course of study for the rural schools of the state and instructed to prepare a set of guiding principles.

Mention of the normal school in the annual report provided Snedden with the opportunity to delineate the distinction between liberal and vocational studies — called "cultural" and "professional" here — which properly divided would produce the efficient person. However, he said, there still seemed to be "considerable vagueness" concerning the procedures and studies to be employed in each type of education. He found comfort in the thought that this problem was not confined to normal schools. Indeed, by his estimate, it was a problem that might well concern both the secondary schools and the liberal arts colleges.

Snedden's major concern at this time, and throughout his subsequent career, was the development of the "efficient" citizen, one whose vocational competence would contribute to his overall efficiency. He believed that this kind of citizen was created through an educational program pointed toward physical, social (moral and civic), vocational, and cultural aims. While the vocational aim was extremely important to him, he gave as much or more space to the cultural aim. Cultural education in his program contributed to the vocational by putting the student's chosen vocation in a larger context of service and making its true significance more understandable to him. Cultural education also contributed to social or civic education by providing the student with worthy avocational interests and understandings that contributed to social sensitivity.

Up to now, his use of the term "vocational education" had lacked clear definition. Frequently in the past he had included all forms of manual activity, including manual training. Now he came to demand "real vocational education," training in the specifics of precisely defined occupational fields, training that would lead to the production of a marketable product. He saw in the immediate future a system of vocational schools parallel to the traditional schools but for the "rank and file" of society.

The portion of the *Seventy-Fifth Annual Report* editor Winship called "the most interesting and the most important section" was prepared by Charles Prosser.[12] It dealt in some detail with the development of a system of vocational schools, his immediate responsibility. Prosser described these schools as "fitting" for industries and adapted to boys of fourteen to sixteen years of age. Abstract or theoretical instruction was found of little worth to these students, for they were assumed to be of a type who learned largely by doing productive work in the shop. The vocational school was a parallel institution to the regular school, but one that "tapped a different school strata."[13] As far as cultural education was concerned, he claimed that the interrelation of mathematics, English, drawing, economics, and civics in shop and classroom resulted in achievement in these subjects fully as great as in the corresponding public school. Prosser reported rapid growth in the number of state-aided vocational schools. From a total of six under the old Commission for Industrial Education in 1908, the number of schools had increased to twenty-one in the first full year of his administration and to forty in the present school year, 1911–12.

The vocational program for pupils over the age of sixteen had not yet been worked out to Prosser's full satisfaction. He thought the best solution lay in "fitting for more efficiency in the actual work of the calling" in a school situation operated as closely as possible to commercial standards. Prosser expressed similar concern for the "mature worker" who might want to advance himself in his calling through evening classes. For this kind of student he proposed brief units of training in a specific skill, "blueprint reading for plumbers," "applied design for granite workers," "sleeve making for dressmakers," by way of example. Short courses, he said, were becoming more and more popular because they promoted "trade efficiency" measured by wage-earning capacity.[14] It was this kind of training Snedden came to call "real vocational education" and he came to expand upon it as the desirable kind of education for all vocations. This approach to education, incorporating the precise definition of aim, describing the specific skill to be developed, demonstrating concrete results, and making a visible contribution to society, was very much in keeping with all he believed about the social efficiency purpose of education.

During 1910 to 1912, Snedden more precisely defined his program for secondary education, particularly as it concerned what he considered "the weakest part" of the American educational program, that provided for children of ages twelve to sixteen. Beginning with the critical twelve-to-fourteen age group, which he would remove from the domain of the normal-school-trained teachers, he proposed "flexibility" in the form of a three-track program providing a foreign language beginning in grade seven for those who would probably go on to higher education and a choice between practical arts or a commercial course for those who were "preparing for life." He expressed the hope that the children of laborers and others of moderate means would find such a program more valuable than the traditional academic fare, which he saw as barren and purposeless for them. Snedden identified the dropout with this group and hoped to provide a two-year high school course specifically for them, one that would provide "opportunities for vital, liberal education" and contribute to their "personal culture" and "civic efficiency." These "flexible" courses for grades nine and ten would all contain a common core of English, science, and social studies, but their desirability lay in the option of "one of the four great fields of practical arts study" — agriculture, industrial arts, practical arts, or commerce.[15] Snedden judged the pupil at sixteen ready to learn a specialized trade in a trade school or on the job. The practical arts, as they appeared in his program for the fourteen-to-sixteen age group, were general in nature to provide a foundation for "whole groups of industries," and all of the academic or "book studies" would have to be related to or growing out of the practical work. Though he was not at all sure what the content of "general foundations" for various groups of vocations might include, Snedden became increasingly more adamant in his demands for "pre-vocational education" and in his insistence that real vocational education could be carried on only in highly specialized trade schools.[16]

In this vein he found occasion to correct his superior of his Stanford days, Ellwood Cubberley, at a meeting of the Harvard Teachers Association in 1911. Cubberley lauded the introduction of courses in mechanical arts, commerce, agriculture, and household arts as means of attracting great numbers to the schools. While agreeing with Cubberley about their value, Snedden took issue with his use of the term "vocational" in connection with these subjects. He contended that most of what was being passed off in the teaching of them under the guise of vocational education was really liberal education, of a general pre-vocational nature.[17] True vocational education was like that provided girls under Miss Florence Leadbetter in a private vocational school in Boston.

At the meeting, Miss Leadbetter had caricatured liberal education and the traditional school as "easy, lazy, go-as-you-please . . . with dances, sports, and all sorts of good times." By contrast, she understood vocational training to mean "long hours, close application, the constant discipline of responsibility and little time for play." While the "cultural schools" emphasized "enlightenment," the vocational schools should stress "service." In the spirit of the day, she reflected, "acceptable service is the fruit of efficiency, . . . efficiency springs from character, . . . character results only from a clean body, mind and spirit." At Miss Leadbetter's school, figuratively and practically, the girls began in the laundry. She felt that the school's recommendation, which the girls expected when they graduated and went out to seek employment, provided the necessary element of control to enforce standards of cleanliness in speech habits and dress. She prognosticated that vocational education would ultimately revolutionize cultural education with schools like hers showing the way in "caring for the individual" according to individual needs.[18]

Snedden acknowledged vocational education a threat to liberal education only to the extent that the subjects as traditionally organized might represent "liberal education." He predicted liberal education would be enlarged in the school program, but in the form of new subjects and the traditional subjects reorganized. Ominously, he observed that if the cultural high school of the traditional sort did not yield to the demands of these changes it was likely to be "in danger."[19]

For Snedden, man had two basic functions in society, that of producer and of consumer. All of education was directed to the efficiency of one or the other of these functions. Vocational education was designed to make man an "efficient producer," and for this reason it had to be hard, serious, and realistic. Liberal education had as its goal the "efficient consumer" and might well be pursued in a less serious, less concentrated manner. Thus the practical arts could be either vocational or liberal depending upon whether they were taught "in the spirit of the amateur" to develop tastes and appreciations or with systematic approach, drill, and journeyman's standards in the vocational school. The problem was one of correct definition of aim. The merit of the different studies was to be measured in terms of results, and by this measure their relative values could be judged. Finding the methods for determining relative values and achieving specific aims was to Snedden one of the pressing and perplexing problems facing education.[20]

He further discussed this problem before the New England History Teachers Association in their fall meeting of 1911. History, he said, had been a subject of "great expectations"; the public expected it to encourage good citizenship and manhood. But history was also one of the great disappointments of education because the hoped-for results had been based simply upon faith rather than on sharply defined aims. Snedden admitted he could find "no real purpose in the study of history" or presumably the study of any other subject as a subject; rather, the real purpose of all education should be to contribute to the individual's "idealized grasp of the social environment." History, he said, was really only the chronological dimension in the study of the social environment and should be handled as sociology. It could only be justified for its contribution to a better understanding of the social environment of the present, and the material of instruction should be selected with this in mind. He had come before the group to explain the plans of the State Board of Education for teacher certification, the means the board had chosen to foster this kind of teaching. He told them certification would be based upon identification of the kind of work they would do instead of the more common written examination.[21]

A few months later, in the fall of 1912, Snedden added Clarence Darwin Kingsley to his staff as the board's agent for high schools. Kingsley was a teacher of mathematics in Brooklyn's Manual Training High School. During the previous two years he had risen to a position of national prominence as chairman of the NEA Committee of Nine on the Articulation of High School and College, and he was currently general chairman of the NEA Commission on the Reorganization of Secondary Education. Serious, dedicated, and hard-working, Kingsley was serving on five of the nine standing committees of the New York High School Teachers Association at the time of his appointment to Massachusetts.

As a high school teacher of mathematics, Kingsley had become concerned with the larger problems of the high school program. He had been placed in charge of programming both students and teachers in the large Manual Training High School, and the problems arising in programming a diverse student body in order to satisfy a great variety of college preparatory and vocational demands proved both frustrating and provocative of schemes for improvement.

Kingsley had noted that most of Brooklyn's 11,667 high school students had to travel a great distance each day to the specialized school of their choice. At the current rate of growth, almost 25 per cent a year, Kingsley expected Brooklyn would need three to four times as many schools within five years. So that these schools could be located within walking distance for most of the enrollment, he urged that first one, then another, of Brooklyn's specialized high schools be built at the same central location. He called this a "university high school" because he liked to compare the complex of schools with a university — a number of separate, semi-autonomous schools. If each of several centers were to offer enough of the different specialized departments it would eliminate the present need for travel to specialized high schools.[22]

During 1908 Kingsley had been named chairman of the High School Teachers Association's Committee for the Increase of High School Accommodations. It was the committee designated to worry over the growing shortage of space as enrollment climbed. Kingsley chose to make the first purpose of the committee the cause of the university high schools. To dramatize the need for this kind of high school, he and his future wife, Miss Elizabeth Seelman, prepared a detailed map locating the homes of all 11,667 Brooklyn high school students in relation to the schools where they were enrolled. On accompanying charts he computed the total cost of carfare and the total hours spent in travel by Brooklyn students over the period of a year. He injected another element into his argument; the moderate size of under a thousand students for each semi-autonomous unit would permit closer work with parents and more individual advice and consideration for the student. Kingsley felt that the excessively large school merely tended to aggravate an evil to which the city child especially prone, that of being able to effectively dodge the results of his own actions through the inability of the large school to hold a student to his responsibilities.[23]

In the formal report of the committee the following year, Kingsley settled upon the term "cosmopolitan high school" to identify the single high school offering many specific courses, the comprehensive high school of the future. The cosmopolitan high school, in the vocabulary of reform, made the "modernized" courses — commercial, practical arts, and household arts — and the traditional academic subjects equally available to all students. He expressed the hope that this kind of school would mitigate class distinctions by bringing into intimate association the children of the rich and the poor, the native and the foreign born.[24]

Like Snedden, Kingsley proposed a differentiated course of study but, unlike Snedden, he could not accept as unavoidable the class distinctions rising out of vocational choice.

Kingsley also had been a member of the New York High School Teachers Association's Committee on Revision of the High School Course of Study. The work of this committee began in 1908 at the behest of John L. Tildsley, then president of the association. The meetings of that year were planned to secure expert opinion on the purposes of the high school program. Guest speakers at the three quarterly meetings were Franklin Giddings on "Aims and Scope of the Public High School," President Woodrow Wilson of Princeton University on "The Meaning of Liberal Education," and David Snedden of Teachers College on "Should There Be a Difference in the Training of High School Boys and Girls?" Giddings seems to have set the tone of the inquiry by declaring that "high school education should make citizens, not learners." Snedden delivered his usual argument for differentiation and specialization in education, and the committee seems to have followed his lead in identifying six types of pupils for whom to prescribe a course of study.[25] Kingsley became chairman of the subcommittee on the high school course for girls preparing to enroll in a normal school.

In his report Kingsley set down six general objectives for the course, four stated in terms of life activities: health of body and mind; well-conceived standards of living; love of the best in literature, art, and music; and a broad outlook upon science, history, and current events. The fifth objective was comprehension of the underlying principles in language, science, and mathematics, and the sixth, "as a by-product," was mental discipline.[26]

To implement these objectives the committee set out a four-year course of study, general enough in the first year to give opportunity for easy transfer in or out of the program and emphasizing in the first two years subjects "fundamental to right living." To provide a useful program for the 75 per cent of the girls who dropped out before the third year of high school, Kingsley suggested placing bookkeeping and "household accounts" and a study of vocations in the first year. A progressively more difficult course covering "current topics" occupied one period of the English course each week for all four years. A course on the city of New York to give understanding of the local environment was presented in the first year followed by a survey history of the last hundred and fifty years in the second year, and history up to the last hundred and fifty years in the third. Science in this course was heavy in content contributing to life activity aims. Hygiene and Sanitation in the first year was intended "to help form public opinion with regard to standards of health." Household Chemistry in the second year reinforced the course in Household Science; the stated aim was to promote "the health and efficiency of the individual and the welfare of the family." The curriculum required only a single foreign language as compared to two recommended by the NEA Committee on College Entrance Requirements of 1899. Geometry was taught in the third year followed by algebra in the fourth. Household science and art, music, and drawing were to be taught each of the four years. Like Snedden's course for the normal schools of Massachusetts, this course was concerned with the future teacher as a homemaker and a member of society, and only collaterally as a future teacher.

The dilemma of providing a program of studies to meet a wide variety of entrance requirements for the few college-bound students in the specialized high schools had come to the attention of the High School Teachers Association in March, 1910, with the appointment of a Committee on Conferences with Colleges; Clarence Kingsley was named chairman. By May of the same year he had a report before the parent organization entitled "Articulation of High School and College, The Reorganization of Secondary Education." [27] It was published for distribution at the NEA convention in Boston the following summer. The attention attracted to this report, more than anything else, projected him upon the national scene.

The statement prepared by Kingsley's committee and adopted by the High School Teachers Association claimed a "wide discrepancy" between the "preparation for college" as defined by current college requirements and "preparation for life" of the kind the New York schoolmen deemed most necessary. It reacted against the dualism that separated students into specialized courses so that those dropping out of the college preparatory course lacked training in citizenship, as well as "industrial and commercial efficiency," while the student "prepared for life" had closed the door to college admission.

Kingsley's report, to which the association had committed itself, called for reduction in the number of required subjects and recognition of all "standard subjects" for credit toward college admission. It also specifically recommended a program enabling the student to confine his study to but a single foreign language, modern or classical, and called for recognition of credit in drawing, music, household science and art, shopwork, the commercial branches, civics, and economics for admission to any college he should choose to attend. At this point Kingsley specified "seven distinct lines of work . . . essential to a well-rounded high school course; to wit, language, mathematics, history and civics, science, music, drawing, and manual training." He considered household science and art a necessity for all girls. In the main, the report said a good high school course, in terms of preparation for life, should also be accepted as good preparation for higher education, except in those subjects where the material of the college course was built directly upon that of the high school.

Kingsley submitted the newly approved statement without delay to college presidents, teachers associations, and school superintendents to solicit their reactions. When nearly a hundred replies had been received, most of them favorable to the statement, he prepared a pamphlet for general distribution at the national convention of the NEA at Boston during the first week of July. Doubtless some of Snedden's guests at his Rockport seaside residence brought copies of the report with them and discussed it over after-dinner coffee. Though this is not reported in either David or Genevra's autobiographical works, the subject was certainly one Snedden would enjoy talking about.

The NEA was moved to action; three departments, manual training, commercial, and secondary education, passed resolutions concurring in Kingsley's statement. The department of secondary education created a Committee of Nine to report on the problem the following year. Snedden's deputy commissioner, William Orr, was among the nine and Kingsley was named chairman. The group took its name from the title of Kingsley's New York report and called itself the Committee on Articulation of High School and College.

The committee's report in 1911 tended to expand upon Kingsley's initial statement prepared for the New York teachers the previous year. It structured his proposals into a total program, requiring a minimum of fifteen units, organized into two majors of three units each and one minor of two units. The student was obligated to select a minimum of eleven units from the academic subjects, leaving four units open for practical work.[28]

At the same time, Kingsley began his own study of the many and varied college admission requirements currently in use throughout the country. A short time after Philander P. Claxton took office as United

States Commissioner of Education, he named Kingsley one of his non-salaried "specialists" and in so doing brought the prestige of the Bureau of Education behind the study. Kingsley spent two months in Washington during the spring of 1912 putting his report into condition for publication by the Bureau. The report analyzed the requirements of 204 liberal arts colleges and found that almost one-fourth of them would accept four units of practical work for admission, as recommended by the Committee of Nine. Kingsley believed the solution to the problem depended upon the amount of flexibility colleges were willing to permit in their entrance requirements. With some flexibility he believed high schools would be able to adapt their programs to "the needs of the community."[29]

When the American Institute of Instruction met at North Conway, New Hampshire, in July, 1912, Kingsley was there to outline the most important problems in the articulation of high school and college. It was an "exceedingly fine program," according to editor Winship. In addition to Kingsley, William H. Allen talked on "Current Tests of School Efficiency," and William Orr presented "The First Year Science Course."[30]

Kingsley went from the meeting of the American Institute to Chicago where the NEA was convening. He had considered his initial report on the articulation of high school and college merely as "first-aid" and in no way a final solution to the problem. Now he was ready for the larger task of the reorganization of secondary education anticipated in the title of his original report to the New York High School Teachers Association. In the summer of 1912 he asked for and got from the NEA the appointment of twelve subcommittees to assay the content of the various subjects, including the new practical subjects. They would function as part of the continuing work of the Committee on Articulation of High School and College. Kingsley saw the forty-eight colleges already in accord with the recommendations of the committee as representative of a trend to wider acceptance of a good high school course as good preparation for college. He believed now more than ever that responsibility rested with the high schools to identify the content of each subject and to justify its presence in the curriculum.[31]

It was at this juncture — as he was drawing his survey of existing admissions requirements to a conclusion and embarking upon the larger study to reorganize the program of the secondary schools — that Kingsley joined Orr on Snedden's staff in Massachusetts.

The position of high school agent in Massachusetts had suddenly come open on August 5, 1912, with the death of James MacDonald, a veteran of twenty years with the State Board of Education. Kingsley had been known to Snedden for at least a year; upon receipt of the report of the Committee on Articulation of High School and College, Snedden had written him that the document represented "a distinct step in advance in the solution" of the high school problem.[32] It will be recalled that William Orr, Snedden's deputy commissioner for general education, had been a member of Kingsley's Committee of Nine for the past two years. That Kingsley should receive this appointment to work under Orr in Massachusetts seems a likely move, but it also gives evidence of aggressive administration on the part of Commissioner Snedden. It was only remarkable that a more important appointment did not come his way.

On the surface Kingsley and Snedden appeared to speak the same language and to favor the same changes in the program of the schools, but fundamentally they held very different views of society and the place of the individual within society. While their differences were fundamental, they were not immediately apparent and did not become so until publication of the Cardinal Principles Report of 1918. Both looked upon education as a means to social efficiency and could support each other with nods of agreement in calling for aims that would be stated in terms of their effect upon the student rather than in terms of subject matter to be mastered. But Kingsley hoped to achieve his social goals by integrating students headed for many destinations into a single comprehensive high school, affording a maximum of social contact and a maximum of academic choice. Kingsley called this freedom of choice and of movement in and out of course tracks "flexibility," and for him it implied opportunity for social mobility.

Snedden placed the larger departmentalized school, where students of several destinations rubbed elbows, at the seventh- and eighth-grade level. In his vocabulary "differentiation" would place students of different economic backgrounds into courses suitable to their probable destination. At age fourteen, or in some states at sixteen, the student would move either to a vocational school for job training in some specific skill or to a "traditional" college preparatory course. He considered the latter alternative preparation for vocational education in one of the professions at the college level. This system of "fitting for a probable destination" was Snedden's definition of "flexibility," and mobility rested in the more adequate preparation one possessed for his place in life — in a word, in "vocational efficiency."

Kingsley came to Massachusetts at a time when Snedden wanted to work a reorganization of education in that state. The rural high schools, small, two- to four-teacher institutions, were recipients of state funds which brought them under the supervision of the commissioner. The subsidy had been legislated to provide children of the state with the opportunity to prepare for college. Snedden alleged this caused these schools to feel restricted in the courses they might offer. He was anxious for them to introduce agriculture, manual training, household arts, and commercial subjects. He hoped that by working reforms in these schools, which he thought of as the feeder schools supplying faculty to the larger city high schools, all secondary education in the state would gradually move away from its present rigid, academic, and disciplinary orientation.[33]

A partial curricular reorganization of the small high school, "adapted to local needs," became the immediate task of Kingsley and Orr.[34] Snedden hoped to use the device of teacher certification to force the teachers in these schools to abandon their academic bent, and publication of a teachers manual was supposed to guide the direction of their efforts. Kingsley and Orr held a series of conferences with high school teachers during the fall of 1912; a total of 407 attended, representing 151 high schools of the state. The preparation of a manual was assigned to Kingsley, whose experience seemed well suited to the project. Before the end of the year a teachers manual was in preparation. It contained a list of subjects to be included in the program of the small high school along with a statement of aims for each subject.[35]

Proceeding apace with the work of his first year in Massachusetts, Kingsley was deeply involved with organization of the subject committees which in the following year were to form the backbone of the Commission on the Reorganization of Secondary Education. For the present they were committees working under the direction of the Committee on Articulation of High School and College. During the year, ten of the twelve committees authorized by the NEA the previous July were organized. His former colleagues in the New York High School Teachers Association, Walter Eugene Foster and A. L. Pugh, were named chairmen of the ancient languages and business committees, respectively, while William Orr assumed charge of the science committee and Frank Leavitt headed the committee on mechanical arts.

Two appointments of which Kingsley was especially proud were those of James Hosic as chairman of the English committee, which was continuing a project begun by the National Council of the Teachers of English, and Thomas Jesse Jones as chairman of the social studies committee. He believed Hosic would produce "a fresh study of English in secondary schools" and develop a course likely "to fit young people" for the life of the school, the home, and the social and industrial community. Jones, a man of broad experience with social problems and "practical sociology," promised to provide the approach to social studies related to the aim of good citizenship. Kingsley looked for a "new civics," a study of "all manner of social efforts to improve mankind," in the pattern of his own course on the city of New York. Not exclusively the study of government, as was the old civics, this subject would aim to develop "appreciations of methods of human betterment." [36] Teachers of the new civics would have to be people conversant with community services and holding to the same viewpoint as the local charity organization society. Unlike Snedden's "appreciation subjects," civics did not imply a "soft" pedagogy or "playtype" methods for Kingsley.

Kingsley put his subcommittees to work immediately. Two joint conferences of all members were held in Philadelphia in December and again in February. Each committee was directed to submit a first report to the NEA at Salt Lake City the following summer. As early as the meeting in February, 1913, if not earlier, this group agreed to take up the project Kingsley had anticipated in his own curriculum work in New York, the reorganization of the studies of the secondary school. To make this clear and to give the subject committees the freedom they needed, it was decided to request the parent organization create a commission on the reorganization of secondary education, incorporating into it all of the subject committees.[37]

With Prosser's resignation, April 1, 1912, to become the full-time executive secretary of the National Society for the Promotion of Industrial Education, direct responsibility for supervision of the system of state-aided vocational schools fell to Snedden. This state of affairs lasted almost a year. The position was still open in February, 1913, when Snedden offered it to his old friend of his California years, Ernest Carroll Moore, then professor of education at Yale University. Moore considered the offer "a great personal compliment" and found himself greatly drawn to what he saw as a "great new experiment" in providing education for the poor; but, with searching self-examination he came to the conclusion, "I do not know as much about industrial processes as I should for that purpose." Snedden had asked him to pledge himself to remain for the full five-year term, and Moore was reluctant to obligate himself for that period of time, so he declined the position.[38] Surprisingly enough, Snedden had again offered this post to a man who knew little of industrial education and had been little involved in the field.

The supervision of the vocational schools added to that of the normal schools presumably left Snedden with little time to pay much attention to what Orr and Kingsley were doing. He did take the time to prepare a detailed exposition on the reorganization of secondary education in terms of its sociological foundations for the *Seventy-Sixth Annual Report* in January, 1913, but it was little related to the actual reorganization being carried out by Kingsley's commission.

While Kingsley was working at the national level to provide a place in the high school program for some technical training, Snedden was working for complete separation of the cultural and the technical in the normal schools "to prevent confusion of aims. . . ." Fitchburg had a course for teachers of manual training open only to men with experience in the trades, teachers who would be "well equipped with practical knowledge." Framingham had a three-year course in household arts, as had Salem in commercial training, both calculated to provide teachers especially prepared to work in the upper grades while the two-year course remained standard preparation for the first six grades. The graduates of these special programs would be prepared to implement Snedden's proposed "differentiated" course of study for pupils over twelve years of age.[39]

In the field of vocational education, his annual report stated the past three years had seen "steady progress away from a large amount of abstract and theoretical instruction, toward the practical—actual productive work of marketable products. . . ." The evening program now offered 99 courses in 40 different subjects; but there were 285 trades practiced in Massachusetts and public education offered training in only 19 of them. Clearly there was much to be done if training was to be provided specific to each trade.

Snedden continued to press for a six-year elementary school close to the children's homes, followed by two years in a large central school offering departmentalized teaching and differentiated courses. At fourteen, the student could enter the conventional high school or one of the state-aided vocational schools "to be fitted for work in the shop, in the home, or on the farm." In the vocational schools, the major portion of the drawing, mathematics, and technical work would be closely related to the practical work. As a further development during the past year, he reported that the pupil was giving considerably more than half of his time to shopwork so as to "become thoroughly grounded in the fundamental processes connected therewith" and as a basis for abstract study.

In 1913, while Kingsley's ten subject committees were working to define the objectives of each study in terms of the effect they would produce in the life of the pupil and as a basis for the selection of appropriate content and method, Snedden held a series of conferences with teachers and principals of the normal schools for a similar evaluation. The result of these conferences with a different department of instruction each week was to make a distinction between those courses purely vocational in nature "designed to prepare for the work of teaching" and those making a contribution to the students' physical, social, or cultural development, or in Snedden's scheme, to "general education."[40]

The content of general education was assumed necessary preparation for the future homemaker and citizen. Snedden dismissed the high school education of his normal school students as "cold storage" information combined with various "abstract statements." He considered it unproductive of "appreciation, culture, or vital power of any sort." He warned that education of this kind would only produce "passive, perfunctory teachers" and said that existing normal school teaching was only more of the same, too much information and "too exalted teaching." He wanted teachers to produce students possessed of "more responsibility" and "self-activity." Never personally identified with any academic field himself, he believed the reorganization of the subjects and the revision of method would produce just such students. Thus, for the normal school teacher, a professional study like the history of education should abandon its "traditional chronological" organization and by the "introduction of rich materials . . . at appropriate time and in an effective way" produce the desired educational perspective and ideals.

The leisure-time activities of the normal school student were supposed to serve the purposes of responsible self-activity. Satisfactory courses of action in behavior, recreation, association, physical training, and general reading should be mapped out for each student, subject only to the "general oversight of the schools." The inability of a student to follow through with such prescribed activities suggested, to Snedden's mind, evidence of an inability to meet the responsibilities of the teaching profession.

Commissioner Snedden made clear his intention to use teacher certification to impose more practical education upon the schools. It would be particularly useful as it affected the high school teachers, usually college trained, and not likely to be aware of what was being done in the normal schools.

Snedden had previously identified four kinds of education to which the several subjects might be made to contribute. In his annual report for the year 1913, he became, for the moment, a practicing sociologist and presented his "educations" as "social utilities" within the larger frame of reference of the social economy and as the basis from which to develop educational aims. He said social utilities were those specific forms of culture, civic ideals, and vocational power "which secondary school studies can produce in and for men and women to the end that they may serve in the world as cultured individuals, good citizens, and competent workers." At this time he added a fifth category, "education in the use of intellectual tools." Like the "fundamental processes" aim of the Cardinal Principles Report, this latter category, based on intellectual skill, was a late addition. The utilities in themselves were not yet aims, but were convenient categories from which aims of a more specific type, related to "social needs," might arise. In the process Snedden believed new subjects would emerge as "instrumentalities" to satisfy the new aims.

Even before the summer of 1913 when the NEA created the Commission on the Reorganization of Secondary Education, Kingsley's plans called for the subject committees already established to define their aims in terms of how their subject might be made to affect the lives of boys and girls. When he asked the convention in July, 1913, to name a reviewing committee, it was for the purpose of preparing a body of general aims, not unlike Snedden's "social utilities," to be used as a platform upon which to build subject aims.[41]

Snedden was already making use of his utilities to plan a reorganization of the studies. He said the field of social education included "all forms of organized educational effort" intended to produce "the habits, appreciations, understandings, and ideals . . . needed for the 'group' life of men and women"; it should be education for life in the family, the community, and the state. He suggested community civics, Kingsley's innovation, as one of the new subjects calculated to make an important contribution to this area. The course he proposed combined various forms of municipal activity with selected content from literature and history intended to "kindle social sentiment and ideals" and "form ideals for civic conduct." Cultural education meant education for "consumer capacities" and was a means of social control intended to force higher standards of production by intelligent acceptance or rejection of the product by the consumer. He considered it a form of "liberal education," like the "so called practical arts," gardening, various industrial processes, household arts, and commercial occupations, taught as a foundation for vocational guidance.[42]

In practice Snedden moved slowly. His plan to standardize and make more flexible the entrance requirements of the colleges in the state drew heavily upon the 1911 report of the Committee on the Articulation of High School and College. He proposed that the entrance requirements permit a "free margin" of three to four units, depending upon whether fifteen or sixteen units were required for graduation, which might include "any units approved by the state board and counted by the school for graduation." Presumably this meant the "new" subjects of practical arts, not presently acceptable to fulfill college entrance requirements. He retained twelve units of academic subjects, eight required units — three of English, two of mathematics, and three of any one foreign language — and four electives.

Kingsley also applied the principle of the "free margin" to the Massachusetts situation in urging introduction of the practical arts on a full-time basis. He had told the Middle States Association in November that aims stated in terms of the effect to be produced on the boy or girl, rather than in terms of subject matter to be mastered, would require the working out of new subjects. Arguing from Snedden's proposal to the colleges of Massachusetts, Kingsley said the "free margin" would provide the opportunity to introduce the new subjects. He included in this group community civics, general science, survey of vocations, and all of the practical arts. By his appraisal, there existed in educational circles a growing desire to organize all subjects to serve the needs of students who did not intend to go to college, or for that matter who did not intend to finish high school; and in this he may have been reflecting his close association with Snedden. For all students, college-bound or not, the aims of education were coming to be stated in terms of life activities rather than subject matter.[43]

In May, 1914, Snedden appeared again before the New England History Teachers Association in Boston. It proved to be one of the most interesting meetings of the association in a long time.[44] He told the history teachers that the educational values of all secondary school subjects needed to be scrutinized in relation to the "new needs" of secondary education. He interpreted "the spirit" of the contemporary social economy as requiring secondary education to be made purposeful and efficient for the new, larger, high school enrollments. Snedden caricatured the chronological organization of history as "cold storage" education and, at least for the "rank and file," he again urged history be taught to satisfy specifically defined aims drawn from functional social needs.

By way of example Snedden identified two major groups of aims for history, those contributing to personal culture and those identified with citizenship; but he expressed some doubt "as to how far the school is under obligation to promote . . . purely cultural interests." According to Snedden, the really great value in the materials of history lay in training for citizenship. "Having once conceived of the citizen as we should like to have him," he said, "we can work back and by analysis find the numberless specific forms of training by which we can produce this type." Here was social efficiency boldly stated.

According to the line of reasoning laid down by Snedden, "pedagogically sound" history was based upon well-defined knowledge of present social institutions. Choice of materials drawn from the various periods of history must be based upon their meaning to the present and the near future. He recognized that he was advocating "a dissected . . . and even fragmentary treatment of history," but he believed it inevitable if any profitable use were to be made of the subject. Not merely organized knowledge but rather "attitudes of mind" must be cultivated through history if the citizen of the future was to be equipped with "ideals of right social action."

Frederick Jackson Turner, who had moved from Wisconsin to Harvard, a Mr. Chase of the Milton Academy, and Cornell's George Burr all rose to express their disagreement with Snedden. Burr's paper was subsequently published in the November, 1914, issue of *The History Teacher* magazine. To him, Snedden's brand of history seemed "like history with history left out." For the Cornell professor, all history was a running commentary of the origin and growth of the civilization in which the child found himself, and its cultural worth lay not in knowing the past but in living the past. To sort out from the present, those things that interest us and to trace them back to their origins, was not history at all, but genealogy. He agreed with Snedden that history dare not be "cold storage knowledge" and for this reason he held the teacher more important in history than in any other subject. History was life, and the teacher alone could make it live with the well-told tale.

Burr focused on the heart of the argument, and perhaps on Snedden's most vulnerable spot, when he charged "sociology sacrifices man" and said it makes man little more than a statistic; to the sociologist, the greatest of statesmen become little more than blind tools of the social group. History, by contrast, focuses on the individual; in its study, the contribution of the individual looms large. The study of history itself, he said, was a liberating force humanizing all other studies.

Even those who professed to support the social efficiency purposes of education at times found it difficult to follow Snedden in all details of his program. It was just such an encounter that added zest to the 1914 meeting of the Department of the Superintendence when Snedden and William Bagley crossed swords over how cultural and vocational education should be handled.

Already considered by some as the "most prominent leader of . . . the extreme in educational innovation," Snedden usually made a sharp distinction between vocational education designed to make a person an efficient producer and liberal education intended to train the efficient consumer. He may have taken this analogy between the producer and the consumer from the report of the Douglas Commission in Massachusetts in 1906. He used it in his book, *Problems of Educational Readjustment*, published in 1913. In review of that book, Superintendent James Van Sickle had found in this distinction "the breath of the pioneer spirit" and a reminder of the frontiers that remain in education.[45] Not so for Bagley; he found in this comparison a weakness upon which he might capitalize.

Before the superintendents, Snedden categorized efforts to produce vocational efficiency when part of the school's program included general education as "sham vocational education" carried on in a "land of make-believe." Not that he opposed the practical arts — industrial arts, gardening, homemaking — in the school program; on the contrary, he firmly believed they would vitalize instruction, particularly for the twelve- and fourteen-year-olds. But at this level they should be taught as "real liberal education" to prepare educated consumers who would use the content of these new subjects "in the spirit of the amateur" to enrich life. He would broaden the practical offerings to include such things as varnishing a desk, cleaning and repairing a bicycle, faucet, lock, or sewing machine, sharpening a collection of cutlery, and half-soling a pair of shoes. For students over fourteen, the work of the vocational school was quite different. The vocational school had the serious responsibility of producing a graduate disciplined to journeyman's standards. This was the place for drill and the systematic approach with the ultimate goal being the production of a marketable product.

Snedden was particularly concerned that these two institutions — one educating the consumer, the other the producer — be kept physically and administratively separate. If the vocational school was to maintain the rigorous standards necessary to turn out the efficient producer it dare not be involved in the less-disciplined education of the consumer. The superintendents did not particularly care for this division of administrative control which was coming to be called the "dual system" and his remarks were not warmly received by what may be called the "rank and file" of their membership.

In his answer to Snedden, Bagley won the support of the audience by insisting that vocational education could be articulated with cultural education under existing administrative arrangements; but he reserved the full vigor of his attack for Snedden's attempt to make a distinction between cultural and vocational education.

Like Snedden, Bagley believed that social efficiency was the desired outcome of the educational process; but he believed it was produced as a remote general aim, rather than as the consequence of many small immediate aims. He, too, advocated concrete aims to make the liberal studies as "definite and tangible" as the vocational studies, but he took issue with Snedden's distinction between education for consumption and education for productive activities. He ridiculed these terms as the property of the field of economics and poorly adapted to education.

Bagley also found "producer education" and "consumer education," over-simplifications and unnecessarily limited in scope. As substitute terms, Bagley proposed "specific education" and "general education." He saw vocational education as one of several possible subordinate types of specific education. He suggested three subdivisions of general education: elementary education, the three R's; liberal education, to make the individual adaptable to changing situations; and cultural education, to prepare him for use of his leisure time.

Bagley opposed a dual system of administration on more fundamental grounds than mere administrative expediency. Snedden had assumed the aims of each kind of education were totally different and his choice of the terms "consumer" and "producer" emphasized this belief. For Bagley, the aims of each kind of education, general or specific, differed only in degree. By keeping both types of education under one administration, the aims of liberal education would become more definite and concrete, while the correlations possible between vocational and liberal education would work to the "great benefit of both." He warned, too, of the social stratification inherently present where separate systems of vocational schools were established, even though it were excused with the euphemism of "national efficiency."

In the *Journal of Education*, Winship was exuberant in proclaiming, "The war is on." He said Bagley brought brilliant, impassioned oratory to his argument. However, the experience had little effect upon Snedden's subsequent thinking.

In a series of articles for the *New Republic* during the winter of 1914 and the spring of 1915, John Dewey allied himself with those who opposed Snedden's separation of vocational education from the rest of secondary schooling.[46] Snedden expressed surprise and shock at opposition from this quarter and accused Dewey of siding with the "academic brethren . . . the beneficiaries of vested educational interests and traditions," and thereby "giving aid and comfort to the opponents of a broader, richer, and more effective education." He quickly dismissed the question of any particular type of administrative organization, be it dual or unit, as being peripheral to the main problem. The aims and methods of vocational education were the fundamental problem, and the type of administration adopted must be capable of realizing them.

Snedden readily admitted that vocational education was "not all of education," but he argued that the right kind of vocational education at the right time meant opportunity for the rank and file of youth, even as the professions had always provided opportunities to the "more favored classes." Opportunity for this class was to be found in the competition of employers for skilled labor. Their "mobility" was the physical mobility of labor attracted by a higher wage from one industry or region to another. The dual system of organization was only incidental to these larger considerations of opportunity, but it was the desirable form of administrative organization because it was "more efficient." Fused into the same system as general education, vocational education would likely be contaminated by the organization and method of the persistent academic tradition. He said that businessmen were generally "suspicious" of the so-called academic mind in connection with vocational education and believed the schoolmaster neither friendly nor competent in this field; for that reason alone separate control was advisable.

Snedden's reply merely confirmed for Dewey the validity of his criticism. Snedden's approach to the separation of trade and general education portended to make both kinds of training only narrower. Anything but a foe of vocational education, Dewey maintained that he would go farther than Snedden to make industrial education more than mere training. He would make it the kind of education that would develop the ingenuity and executive ability of the worker and make him the master of his "industrial fate." He categorized Snedden's "narrow trade-training" as "social predestination," and Snedden was made to appear naïve for putting himself in support of the scheme of "less well-intentioned men." Dewey concluded, however, that their differences were not educational but political and social. Snedden's vocational education would adapt workers to the existing industrial system, while according to Dewey, his kind of education would ultimately transform the system.

Snedden's annual school reports for 1913, 1914, and 1915 continued to have the appearance of textbooks in educational sociology or, using his term, "practical sociology." He sent a copy of the *Seventy-Seventh Annual Report*, which contained a "Survey of Three Years" of his administration, to his old mentor Samuel T. Dutton. Dutton encouraged Snedden by saying that re-evaluation of aims in education was a tremendous subject, well worthy of his attention; but he thought the report itself would accomplish little. He doubted if one in twenty high school teachers would see the report, much less read it; and of those who did, only a few would understand Snedden's ideas, and fewer still would accept and utilize them. Dutton suggested that Snedden "kindle fires in various parts of the state" by singling out the best teachers, whom others might be advised to observe and emulate.[47]

One of Snedden's suggestions, one Dutton had not heard before, he thought "most excellent." It was that the College Board examinations be based upon ability rather than the mastery of subject matter alone, as was then the practice. Just such an examination, in the form of the Scholastic Aptitude Test, made its appearance only three years later.

Snedden may have found some of Dutton's criticism useful, for the

Seventy-Eighth Annual Report was presented in much more direct and concrete terms. He presented his case for the reorganization of studies via a rather detailed exposition of the reorganization of the normal school course. Above all, the final test of the normal school was "the ability of graduates to enter on work so as to show from the start good results as teachers." With this as his point of departure, he then expounded upon the program of the elementary schools and the practical course of the high school as well as that of the normal schools, and in all of them related the educational program to practical aims.[48]

There seemed to be no consensus among normal school faculty about whether commercial teaching was primarily vocational or primarily general education. He proposed that students preparing as commercial teachers at the Salem Normal School spend a year in a "wage-earning commercial occupation" as a prerequisite to the final year of the course.

He reported that the normal school of art in Boston was experiencing many difficulties in defining aims for art education. What they finally came up with looked something like Snedden's own solution to the problems of art education. It provided "teaching the talented" for "special callings" in art and "systematic education of all children in all grades towards higher and sounder standards of appreciation." [49]

Snedden also said that English expression needed more emphasis at all levels, particularly since a majority of the people of the Commonwealth were now the descendants of non-English-speaking immigrants. Some subjects should be taught for direct results, others for indirect results. English literature, the single most important cultural subject, fell into the latter category, "to effect the formation of moral ideals."

Lack of clearly defined aims worked a handicap on the practical arts and accordingly made difficult the normal school's efforts to determine the scope of teaching in this field. Snedden felt that science was the victim of "over-elaborate" instruction in the normal school and, with better definition of aims, instruction could be made to relate to the environment. History was an "over-loaded subject . . . taught too elaborately." Since the state was populated largely by descendants of recent immigrants, more "practical civics" needed to be taught. He had little use for any mathematics other than arithmetic in the normal school, and arithmetic only needed to be taught for its "practical utility."

Snedden had put his agent for elementary education to work on a second course of study for grades one to six in cooperation with committees of superintendents. Presumably, it was to replace the similar document he had had committees of normal school teachers prepare in 1911. This time the course was to specify pupil attainment in terms of minimum requirements for each subject in each grade.

In the *Seventy-Ninth Annual Report,* for the year 1915, Snedden proposed another step in the direction of increased control over local high schools by the State Board of Education.[50] Following the certification legislation of 1911, affecting teachers in state-subsidized high schools, he had gotten a bill through the legislature in 1914 empowering the State Board of Education to define the standards of a legal high school for towns required to belong to a state-subsidized superintendency union. The staff of the board also performed a certification function in identifying those high schools whose graduates the normal schools would accept without examination. Since twelve hundred students were admitted annually to the normal schools, the board had the opportunity for wide supervision. With this report he proposed a bill providing for state certification of all public-school teachers.

The expanded system of certification was but one step in a larger program, credited to Kingsley, for improving instruction in Massachusetts high schools. The other parts of his program included a week of institute work at the beginning of the school year, an increase in staff to provide supervision in the various subject fields, and teachers manuals in the various subjects. Kingsley had but recently completed a teachers manual on "community civics" for use in the state and he had others in preparation for the commercial subjects and the household arts.

Much of the report was defensive in tone, an effort on Snedden's part to justify his administration of the past six years. The irony of the situation was unique. Snedden had been judged harshly by the State Commission on Economy and Efficiency. A creation of the 1912 legislature, the commission had been established to inquire "into the laws governing the financial transactions of the Commonwealth" over the period of the next two years. As implied in the title, the inquiry was largely concerned with fiscal efficiency, and the state auditor was an *ex officio* member of the commission. The commission was given the power to take testimony under oath and to investigate the records of government agencies. It was expected to recommend legislation that might lead to "consolidation or coordination of departments and institutions."

The 125-page report on the normal schools of the state, fresh from the press and placed into the hands of Governor David I. Walsh by the commission on January 15, 1915, was an expression of this brand of efficiency. It was critical of Snedden's attempts to prepare teachers specifically for rural schools. The Commission on Economy and Efficiency criticized the course offerings at the North Adams Normal School, which specialized in this function, for duplication of the offerings of other normal schools. In another place they were critical of his efforts to produce the socially efficient teacher, capable of making a contribution to the community, because, they said, this brought "non-functioning" courses into the curriculum, courses that made no direct contribution to a teacher's vocational efficiency.

Snedden answered his critics with another of his sophisticated discussions relating all of public education to the general social economy. He defined the term "social economy" this time as being all of the many and varied efforts looking toward a better development of individuals and social groups. Education, called one of the great enterprises in social economy, would make progress in the future only through a more extensive use of expert knowledge, a greater division and specialization of effort, more scientific research, and increased financial support. The public, he argued, must be made to regard money, time, and energy spent on education as a "social investment."

There is little doubt but that Snedden felt piqued by what he must have considered unfair criticism. He addressed each point of criticism with such statements as: "The commissioner believes that many of the comments . . . are more severe than the situation . . . warrants"; or simply, "This is a very much exaggerated statement." He made little direct reply to the commission's recommendation that the teaching of sociology be eliminated on the grounds that it was an "academic incumbrance," but in his introduction he made it clear sociology would formulate the exact definition of aims to make education as scientific as medicine or engineering. In rebuttal to the commission's report, he expressed less concern for the non-functioning studies, which after all contributed to the social control of the individual, than for the "partial or incomplete function of the so-called 'functioning' studies." Pressed to be more definite, he doubtless would have resorted to his already well-worn formula promising appropriate educational methods only after adequate aims had been found. The commission seems to have understood "efficiency" as related to a system of organization free of duplication of function, a type of business efficiency. To Snedden, "efficiency" was concerned with the individual's effectiveness in society and how such social efficiency could be produced through education.

A reaction against Snedden's use of centralized administrative control, rather than opposition to his educational reforms, seems to have been developing as early as 1913. In the Christmas edition of the *Journal of Education* that year, Edwin Kirkpatrick, director of the child study department in the Fitchburg Normal School, delivered a broadside against Snedden under the title, "The Drift from Town to State Administration of Education in Massachusetts." Kirkpatrick came from the Clark University "school" of child study and had gained a wide reputation as the author of several books on the subject. He charged Snedden with imposing the debilitating force of administrative red tape upon the schools with claims that "where the state's money goes, there must go the authority of the State Board of Education." He accepted Snedden's claim of the need for more experimentation in education, but concluded that the commissioner was better prepared by his training for that kind of work than for the supervision of details with which he seemed encumbered. Kirkpatrick charged Snedden was so overburdened with the administration of board rules that he had ceased to be "the educational enlightener and leader of the State." He found the resulting educational climate a "leveling, stupifying, deadening drift toward uniformity and bureaucracy."

Snedden listed eleven conditions adverse to effective educational administration in Massachusetts in the *Seventy-Ninth Annual Report*, his last as commissioner of education. He placed as first the large extent to which control and direction of educational affairs still rested with local authorities.[51] Two years before, he had reported that his attempts to reorganize the normal school program resulted in "a measurable unsettling" of the lifelong convictions held by many of the staff members; but, at the time, he believed the condition temporary.

Another sort of criticism, different from that leveled by the Committee on Economy and Efficiency or that of Kirkpatrick, may have been registered privately, though Snedden nowhere alludes to it. Ernest Carroll Moore, now a member of Paul Hanus' staff at Harvard, described for his diary Snedden's approach to teacher education as "teach them the best tricks . . . and send them out to use them," but said this did not educate them to critically evaluate and improve their work. Apparently Moore had discussed the normal schools of Massachusetts earlier in the evening, as he recorded with firm conviction that one day it would all have to be undone. He feared Snedden's program would make teachers slaves to subjects.[52]

Professor E. A. Strong of Ypsilanti Normal School directed similar criticism against Snedden's position on the teaching of general science. In February, 1915, speaking before the Science Teachers Club of Teachers College, Snedden had proposed that this new subject, "general science," ignore the historical subject classifications, as set down by mature and trained scientific minds, in favor of "working classifications" based on the interests of the learners or the local significance of the phenomena. Theoretically, all human knowledge was within the area of study appropriate to this subject, and the teacher had merely to organize the learning materials in a way that seemed most desirable to the needs of the group. This subject, as he conceived it, would be taught primarily for "appreciation," using as content the easily comprehended applications of science to human well-being. "Learning standards" in this subject would be comparable to those set for the reading of literature. The study of the sciences, as traditionally organized for purposes of mastering the principles of each area and attainment of scientific method, should be reserved for the later years of high school and for those who intended to go on to higher education.[53]

Strong took issue with what he supposed to be Snedden's inference that the teacher of general science might safely be ignorant of the sciences and neglect them in her own preparation. Such teachers, he maintained, far from being free of previous bias, are the very persons most lacking an open mind and under "the tyranny of words" — the organizations and explanations of others. He would insist the teacher have some knowledge of several sciences and thorough scholarship in one.

As was his custom when confronted with adverse criticism, Snedden replied by bringing his critic into seeming agreement with his own position. He gave assurance that only the "exceptionally qualified" could administer the program of general science education. Strong had said that general science would never be highly thought of since it gave the student nothing to build upon in the later years of high school, and could never be accepted as a college examination subject. In his reply, Snedden offered the hope that one day the senior high school and the college would accept general science for its cultural contribution.

The Snedden-Bagley encounter before the Department of the Superintendence in 1914 was not quickly forgotten. Winship believed Bagley
had come away with much the best of it. In 1916 Superintendent John D.
Shoop of Chicago, chairman of the department, endeavored to stage a
rematch. Unfortunately, the question finally settled upon proved so
tame the "star act" fell short of expectations.

However, the following month Snedden rose in reply to Bagley's
paper, "Some Handicaps to Education in a Democracy," at the Harvard
Teachers Association and renewed hostilities.[54] According to him, Bagley had emphasized the need for more and richer liberal education in
competition with vocational education. Snedden also wanted greater
quality of liberal education, but this did not mean more Greek or any
of the "traditional studies." He pegged the underlying theory of the
existing "historical liberal education of high school and college" as
wrong both in orientation and purpose.

The reply to Snedden was delivered by George A. Brown, a fellow
editor with Bagley on *School and Home Education*, in a lengthy and
scathing editorial. He took issue in particular with Snedden for ridicul-
ing as "faith aims" such large encompassing educational objectives as
"culture," "citizenship," and "intellectual power." Brown maintained
Snedden's multitude of specific aims would result not in a school but
in a kind of apprenticeship. He charged it was really the old "fitting
school" idea applied to many more activities and, Brown contended,
the "plain people" had always opposed the fitting school. He called this
"Snedden's un-American theory of educational administration," not
because it was un-American to be efficient, but because it was un-American to be *only* efficient. Give the children "a real teacher," he said, and
one need be little concerned about what subjects were being taught.

To document his attack, Brown used one of Snedden's papers, "New
Problems of Secondary Education," given before the Academic Principals Association of New York the previous December and subsequently
published in *American Education*.[55] On that occasion Snedden had expanded upon what he called "concrete aims," as opposed to "faith aims."
Concrete aims were those "with some degree of scientific exactness,"
and he had used the study of French to illustrate his point. France was
remote, an ocean away, and French cultural and scientific contributions
were readily accessible in translation. He saw no pressing need for "a

smattering of French to be taught to so many." He had suggested instead that a few carefully selected students should be taught a great deal about the French language and given the opportunity to live in France to gain a real mastery of the language, literature, and culture so they might become translators and interpreters.

In reply to Brown, Snedden expressed some doubt that the article in *American Education* had been an adequate treatment of his position. He spoke from the viewpoint of the "student of sociology" and professed that his greatest concern was for "liberal education," more so than for vocational education. He was greatly interested in the humanities, "those studies in any age and among any people, that enlarge human visions of fellowship, develop wide and eventually world-wide sympathies and understandings." At one period in the evolution of Western civilization, he asserted, Greek and Roman literature, art, history, and philosophy were the humanistic studies par excellence, but for the modern world, the social sciences, travel, geography, and the motion picture contributed valuable humanistic elements.

Without directly addressing the charge that he was un-American, Snedden related his argument to the efficient teaching of citizenship. To do so efficiently one must define good citizenship and the specific and purposive means of producing it. He cited especially a quote of Brown's that "human values" did not mean to Snedden "the influences which bring people together and cause mutual appreciations." To the contrary, he protested, he attached "great values to the socializing means and agencies of education," as these were the means to "efficient groupings." He wanted it understood that it was on these grounds he criticized much of the work of the liberal arts high schools.

In February, 1914, Dean Russell had asked the Sneddens to be his guests in New York for the annual meeting of the Teachers College Alumni Association, held just prior to the annual meeting of the Department of the Superintendence. The reception and dinner at the Fifth Avenue Hotel with some eight hundred alumni in attendance proved a memorable experience for Snedden. As one of the speakers of the evening, he was introduced as the first Alumni Trustee appointed to the Teachers College Board. This was the twenty-fifth anniversary of Teachers College, and the trustees chose this way to honor the alumni for their contribution to the continuing welfare of the College.[56]

As Snedden's two-year term on the board of trustees was drawing to a close in the fall of 1915, Russell offered him a new chair on the Teachers College faculty. It was in vocational education and educational sociology, two of Snedden's major interests, and seemed to have been created especially for him. He accepted the appointment in February, to begin his duties at Columbia on July 1, 1916. In the *Journal of Education*, Winship professed no surprise at the appointment because, as he put it, Snedden had always been "foremost in the esteem of the administration of both Columbia and Teachers College." Winship claimed to have known Snedden since he was a country teacher in California and said that during this time scholarship — not "in the scholastic, but in the educational sense" — had always been his first love, certainly never administration. "Completely intellectually abstracted" no man was "more confident of his argument"; yet it seemed to Winship that Snedden, as few men, was "little inclined to assume superiority." Massachusetts' loss, he concluded, was Columbia's gain.[57]

Snedden had signed a contract for a second five-year term as commissioner of education for the state of Massachusetts, but had completed only a little over a year of his new term when he announced his intention to return to Teachers College the following July. Like the first contract, it could be abrogated at any time by a majority vote of the State Board of Education. During the previous three years in particular, he had become a controversial figure in educational circles of the country, while in Massachusetts his administrative procedures had come under question both for reasons of excessive centralization and lack of "efficiency." A controversial person, likely to excite thoughtful discussion and argument in the academic world, could be as much of a liability to the body politic as an asset to a university. His legislative requests, for better enforcement of the compulsory attendance laws through the agency of the state board and for extending certification of teachers, would suggest he was committed to even greater centralization of authority in the State Board of Education.

Clarence Kingsley, his agent for secondary education, upon whose shoulders he placed much of the responsibility for those changes the board was currently requesting, had already achieved a national reputation in secondary education; but Kingsley's approach to reorganization, not yet in print, was based upon the "vague," "general," "faith aims" Snedden had attacked the previous year. Here was another source of possible tension and controversy. For Snedden educational administration had never been an end in itself, but always a means to realize the sociological ends and purposes of education. The details of finance and the legislative procedures were tedious necessities, not at all congenial to his more enduring interests. To Snedden the time may have seemed right for a change of "work."

On the evening of Friday, May 19, 1916, two hundred of Massachusetts' educational leaders gathered at the Hotel Brunswick to honor the departing commissioner with a testimonial dinner. Ernest Carroll Moore, Frederick Fish, James Van Sickle, and Charles Eliot were among the eight speakers on the program who "left nothing unsaid" in expressing the "appreciation of the state." [58] Snedden professed that, except for the position offered him in Columbia University, no other work, no place, was preferable to the Massachusetts office; but he may well have been transported for the moment by the emotion of the occasion.

Snedden brought together some of his pet ideas and most cherished prejudices for the major address of the evening.[59] He acknowledged the lack of interest in history of which he was suspect, pleading that his interest lay instead in the "present and the prospective." He pictured the institutions of society as individual rafts piloted in the swift current of life. The education raft was especially large and in the process of being rebuilt. He observed, almost with envy, some of the rafts had developed techniques of steering that made possible control of both their own and their neighbors' course. Perhaps he was alluding to personal difficulties when he declared education had not yet learned the cooperation and coordinated effort so necessary in steering its raft. Again he touched an apparent source of irritation in urging the problems of lay-versus-specialist leadership and central-versus-local authority be avoided through sharing "complementary" responsibilities. He prophesied the future would see local school officials placing fewer obstacles in the way of the development of central agencies. Aside from the symbolism of the "rafts," much of the address was a restatement of his article "What of Liberal Education?" prepared for *Atlantic Monthly* in January of 1912.

In what was probably Snedden's last official act, he composed a brief letter of appreciation, on behalf of the board, to his deputy commissioner William Orr. On June 15, 1916, Orr announced his own resignation in order to accept a senior secretaryship with the YMCA, in charge of educational work. For Orr, this was a new opportunity to promote "educational efficiency" with the additional appeal of an increase in salary.[60]

The new chair at Columbia offered the opportunity to work in an area of absorbing interest to Snedden and he said he "jumped at the chance." Ross had left him with a desire to do further work in sociology. Even on his last Columbia-sponsored trip to Europe in the spring of 1909, he had "stolen time" to dip into French sociology at the Sorbonne. The bulk of his writing during his Massachusetts years, and even before, had claimed the support of the supposed discoveries of the new "science" of sociology. Now he felt himself "a sort of frontier explorer" in two areas, vocational education and educational sociology, both rapidly developing in importance. As he viewed it, vocational education was but one branch of the larger subject of "educational sociology."

During the winter of 1916 Genevra went to New York to find a house preparatory to their impending move. She finally settled upon a home in Yonkers. Large and not especially attractive, it was never an object of their affection, but it was in a community she believed had a better school system than that of New York City. The Snedden's next-door neighbors there were the Paul Monroes and the Thomas Briggs. Within two or three blocks the Frank McMurrys, the Hosics, and the Ruggs all resided, placing the Sneddens in a small enclave of Teachers College personnel.

Snedden returned to Columbia and to the "most satisfying period of his life" in July, 1916. He returned a much more secure member of the profession, holding a position of prominence in the councils of the NEA's influential Department of the Superintendence, a name to be reckoned with. Snedden was now a full professor with tenure and a salary equal to that he had received in Massachusetts.

Upon entering into the responsibilities of his new appointment Snedden brought with him well-defined views. Education should be related to a new body of aims based upon "demonstrable worths" as evidenced in the lives of successful practitioners. These aims differed from others based upon life activities in that they were to be precisely stated in terms of specific kinds of abilities, skills, understandings, and appreciations. He opposed broad generalizations which, while based on life activities, were so broadly stated as to constitute "faith" aims; above all, he rejected the study of a subject for its own sake. He had already described sociology, his new field, as an empirical science, and saw it as the basis for aim development in education. He had already begun this process by dividing all of education into producer education and consumer education, depending upon the broad purposes to which it would be put in the life of the learner. He had also identified four kinds of education, cultural, physical, vocational, and social — terms not unlike the "faith aims" he found inadequate. They were to him but broad areas, "social utilities," from which more accurately defined aims would come. He justified the entire procedure as contributory to the "general social economy."

Chapter VI

EDUCATIONAL SOCIOLOGIST

The next two decades at Teachers College — for David the "satisfying years" — were a period of consolidating, refining, articulating, and defending the theories he had already developed concerning education for social efficiency. They were satisfying years because he was teaching his favorite subjects, educational sociology and vocational education, and because his "hundreds" of students "seemed no less interested in those subjects than he himself." [1]

In the days immediately ahead David again found himself before various groups of teachers as the featured speaker, a role he thoroughly enjoyed. For Genevra, this was little different from their life in Massachusetts. There he had been gone six nights a week, lecturing to various groups, and never came to know the Brookline home and neighborhood, even as he came to know Yonkers but little. Dean Russell expanded the work of the Alumni Association in the fall of 1916 by the establishment of local alumni clubs throughout the nation. He frequently called upon the gregarious, affable Snedden to represent Teachers College Board of Trustees and the fluency of presentation Snedden was a wise choice indeed. He was able to combine the urgency of his demands for reform with the insight bred of his two years on the Teachers College Board of Trustees, and the fluency of presentation acquired before a multitude of teachers institutes in rural California with the polish gained on hundreds of Massachusetts lecture platforms.

When the first of the new locals, the Teachers College Club of Maryland, was organized in the fall of 1916, Snedden appeared at Baltimore to speak on "Some Current Problems in Education." The meeting was thrown open to the public, some three hundred enthusiastic friends and alumni turning out to attest by their presence to the growing prominence of Teachers College upon the educational scene. Fifty of those present turned out to be bona-fide members who clustered about Snedden at a reception later in the evening, eager for news of the college. Later in the school year he addressed other new locals in Cincinnati, Kansas City, and Buffalo. He remained a popular speaker before the alumni clubs in the years that followed, but it was not primarily before these groups that Snedden appeared; instead, he seems to have become almost a roving ambassador of Teachers College. During the three winter months of December, January, and February of the 1921–22 school year he appeared before no less than eight, widely varied, professional groups.[2]

Snedden now found himself in the topmost echelon of the new educational leaders. When Charles Judd, Edward Elliott, and Leonard Ayres organized the Cleveland Conference in 1916, he was chosen along with Paul Hanus, E. L. Thorndike, George Strayer, Ellwood Cubberley, and Abraham Flexner to be among the select twenty invited into membership. Although Snedden had once found the Scholia Club of California a stimulating professional experience, he alone failed to respond to his nomination and after two years of inactivity was dropped from membership.[3] Seemingly he was so permanently placed and so engrossed in his sociological ruminations that the honor meant little to him.

He was also getting another "image," unfortunately one he could not always live with comfortably. He had become the symbol of irresponsible reform, the enemy of scholarship, and frequently found it necessary to explain, clarify, and at times justify his position. Perhaps Cassius Keyser did not realize he was using the name of a new colleague on the Columbia faculty when he mentioned Snedden in a review of G. H. Miller's *Historical Introduction to Mathematical Literature for Science* in July of 1916. He pictured Snedden as the kind of "agitator" whose "nationwide depreciatory utterances" concerning mathematics Miller was addressing in rebuke. The author, he said, "believes that 'shameless ignorance' of mathematics 'does not represent a normal condition on the part of those interested in the history of the human race.'" Supposedly Snedden did.[4]

Snedden made a direct and immediate reply in *Science* the following month. He wished to make clear that he himself had once been "a

moderately successful teacher of high school mathematics," as indeed
he had in his native California. And it was from the unassailable position of experience, rather than that of sociological speculation, that he
attacked the highly "protected" position mathematics enjoyed simply
because it was assumed to be especially useful to train the mind. As a
teacher he had found "a substantial percentage of students, otherwise
of good ability and promise, who did not 'respond' to mathematics
teaching," but who nonetheless possessed "artistic or literary bent."
For students anticipating certain vocational pursuits, the study of
mathematics would serve a useful purpose and should be pursued vigor-
ously, but not otherwise. Snedden wanted education to be useful on
the most immediate practical terms.

The following year, the Chicago Mathematics Club came to the
defense of their specialty against "would-be reformers." In this cause
they solicited testimonials from doctors, lawyers, merchants, bankers,
and other men of local prominence. The overwhelming majority responded by telling the important part they believed mathematics had
played in their own success; thirty-five believed its contribution was
primarily in some form of mental training, ten cited practical applications.

Perhaps Snedden felt himself one of the "would-be reformers" to
whom the article made reference. His reply was received by *School and
Society* in time for publication just two weeks later. As "a scientific
student of pedagogy," he said he found a certain charm in "the dogmatism and naïve psychology" of the replies the committee chose to
print. He quickly dismissed them as ex-cathedra utterances based upon
no real knowledge of the subject. He suggested the committee should
go to the classmates of the prominent men, to those who had *not* suc-
ceeded and who cursed their teachers for not giving them practical
knowledge. He did not claim that this class of witness would provide
more valid testimony, but only a more balanced appraisal. He continued
to plead that the subject no longer be required of those who were unlikely to find practical use for it.

At this point Cincinnati's Charles Moore moved in to attack Snedden
on his own ground, science. He took issue particularly with Snedden's
stand as a scientific critic. He said that a scientific jargon quoting "bio-
metricians" and speaking of "selected groups" and "random samples"
was only camouflage intended to sound imposing but hardly likely to
fool anyone with real scientific training. Moore believed the arguments

already advanced by teachers of mathematics in support of the disciplinary value of their subject had been carefully worked out and remained valid. He saw nothing scientific in a random sample that gave equal weight to the opinions of the admitted failures along with those of the successful. He said Snedden had presented "another illuminating example of the essentially unscientific nature of many of the recent, so-called scientific discussions in the field of education." And as for Snedden's comment about "dogmatism and naive psychology," Moore recalled a statement before the NEA at Cincinnati by a certain gentleman who considered himself one of the "scientific students of pedagogy" that "of course nobody nowadays believes there is such a thing as transfer of training." The statement might easily have been attributed to Snedden, but Moore did not do so. In his estimate every psychologist who had investigated this question came to the opposite conclusion, and here was a clear case not only of "dogmatism and naïve psychology," but ignorance of psychology itself. The article fairly bristled, and this time Snedden chose to make no reply.

The following October, *School Review* published one of Snedden's papers, "Liberal Education Without Latin."[5] Much of Snedden's argument was concerned with what he called the inadequate contribution of the traditional liberal studies to the spiritual and intellectual preparedness of wartime America. He scoffed at the supposed ability of these studies to produce "a kind of magic mental discipline" and ridiculed their substantive contribution as being drawn from a civilization of marked moral degeneracy, poverty, and slavery, all "concomitants of low efficiency." He looked to a new type of schoolmaster, one who could "comprehend the significance in true cultural education of self-inspired work, leisurely development of tastes . . . and the richness of inspired social intercourse." In a democracy, he believed, it was the right of each one "to be socially efficient in all ways — culturally and morally — no less than physically and vocationally." He mentioned mathematics only twice, but when he said, "the dead hands of Latin, Greek, and mathematics . . . paralyze the aspirations of our youth," he brought Charles Moore's wrath down upon his head once again.

This time Moore was blunt in questioning the degree of common sense Snedden brought to the argument. He numbered Snedden among the "ill-advised agitators" of the educational world who were "unconsciously perpetuating an injustice on the youth of the land" and called their activities "a menace to national security." Didn't Snedden recognize the crying need for minds trained in mathematics, not only for navigators and artillery officers, but as "an essential requirement for efficiency" in many other important war tasks? In Moore's eyes, Snedden's "hopelessness" lay in his failing even to realize how much he didn't know.

This time David replied, not in kind, but in apologetic tones for having "seriously failed to make clear all phases" of his position. He believed the war really served to emphasize the need of training for a specific function, and so it probably had. Girls did not usually become artillery officers or navigators, so why should they be forced to learn mathematics? He felt it should be required only as preparation for those vocations in which it was necessary. Frustrated, he asked, "Can educators not realize the importance of distinguishing between general (cultural and civic) and vocational aims in education?" He had referred to the "dead hand" of mathematics only in general education, but he explained that as a vocational study it was "decidedly a 'live one.'"

A paper prepared for the Central Association of Science and Mathematics Teachers meeting at Chicago, December 1, 1916, only a few months after he had returned to Teachers College, may have served to focus the attention of Moore and others upon Snedden.[6] Always anxious to prescribe for the future, Snedden chose on this occasion to describe the high school of 1925 for his less sociologically sensitive audience.

In that distant day, nine years hence, the efficient high school would not attempt to fuse general and vocational education and have to settle for "denatured" vocational education. Rather, all signs pointed to vocational schools that would fit the student to a lifetime occupation by working with him seven to ten hours each day and leaving to the high school the task of general education. General education encompassed three of Snedden's four basic educations or "social utilities" — cultural, physical, and social-moral-civic — all contributing to "a thousand definite educational objectives the realization of which will have demonstrable worth to society." Some of the studies offered, called by him "alpha subjects," would be hard work; others, called "beta subjects," would be high-grade play. All would be tailored, with the help of a counselor, to the student's individual program.

Among the alpha subjects, Snedden listed algebra, plane geometry, chemistry, physics, mechanical drawing, technical machine metal work, and instrumental music. These kinds of subjects would be studied on a pre-vocational basis, with drill for proficiency. The beta subjects, high-grade play, contributed cultural "appreciations" — development of leisure time interests — and here Snedden exercised some imagination in suggesting as possible courses: school government practice, social ethics, contemporary fiction, industrial arts, commercial arts, field sports, general hygiene and sanitation, and general mathematics. The distinction he intended to make is more clearly seen by his division of "mental science" into "general mental science," a beta subject, and "methods of study," alpha study. In language study, general classical language and literature was offered as high-grade play as was French and German literature, but courses like Latin in Relation to English, French Reading, Spoken German, and Prevocational Spanish Reading, all were hard, alpha studies. Two of Clarence Kingsley's course innovations also appear on the chart, Study of Nations as a beta subject and Community Civics offered as either "work" or "play."[7]

Snedden expanded upon this means of valuation to the New York Physics Club in November, 1918.[8] He told the physics teachers he believed it was as hard to find justification for the teaching of physics, as then taught in 90 per cent of the high schools, as to justify Latin for boys or algebra for girls or ancient history for either. He called for several physical science courses, some purely cultural, others of general utility, still others integrated with social studies along with several different pre-vocational physics courses. The cultural courses would be easy, and elective, to develop appreciation, while the general utilities courses would cover the applications of the knowledge of physical science to the everyday activities of man. This latter group appears to have anticipated the life-adjustment approach of the mid-forties, which was also practical, substantive, and frequently involved the functional reorganization of traditional subjects. Pre-vocational physics, the third type, would be of many kinds, some preparatory to the study of engineering, others preparatory for gardening, "dryland" farming, stenography, and even a special course for homemakers who expected incomes of less than two thousand dollars a year and who had accepted this fate.

Snedden told the physics teachers he was certain that all of the "standards of value" behind the high school subjects needed to be reconstructed. Useful attainments as demonstrated by above-average men and women, he said, should set the guiding standard; he seemingly forgot for the moment his criticism of the Mathematics Club's survey. He urged, in fact, "the consensus of judgment of competent critics" — the above-average members of society — be used to determine what was "good for the individual and good for society." Snedden may have borrowed this approach to the problems of curriculum reorganization from the work of the National Institution for Moral Instruction, with which he became quite intimately associated at about this time.

The NIMI was organized by E. Milton Fairchild in 1910 as an outgrowth of his "Educational Church." Fairchild, a disillusioned Unitarian preacher, was attracted to Edward A. Ross with the publication of Ross's first article on social control in the *American Journal of Sociology*.[9] Fairchild's "system" of moral education employed a series of illustrated lectures, "What Men Think of Boys' Fights," "The True Sportsman," "Personal and National Thrift," and others, each based upon certain specific elements of moral character.[10]

Fairchild presented his lectures to school assemblies. The pictures were his own, captured from life situations with the aid of a unique, high-speed camera, also of his own invention. His wife, Salome Cutler Fairchild, prominent in library circles, wrote the narrative. The moral position taken was supposedly that of "good judges of conduct."[11] A decade later these judges of the best in moral conduct were institutionalized as Educational Directors of the Moral Education Board, and David Snedden was honored as one of this select group of twenty. All were of the new breed of professional educators including Ernest Carroll Moore, Pennsylvania's A. Duncan Yocum, United States Commissioner of Education Philander P. Claxton, and Wisconsin's Michael Vincent O'Shea. It was especially fitting for Snedden to identify with Fairchild's approach, for Fairchild, like Snedden, sought to identify specific "appreciations" to be learned apart from the studies as traditionally organized. Furthermore, Fairchild's approach to moral education as a separate subject field was analogous to Snedden's "social-moral-civic education," one of his four "social utilities." His definition of moral education gave plenty of space to civic and social responsibility.

The illustrated lectures reached their peak of popularity about 1911. According to Wyllys Rede in the *Independent* that year, Edward A. Ross, Charles W. Eliot, John Dewey, and Henry Churchill King all gave their endorsement to the lessons. Gradually as the novelty of their presentation began to wear off, as student audiences became less easily charmed by innovation, and as some of the new men in education — especially Charles Judd and Charles Hughes Johnston — became skeptical of their value, the lectures rapidly declined in popularity. During this period, late in 1915 or early 1916, David Snedden moved up to the presidency of the NIMI. With this move the organization became more firmly committed than ever to the principle of specialization of aim and less tied to a single method of presentation.

The institute turned now to the definition of objectives and set about a search for a code or inventory of desirable behavior. The search was conducted on a grand scale. A prize of five thousand dollars was offered for the best morality code, and the contest was open only to professional educators, so the judges would not be "swamped with worthless codes." The various state superintendents were asked to name seventy code writers, at least one from each state. The time limit for the contest was from Washington's birthday, 1916, to Washington's birthday, 1917. Professor William James Hutchins of Oberlin College won the contest.[12] It was intended that the forty-eight codes, one from each state, should be used "to assist teachers and parents to decide what moral ideas ought to be inculcated."[13]

The *School Review* printed Fairchild's own "School Character Chart" in its column of news and editorial comment for February, 1916. There he listed six areas of character development, each amplified with specific details of behavior. He urged that the diagnosis of the strength and weakness in character of any pupil be used remedially as a basis for planning his or her character education. His six phases of character development — intellectual, vocational, personal, social, emotional, and physical — closely approximated Snedden's four "social utilities," still useful to the latter after a decade.

Snedden, in turn, some years later called for the teaching of "moralities" in preference to "morality," because, he said, there were "thousands of kinds, like manners." They needed merely "to be analyzed for specific types."[14] The character chart and the national and state morality codes were each attempts in their way to give definition to the more specific and satisfactory aims in education, and as such were characteristic of the social efficiency movement and of David Snedden.

The aims having been defined, at least for the present, the "next great step" for the NIMI was a search for the best method of instruction. Accordingly, the institute sponsored another national competition and a prize of twenty thousand dollars was offered by an anonymous donor for the best method of character education. Again it was a closed contest. At the same time, David Snedden called attention to the "need for research into moral and civic education," two categories, he said, "otherwise expressed as character education." He observed that "the means and methods of moral education" would have to be learned and he saw this as the real justification for the inquiry and research of the NIMI, especially the Interstate Character Methods Competition.[15]

Finally in 1925, in what was perhaps its last significant endeavor, the institute urged high school administrators to introduce, "as a part of high school character education, a course dealing with the personal rights and obligations of the citizen." The course content was described as constituting "those established social regulations which the young people can depend upon as establishing their own rights and also the rights of others." It was intended "to take the place of civics and sociology" and should draw upon such material as would enable the teacher "to exercise full freedom in leading the class to positive decisions."[16]

Coming at a time when Fairchild's illustrated lectures had lost much of their appeal, it would appear that the work of the institute was much augmented by the viewpoint of David Snedden. Instead of commitment to a specific method of instruction, it concentrated upon the reorganization of subject matter as the means to social efficiency in this area.

The work of the NIMI was in marked contrast to that of the Commission on the Reorganization of Secondary Education, the CRSE. The commission recognized "ethical character" as one of the seven aims of its Cardinal Principles Report. Henry Neumann of New York's Ethical Culture Society and a member of the Reviewing Committee of the CRSE served in the unique capacity of a committee of one to prepare the commission's report on "Moral Values in Secondary Education." It was essentially a restatement of the program of the Ethical Culture School as its work might be applied to the comprehensive high school. In broad outline it was in direct opposition to the Snedden-Fairchild doctrine. Neumann observed that while separate courses in moral education might seem desirable, they were difficult to maintain and had the added disadvantage of shifting responsibility to a specialist, with the result that other teachers missed opportunities for such instruction natural to their courses.

Neumann went on to say that every school might develop a positive program of moral education if "all of the activities, both in the regular day's work and after school hours" were "employed to widen and deepen the pupil's understanding of right living, to encourage a genuine abiding love of the finer modes of behavior and to form right habits." The problems from life, as found in the content of history, literature, and foreign language, provided ample opportunity for consideration of moral values. Household arts, he said, were "rich in ethical values — i.e., thrift, beauty, responsibility, industry — to provide the moral atmosphere for the good home." As for physical education, the habits of automatic obedience inculcated by gymnastics could hardly be viewed as consistent with the ideals of education in a democracy unless athletics were included "as a corrective." Art, mathematics, the sciences, vocational guidance, all provided an opportunity for presenting moral values. The extra-class activities had special value in providing the opportunity for habitual performance of certain kinds of deeds rather than others, and he noted, "character is a matter of action." Neumann seemed to be reacting to Fairchild's promotional activity when he counseled: "It would be a mistake for a high school to place its main reliance upon any single method, as if character could be developed chiefly by imparting moral wisdom or even by instilling special habits or holding up lofty ideals."[17]

The report came before the Reviewing Committee in July of 1916 when Snedden had already returned to Columbia. The reforms urged in this report, as in the Cardinal Principles Report itself, differed substantially from Snedden's approach. For him, the "values or objectives included under such categories as health, home membership, vocations, citizenship, use of leisure," need be much more specifically defined and would be achieved "through quite other means than the subjects traditionally established."[18] Instead, Neumann reinforced the traditional subjects by proposing that each contributed its share to at least one of the seven aims.[19]

Although the reorganization of secondary education under Clarence D. Kingsley had proceeded literally from Snedden's own offices in the Ford Building since the very inception of the CRSE and he himself had associated with most of the members of the Reviewing Committee at the regular meetings of the Department of the Superintendence,[20] Snedden seems to have been singularly removed from its work. Rather, he sought to work his own "reorganization" and did not blush to use this word, otherwise so generally associated with the CRSE. Indeed, Snedden seemed to disown his association with Kingsley.

Looking back on his six-and-a-half years in Massachusetts, Snedden listed his chief accomplishments there as the introduction of a statewide teacher pension system, the codification of the state's law pertaining to education, and advances in agricultural and home economics education, the latter with the aid of Charles Prosser and Charles Allen.[21] They were a curious combination of what one would otherwise have considered the side issues of those years. The teacher pension law had the popular support of the State Board of Education and Snedden's contribution lay in the addition of a clause making the teachers themselves partial contributors, on the theory that in so doing they were less likely to abuse the system. The codification project was assigned to Prosser who had a legal background, and Snedden took little part in it. His third area of accomplishment, in agricultural and home economics education, recognizes a field of activity that received much of his attention during his Massachusetts years; but his statement is more eloquent for what it neglects to say than for what it recognizes. Snedden always looked upon the problem of vocational education as a part of the total educational program and as an aspect of the social economy. Nowhere does he acknowledge his association with Kingsley, who was otherwise so significant to secondary education.

Shortly after leaving public office in February, 1917, Snedden had told the high school principals the kind of reorganization they must effect. A sharp distinction would have to be made between general education and vocational education — the old distinction between "producer" and "consumer" education again. Of the two kinds, he thought the high school was responsible only for "general education." In this area a distinction should be made between those studies that contributed to one's later adult life in the community and those studies concerned primarily with the development of one's own native powers.[22] The end result, as he saw it, would produce many kinds of mathematics, history, English, and other subjects, each dependent upon the "probable destination" of the pupil and the probable use to which he would put the content.

Snedden discussed the basic differences between his position and that found in the Cardinal Principles Report only after the report had been published. He wanted to make clear this disagreement was not of a personal nature and prefaced his remarks with a complimentary, though probably accurate, description of Kingsley as a man of "quiet persistence, patience, and insight, and certainly one of the exceptional educational leaders." As for the report itself, he said, it was "almost hopelessly academic," produced in an atmosphere of "serene scholastic aloofness."[23]

Snedden's principal criticism of the Cardinal Principles Report centered upon the commission's failure to use what he called "sociological guideposts," and this he said led to unnecessary confusion. Applying his "sociological analysis" to the seven aims, he found "health" and "vocation" were "serviceable" objectives, while he preferred to group "worthy home membership," "citizenship," and "ethical character" into his own third "utility" of social education. He did not appear troubled when he failed to find evidence of his fourth utility, cultural education, but instead chose to focus upon the report's approach to vocational education.

The vocational education movement became an important part of Snedden's life during the years from 1916 to 1925, especially as it was bound up in the work of the National Society for Vocational Education. It was not the all-important cause of his educational career but was significant in that it provided a context for his larger sociological synthesis.

Shortly before leaving Massachusetts, Commissioner Snedden had spoken to a conference of vocational teachers on the achievements of his tenure there and his prognosis of the future. He looked with disdain upon the former ideal of a vocational school, "housed in palatial buildings . . . generously equipped with all sorts of well-kept wood and metal working machinery," and typed this nothing more than a means of maintaining "a splendid bluff." He believed vocational teachers had come a long ways and learned a lot. To prepare workers for the "hire and fire" methods of the working world, they had learned to keep technical training closely related to the practical work; in practical vocational education the product produced by the student must be "good enough to sell"; experience had shown it was futile, even harmful, to mix "a blend or hash of general education into the work of the vocational school." Still to be achieved was the adoption of a school day similar in length to the "workman's day," and hopefully, a system of "unpaid foremanship" among senior students to reduce the amount of personal instruction required of the teacher. He thought the Boy Scout movement might provide some helpful suggestions in this area.

In Snedden's estimate, the Reviewing Committee of the CRSE lacked experience with the "recent movements for vocational education." With this observation he dismissed the experience of Principal Milo Stuart of Indianapolis' Arsenal Manual Training High School, a member of the committee, and in Snedden's opinion, a representative of "denatured" vocational education. He expressed some doubt that the chairman of the vocational committees had "scrutinized the 'Cardinal

Principles' " before approving them. Snedden said that, lacking the "sociological point of view," the report had confused real vocational education with courses about vocations. Illustrating his point, he called for "special schools for special qualified people to be trained . . . for such vocations as tailoring, jewelry salesmanship, poultry farming, coal cutting, stationary engine firing, . . . teaching French in secondary school, . . . raisin grape growing, general farming suited to Minnesota, . . . streetcar motor driving." In a similar vein, a half dozen schools should be established throughout the country for the training of "locomotive drivers." These schools, "no less effective than schools for dentists," would be equipped with "a few score miles of track, a hundred locomotives, a couple of repair shops, a half dozen classrooms and working part-time arrangements with a few neighboring railroads — that would be sufficient. "Clearly these arrangements were a thing apart from the program of the comprehensive high school and would require facilities of a highly specialized nature; but, he insisted these were the only vocational arrangements that would "meet the economic tests of our times."

By his estimate, vocational education was one of the larger movements attempting to meet the demands of the contemporary social economy. The determination of detailed, valid, educational objectives, he said, would require "sociological analysis of the kind that Ross, Tardé, Sumner, Small and Giddings might provide." Significantly, two of these men, Ross and Giddings, had been Snedden's teachers, and he frequently drew upon Small's writings. The suggestion is strong that Snedden regretted not having had a part in the work of the CRSE.

Kingsley replied to Snedden with measured phrases in strong defense of the comprehensive high school and paid tribute to the thoughtful work of the Reviewing Committee. The ideal high school of the commission was one "where the pupils mingle freely, . . . and where the interrelations of different vocational groups find expression in the school itself." Perhaps in reaction to Snedden's implied rejection of the work of Milo Stuart and the program of the Arsenal High School, he named this school in particular as an example of the CRSE ideal. Here many specific trades were taught in two-year curriculums side by side with others that prepared students for the state university. Here the "interests of American society" were best served as pupils in all curriculums mingled freely. For Snedden, reorganization involved defining the school's role in the social control of the individual and implementing this role through a differentiation of program. Kingsley noted that it was not so much the question of specific aims as opposed to general or "faith" aims separating the CRSE approach from Snedden's, but rather, concern for the consequences to a democratic society of an education for a single specific function.

Snedden held to his position. The following September in the *American Journal of Sociology* he said that upholders of the traditional studies feared the early introduction of vocational studies, at age fourteen, would drive out the old studies, as Gresham had shown bad money would drive out the good. It was a fear he shared with them if the CRSE should have its way. Against this apparent hazard Snedden urged "valid aims" in the form of specific objectives be found for the "non-vocational" studies so as to make them competitive. For this educators would have to turn to sociology and draw upon "its knowledge of social controls, social ascendancy, and social progress." By way of example, sociological methods could "discover the scope and character of mathematical knowledge now used in any given 'standard of living,' class, or group."

In the years ahead, the early twenties, David Snedden continued to ridicule what he regarded as the "half-hearted" work of those "anemic little vocational departments" in the comprehensive high school. He called all the more for schools of "real" vocational education located with optimum accessibility to the facilities of productive work rather than to the homes of the student.[24] This had been the ideal of the National Society for the Promotion of Industrial Education.

With the passage of the Smith-Hughes Act in 1917, the NSPIE became the National Society for Vocational Education, and David Snedden was elected its first president at the eleventh annual convention in 1918. He was re-elected the following year. However, in the main, vocational educators were not in agreement with Snedden's demands, and it is likely that most often he was addressing his remarks especially to them. His persistent predictions of the impending total victory for his kind of vocational education seemed intended to demoralize their opposition.

The conflict between the point of view supporting the comprehensive high school and that supporting specific vocational education may be noted as early as 1914 with the publication of the preliminary report of the CRSE Manual Arts Committee. In many details Chairman Leavitt expressed agreement at this time with positions Snedden held. The tentative conclusions of the report called for shorter courses, longer school days, and earlier differentiation. It promoted industrial arts as best suited to the student who would not reach the high school, and it held as the "major purpose of instruction . . . vocational efficiency," all of which was far more extreme than the final position taken by the CRSE. Leavitt stated his point of disagreement with Snedden in blunt language. "We are committed," said he, "to the proposition that *complete* separation between vocational and general election is impossible, unnecessary, and undesirable." The committee believed technical courses should be open to all students and could form the basis of later vocational work for some, though this was not necessary. The question, he averred, would never have been raised had not the demand for separation of cultural and vocational courses been so persistent. In a spirit of charity he sought to find excuse for Snedden's position in the necessity of state-supported vocational education to find a workable definition upon which to base its payment of subsidy. But, Leavitt argued, efforts of "such officials" should not be used to judge the work in progress.[25]

Also in opposition to the rigid separation of function typified by the Snedden-NSPIE brand of vocational education, middle-western vocational educators formed their own organization, the Vocational Education Association of the Middle West, in February, 1915.[26]

United States Commissioner of Education Philander P. Claxton was at best lukewarm to the Snedden approach. Asked by Edward A. Ott of Waukegan, Illinois, to name "the ten foremost things in education," he listed as number eight "specific training for vocations" built upon a foundation of "more definite and more practical" education at the elementary and junior high school level. It appeared with a noticable lack of enthusiasm and paucity of detail. The following year, in a spirit of resignation, he confided to the NEA his own "shudder of abhorrence" for the "brutal efficiency" implied by the new and more effective vocational education.[27]

At this time Claxton made a move to bring both organizations of vocational educators together at a single meeting, perhaps to temper the extreme approach of the Easterners with the more moderate views of the middle west association. Both associations arranged to hold their annual conventions simultaneously in Chicago in 1920 with a single joint membership fee.[28] Five years later the two associations merged.

In September, 1922, David Snedden was named editor of the new

Vocational Education Magazine, the official organ of the National Society for Vocational Education. Its purpose was to represent the point of view of the Eastern association, and it ceased publication only after the merger in 1925. In his initial editorial for the first number, Snedden recognized the two existing journals of industrial arts, *Manual Training Magazine* and *Industrial Arts Magazine,* as "excellent," but quite different in function from the *Vocational Education Magazine* in that they were concerned primarily with "general education."[29] This distinction of itself was reason enough for him to spend his time in this venture. But just so there would be no misunderstanding, he assured his readers his magazine was concerned with "genuine vocational education." He claimed for his cause those social workers who saw in this kind of education the means of correcting many of the problems arising as by-products of the "specialization of work," including the "depletion of rural neighborhoods, mobility of workers, and competition of men and women."

In the editorials of the succeeding months Snedden promoted with great fervor his program of vocational education for specific functions separate from general education and at all times related to the total plan of education and to the social economy or its "sociological foundations." George Counts, then at Yale, argued that "the rank and file of workers" should be given a breadth of view to enable them to see their industry as a whole. Snedden agreed, but asked, why was this the responsibility of the vocational school? What was general education for, if not for this?

After four months as editor, Snedden was calling for the membership to help in the cause. He was forced to admit that the large majority of American educators, manual workers, business men and editors were still "honestly ignorant" of genuine vocational education. Publicity of the right kind was needed. He called for "brief telling statements" prepared by members, each related to a specific vocation, to win support, especially of parents.

At the annual convention of the vocational educators in 1922, the first steps were taken to merge the separate organizations that had been holding joint membership meetings since 1920. The motivation seemed to have come from an awareness that school administrators were less than enthusiastic about vocational education. In the year that followed, Snedden mounted a stout defense of direct vocational education via his editorial page. He blamed the lagging development of full-time day industrial schools on the laymen and educators alike who refused to accept the idea that good vocational education must be "basic rather than merely 'technical,'" not mere knowledge, often textbook knowledge at that, but actual training in basic manipulative skills. He chided them that too often they taught only those subjects for which existed a body of literature when they should be making progress toward specific vocational education, "by working back from demonstrated standards of proficiency in the vocation itself." The industrial school, he insisted, should be a haven where "direct, efficient learning" could take place under job conditions, free of the "easy-going, energy-wasting" methods that typified "on the job" training.

The illusion that there was cultural possibility in vocational education was, to his estimate, the invention of the academic mind and for reason of its persistent reappearance needed to be dispelled. Paternalistically Snedden suggested that in the after-hours the "farmer, bookkeeper, and shoevamper" might properly devote his time to "music, literature, art, craftsmanship, or sociability"; but such cultural interests must be the product of self-education once the youth started his vocational training. The single-purpose struggle for vocational efficiency was grim business indeed.

Snedden believed lay opinion commonly failed to make the proper distinction between practical arts work and genuine vocational education, especially at the junior high school level. He considered the two competing industrial journals as devoted to practical arts and contributing to this confusion. In seeking to justify industrial arts work for children under fifteen years of age, he dismissed most of the usual arguments, that it was prevocational training, an exploratory experience, useful to motivation, a means of increasing technical knowledge, and settled upon one — the "developmental experience" afforded by these studies, especially for urban boys. He observed, perhaps recalling the satisfaction his own son took in working with tools, that the boys from twelve to fifteen took keen delight in the manipulative experience of the workshop. He considered this use of practical arts courses for boys of urban environment the means of fulfillment of valid social demands.

During 1924, the National Society for Vocational Education and the Vocational Education Association of the Middle West were drawing closer together. Snedden appears to have done what he could to forestall the merger short of placing himself in open opposition to it. Editorially, he reasoned that professional organizations were especially important to the maintenance of an *esprit de corps*, especially in pioneer fields like vocational education. For the average teacher, the state association, of all professional organizations, was most important. Few regional associations could be successful; but the midwestern association, organized for the region within twelve hours travel time of Chicago, was unique in this respect and presumably for this reason should continue its independent existence. The national associations and national conventions, after all, were for "policy-makers" and what was really needed, in his estimation, was a national council of spokesmen from all the existing societies.

On the surface Snedden gave little evidence that he realized his type of specific vocational education was being rejected by the profession. Instead he registered frustration over lagging progress and continued to predict its inevitable triumph. In the fall of 1923 he noted that fewer industrial schools were being etsablished; in the fall of 1924 he observed that agitation and promotional publicity for vocational education had diminished, that it had been in a slump for the past two or three years.

He found the 1924 convention altogether too peaceful, too ladylike, too complacent, and too remote from the present-day realities he associated as synonymous with his approach. There were still three fundamental issues with which the association needed to grapple: "the relative efficacy of non-school industrial vocational training and . . . non-school practical experience supplemented by extension instruction, the . . . expected scope of industrial training in special schools, [and] public support of such school industrial training." He reminded the profession that there were hundreds of distinct industrial vocations and separate vocational schools had been established for only a few of them. These were the "critical issues" he believed needed to be "fearlessly threshed out."

At the national convention in 1925 the two associations merged, and in the eyes of William T. Bawden, one of the "Eastern leaders," this meant that the NSVE had "come around" to the more moderate views of the middle western association.[30] Snedden quietly stepped down as editor of *Vocational Education Magazine*, and it ceased publication a few months later.

"Education, social control, and domestic life" were still in the hands of "traditions, faiths, beliefs, and customs," Snedden had said in 1919, even as medicine and the mechanical industries had been in the eighteenth century; but the time was right "to begin a careful examination of the possible contribution of sociology and social economy to education." [31]

Early in 1921 Snedden took it upon himself to suggest some "practical next steps" in high school reorganization to the New York State Academic Principals Association. He turned again to the distinction he liked to make between vocational education and general education on the secondary level. He argued pessimistically that 50 per cent of the pupils entering a high school could not, should not, remain for the full four-year course. High schools should concentrate on truly liberal education for these children during the years from fourteen to sixteen, on laying a broad foundation of "personal culture, civic insight and physical well-being," on providing "educational bread," not stones, to use Snedden's biblical analogy. The "bread" was to be made up of elements taken from existing offerings in literature, practical arts, history, social science, and English, most likely to fit the "needs" of the group; the "stones" were the traditionally organized studies.[32]

Snedden thought the social studies teacher was in a position of special responsibility for the teaching of social values. Teaching in this area was quite different from the teaching of Latin, algebra, geography, handwriting, or a trade. He said, "To 'teach' various social values means inevitably to 'advocate' them, to seek to shape appreciations, ideals, sentiments, attitudes of learners toward them." Bluntly he stated, "Successful teaching of social values necessarily means that the teacher shall be an advocate, a pleader, perhaps a partisan." [33] In this connection the teacher needed to remember that he was a public servant and had no special right to teach what seemed good or true primarily to him. Rather, he was under "heavy obligation" to present "the collective opinions and valuation" of the controlling majority or withdraw from their service. Minority opinion must yield to the will of the majority and if the teacher held such opinion, in his public capacity, he must conform to majority opinion.

Percy Davidson, Snedden's successor on the Stanford faculty, proclaimed his "emphatic dissent" at this article. Snedden had described "precisely what sound teaching *is not*." Instead, the teacher should be wary of betraying his own sentiment, avoid indoctrination, and seek the truth by presenting all sides of an issue. As a public servant, Davidson went on, the teacher must side neither with the majority nor the minority. It seemed to him that "a teacher has 'arrived' when he unmistakably exhibits a conscience that smites him when he falls into pleading and partisanship."

Snedden came back with an immediate reply. He stood firmly behind the principle of indoctrination, which he believed was the basis for the political, religious, philosophical, industrial, and educational progress of the day. Davidson had charged Snedden would make the teacher nothing more than a paid propagandist. Snedden begged the question by urging every teacher be a "propagandist of the best moral and civic values" of the day.

In 1923 David Snedden joined Walter R. Smith of Kansas, Charles C. Peters of Ohio Wesleyan, Ross Finney of Minnesota, and others in founding the National Society for the Study of Educational Sociology. The purpose of the new society was to assist in standardizing the content of educational sociology as a teaching subject on the collegiate level and to develop a technique of research in the field. The new organization elected to meet annually in December with the American Sociological Society and again in February with the Department of the Superintendence. Smith was the first president, Peters became secretary-treasurer, while Snedden, Finney, and E. George Payne of New York University composed the first executive committee. Four years later the society began publication of the *Journal of Educational Sociology* with Payne as editor.

During the period of the early twenties Snedden introduced the designation "case group" to his system. He found it particularly useful in prescribing the program of schooling for the twelve-to-fifteen, later the fourteen-to-eighteen, age group. Identification with a particular case group was based upon native ability, environmental background, and future prospects as imposed by the socioeconomic group from which the student came. By this line of reasoning, ability alone was not enough to warrant a child take an academic program if his "prospects" made four years of college an unrealistic goal.

Snedden considered it reprehensible that high schools should require algebra and plane geometry of all and by his estimate their instruction in foreign language was superficial at best. He said, "The central curse and the anti-democracy of traditional education is, of course, its postulates of uniformity of individuals and of a static social inheritance." [34] Instead, once a study could be made of the school histories and subsequent life histories of several generations of secondary school students, various homogeneous groupings, the case groups, could be designated and educational programs planned to meet their needs.

Snedden took great satisfaction from the supposedly successful experience of sociology in the area of social pathology as it met the demands of society in dealing with the defective and potential delinquent. "The sociologist thinks constantly in terms of social groups" as well as "of individuals composing these groups," he said, in explanation of educational sociology. Some thought his approach, implemented by his "case groups," undemocratic. Brushing aside such criticism, he promised sociology could be expected to establish the valid aims of education, and, indeed, educational sociology was poised to produce a large literature to this end. He himself published four books in this field, with four different publishers, from 1920 to 1922. Educators, he said, should be compelled to go to sociology for the help it had to offer.[35]

In 1922 Snedden expressed his criticism of the numerous progressive experiments in education, which were often based on the optimistic teachings of Friedrick Froebel. He said, "The philosopher who gave the world the kindergarten so overloaded its underlying theory with mystical assumptions as to the practicability of making angelic silken purses out of the biological sow's ears of human nerve tissue as to make his educational metaphysics the despair of practical educators ever since his day." [36]

He had little hope that the children of the rank and file would get through the high school course, and the upper grades of the elementary school had little to offer them until a differentiated program to meet individual needs was initiated. But the little one-room rural school was the worst of all with its "motley processions of teachers which passed term by term through these schools — an occasional rough diamond, not infrequently a vile mountebank, and commonly only youths, or disillusioned elders of more than doubtful competency." Fortunate were the youth of "intellectual inclination" who might be "inspired by devoted and zealous mothers." Perhaps he was thinking of his own youth, of the procession of schoolmasters who came to the little log school in the Lockwood Valley, of Mr. Aram and Mr. Vance and his own mother. To alleviate the "dull routine" of the upper-grade classroom, he urged educators to take a lesson from the Boy Scout movement, which had demonstrated its ability to attract and hold "the most dynamic of boys."

He insisted that in the spirit of true democratic education the schools must cease providing the kind of liberal education best suited to an aristocratic leisure class, "complex" studies that were "nauseating messes" only driving out the children of the "rank and file." At this point Snedden found himself again confronted by Spencer's query "What knowledge is most worth?" or, as he preferred to rephrase it, "What knowledges (habits, ideals, appreciations, skills, aspirations, working powers, self-confidences, persistent interests) are most worth?" He concluded that the answer to this question would be different for each "case group."

Snedden reacted to Bobbitt's curriculum, prepared in 1922 for the Los Angeles public schools, from this viewpoint. He found much to praise in Bobbitt's multitude of specific aims, but to his mind they fell short of his ideal by assuming that the same aims were applicable to all youth. Snedden feared Bobbitt was trying to create a "sociological Utopia" and was assuming all could achieve the same level of efficient, intelligent behavior. In this he said Bobbitt was no different from the "aspirationists." [37]

"Aspirationists" was Snedden's label for those educators who believed all men could be made equal through education. For him this was Utopian and unrealistic. He also defined some educators as "general prescriptionists," that is, those who required the same set program of "cultural" studies for all; an "aspirationist" could as easily place his faith in a freely elective program. He considered the uniform prescriptive program worst of all because it supposedly resulted in an appalling aimlessness and superficiality of instruction. He saw the result as a "leveling down" of all to the same standard of achievement. [38] The next worst method, according to Snedden, was that of free election. He believed children would use little intelligence in the selection of courses, and the school program would lack in depth. Prescription itself, whether by legislative decree, school rule, or by instigation of the teacher, he said, was sound policy so long as it was "personal and concrete." At best only 2 per cent of the youth, he thought, could attain real mastery in a traditional academic study like algebra. Similarly, the average man might only aspire to "civism" in the area of social education, while the above-average man might attain a position of statesmanship in leading and coordinating the efforts of others. The "rank and file" could be trained to be followers and to follow well; like an athletic team or a submarine crew, society also had to rely upon followers as well as leaders. The two kinds of men, fulfilling their proper function, would make an efficient society.

Snedden built his case upon the argument that society was made stronger by a specialization of function analogous to team organization. Both the "team group" and society of which they were part were constantly threatened by inefficient uniformity of "herd-groups." Educators who failed to provide opportunity for differentiation, and indeed, insisted that all take the same program, were branded "herd-minded" — a title synonymous with "aspirationist." He blamed the uniformity of school programs on "the pressure of educational factory methods" because of the economies that accrued from "quantity production of standardized parts," and also on the "rank and file" themselves who seemed to find a measure of status in enrolling their children in the traditional course.

Nonetheless, Snedden conceded some "herd-like uniformities" were inevitable. He was referring to those imposed by his own "genuine" vocational education, and he felt he could justify them because they grew out of the "realities of the vocational world." In the fields of cultural, civic, and physical education, the "herd-making practices" were supposedly worse and could not be so easily justified.

Snedden set himself apart from others who would adapt education to individual differences on the basis of method, holding instead that the aims themselves should be different. For him "educational equalitarianism" was a "gross superstition," likely to deprive a large number of children and youth of the educational opportunities they deserved. He felt that educators under the spell of this belief provided mere sameness of educational opportunity in the confused belief they were providing equality of opportunity. Instead, he argued, the student should be fitted to achieve optimum success in the environment in which he found himself so far as his natural endowment would permit. He recognized differences in endowment and opportunity as "immutable facts," and his program of education was intended to develop the individual to live within his predetermined limits. In this way the needs of a "team society," based upon the "coordinate complementary contributions" of all its members, would be satisfied.

In cultural attainments the team society needed its amateur specialists, those who followed a cultural interest in depth, as their natural ability allowed, but as a leisure-time activity and possibly with the full knowledge that their station in life certainly would preclude its professional development. Thus a boy might be permitted to study a language if he really enjoyed the subject, so long as he did not do so out of the "inflated notion" that he would use it for admission to college when he could not possibly afford the expense of higher education. Youths with superior musical talent were to be encouraged in junior high school, even though shop work or mathematics should have to be waived to provide the time for this instruction. The amateur naturalist should be encouraged, not only for his own satisfaction, but also so he might "radiate" some of his interest and knowledge throughout the community. For the same reason every community needed a few persons of superior talent to master the Japanese language and become local authorities on Japanese civilization.

In answer to Sinclair Lewis' caricature of contemporary American culture, *Main Street*, Snedden provided a far more optimistic view in "Gopher Prairie — AD 2000," published in 1923.[39] Perhaps comparing present-day Gopher Prairie with Santa Paula and Paso Robles in the nineties, he found cause to congratulate Lewis' Mid-America for the high comparative level of culture achieved in but a few short decades. He held it was a matter of first importance to plan the educational program in advance for the cultural level Gopher Prairie should attain by the year 2000. For the moment he was willing to yield to a certain degree of "blanket prescription" so that all might have in common the same "small but significant amounts" of knowledge and data drawn from the traditional subject fields, as well as manners, morals, appreciations, and essentials of dress. Upon this base, he would build "individual and 'small group' culture" with differentiated prescribed programs. Gopher Prairie would have its Japanese Society, its Modern Poetry Lyceum, its "select club" of amateur violin players, and even a small study group to delve into Greek classics. Membership in these various groups would not be restricted to any single social class and supposedly would include professional people, the skilled, and the unskilled. Education for the "*common* culture" would have to be accomplished largely before the age of twelve, and therefore education in personal culture would remain for the junior high school years. Seemingly, the school would determine who should belong to each of the social groups by prescribing, making available, or denying entrance to the course content upon which group membership depended.

Snedden acknowledged the school would permit only a very small percentage of the youth to gain an "intimate acquaintance" with the language and literature of the ancient Greeks, certainly no one "of inferior intelligence or of straitened economic circumstances." [40]

Development of the program of the junior high school especially interested Snedden because, according to his plan, it provided the last opportunity for children of the "rank and file" to appropriate liberal education before beginning full-time vocational education. In 1925 he suggested three kinds of courses, each descriptive of a different type of practical attainment. To get a diploma upon completion of the three-year junior high school program the student would have to present twenty-four units each of "developmental" and "projective" studies and twenty-seven of the "recreational" order.[41]

Snedden's basic unit of measure was the "lotment" calculated in clock hours, as had been customary in vocational education. Each lotment amounted to sixty hours of work, accumulated in one of several different ways. It might be earned one hour per day for twelve weeks, or two hours per week for thirty weeks, or one hour per week for sixty weeks — divisions of time that could be made to fit the quarter, the semester, or the academic year. The work of each lotment of credit was based upon what "learners of modal characteristics" could be expected to accomplish in the particular kind of activity. Perhaps in anticipation of criticism that a standard established in this way would have a leveling effect, he said his plans were primarily for the "common people," the 60 per cent of the population who were neither "gifted" nor "unable minded."

"Lotments," Snedden said, were really "a measure of the 'amount of a specific type of objective'" in a great many different areas of activity. For instance, a course in Pronouncement and Enunciation would earn one or more "projective lotments." Public Speaking might earn as many as nine lotments. Two or more could be earned in Friendly Letter Writing, while lotments were also suggested for Make-up Penmanship, Make-up Oral Syntax, and Stenographer's Spelling. He proposed "developmental lotments" in Appreciation Mathematics, General Science, Scientific Method, and Current Events, to note but a few. Some lotments might be earned during out-of-school hours in such varied areas as library reading, woodchopping, bedmaking, furnace tending, child care, and newspaper selling.

Lotments were but part of Snedden's larger scheme of educational reorganization. He proposed the "peth" — from an old Welsh word meaning "little piece" — as the smallest particle sorted out of the curriculum for purposes of analysis. Each "working unit" in the curriculum was a "peth." It might be a single spelling word, the multiplication table of nine, or the proper pronunciation of a particular syllable. "Serviceable peths of learning" were in fact anything that could be separated out as a unit to be evaluated for its usefulness. He said this was not unlike current practice in "job analysis" for vocational education.

"Strands" were recurrent life activities that would have to be disentangled from the composite of life activities by the process of "strand analysis." He said this was already being done in vocational job analysis, but that perhaps eight hundred to two thousand strands might be found for the non-vocational life activities of adults. Strand learnings might be the result of either in-school or extra-school activities. The individual peths of learning were significant to the school only as they contributed that which could not be learned elsewhere. Once identified they were to be classified according to the life strands to which they belonged and then organized into lotments in the curriculum.

Social efficiency required "making the most of each individual, along lines of his major potentialities." It called for "team efficiency" as opposed to "herd standards." No single study or group of studies was prescribed for all, but all would have to meet certain minimum attainments in English and social studies. Work in spelling, handwriting, oral syntax, silent reading, and "utilizer's arithmetic" would be prescribed in amounts to bring all to their maximum potential achievement in these areas. With the same end in view, developmental physical work might be prescribed for a person in need of body building, while for others it could be used as a recreational lotment.

Beyond this, the school would be expected to prescribe a program "best ministering to desirable ends." He now believed that differentiation might well begin in the lower grades or even in the kindergarten, but it was most needed in the high school. In the interest of proper prescription the school might be expected to amass detailed files on each student. Snedden believed they should include, in addition to the usual content, information concerning parental ambitions for the student, the financial circumstances of the parents, and the opportunities afforded by the student's environment. He urged educators to take their cue from the field of public health, working back from practical situations to their causes, just as he had advocated in providing for vocational education.

It was apparent to Snedden that there was an obvious similarity between his approach and that of Bobbitt and Charters, each of whom was also concerned with defining precisely stated objectives of education covering a broad range of human activity. He felt that Bobbitt's objectives closely resembled his own strand activities, but said they were qualitative only and failed to identify the optimum achievement for each case group of learners — the quantitative requirement. The same held for Charter's work, with the additional limitation that it was based entirely on what Snedden considered "the traditional organization of subject matter."

Snedden liked to view the work of the curriculum-maker as analogous to that of the city planner or the head of the municipal health department, either of whom fit his "eudemic" role for educational sociology. Educational sociology, as it was concerned with the amelioration of human ills, was termed "applied sociology," "welfare sociology," or "eudemics" by Snedden, and he felt it was the responsibility of the educational sociologist to make the importance of this field apparent to educators. They should be forced, if necessary, to study this subject in order to provide the specific kinds of education to correct such social ills as "irresponsible fecundity" and "delinquency." Educational policies should especially take into consideration the special education needed by "rural renting folk," "offspring of mixed Indian and white stock," "men without a country, e.g., American-born Japanese, . . . neither Japanese nor Americans," "adolescents in the 'flitting season,'" and "children of divorce-sundered families" — all potential "case groups."[42]

To illustrate this point and as a class exercise for his graduate students, Snedden created the mythical Province of Zond as an ideal of the "socially efficient community." It was, of course, a society of "team formations," of highly specialized workmen who would refuse to attempt any job for which they had not been specifically trained, and of "case groups" trained to specialized "civic behaviors" and "cultural utilizations." The "eudemic programs" of Zond required that children fill "getting ready roles," learning much of superior "utilizations" in superior homes. In consequence kindergartens and primary schools were unnecessary, and children did not see the inside of a school until the age of nine or ten. All minors were expected to supplement "physical play" with physical work of "primary kinds," like digging, walking, building, and chopping. The men of Zond learned to prefer "freely developed, muscular, thriving, health-ridden women, made such by hard farm, forest, mine, or other 'outdoor' heavy work," who would save the stock from "dry-rot."

In Zond, only a very few men of "higher native ability" would be permitted to prepare for the professions. All would be trained in the "useful conformities" to law and order, but one might expect 2 per cent to become "habitual or confirmed offenders." These would have to be destroyed painlessly, "not as punishment, but as 'social surgery.'" In another place, Snedden said the "useful conformities" should be based upon a series of concrete objectives, "hardly less tangible than . . . the multiplication tables," and these would be instilled as part of the more efficient education. Apart from this basic minimum, the civic education of each individual would vary according to his "ascertained potential" and would be strenuously taught between the ages of fourteen and twenty. Some would continue to be trained for "the conformist civic relationship," in behaviors of "yieldings, obediences, and assentings" to the will of the majority. Others would be prepared for "dynamic civic relationships," as initiators of political action. Cultural education would be similarly calculated to prepare all for a desirable level of "utilization" of food, medicine, recreation, good literature, fine manners, social courtesies, while fostering a high level of specialized "connoisseur appreciations."

Snedden prophesied the science of educational values would develop only after fairly concrete objectives were formulated for school achievement. He thought this development would be comparable to that in the field of medicine following Pasteur's discovery of the bacterial causes of disease. Presumably educational sociology was on the verge of making just as important a contribution and one might infer that David Snedden could be its "Pasteur." Elsewhere he had warned his readers that only rarely had frontier thinkers, like Socrates, Galileo, and Pasteur, been recognized by their colleagues during their lifetime.[43]

For Snedden there was only one approach to an educational problem, the "scientific." He had only scorn for those who were prone to look to the past for the "background" of a problem. Any solution based upon the history or philosophy of education was as passé as insisting upon the logical organization of subject matter, which he said was also "pretty generally blacklisted." He was particularly critical of programs of teacher education that included large portions of traditional subjects. Rather, education, as an "applied science," should draw what it needed from various sources, like medicine.[44]

With embarrassing irony, E. George Payne criticized Snedden's book *What's Wrong with American Education* as an unscientific contribution in reviewing it for his *Journal of Educational Sociology*. Nonetheless, he predicted it would stimulate discussion and recommended the book to those "who want a sleepless night replete with unpleasant dreams." The next year, when Snedden published *Educational Sociology for Beginners,* Payne found the book excessively verbose and again thought the major weakness lay in its "unscientific" approach. The editor said it belonged with other books that used "the older approach to the study of educational problems," one based on common observation. Delivering his coup de grâce, he suggested perhaps the book should have been done by one of the "younger men in the field who have had modern training in the best sociological techniques." [45]

Harsh as these reviews were, it was with Boyd Bode that Snedden seemed most often to find occasion for argument. Bode attacked him for his assertion that the "scientific approach," as he interpreted it, was the only valid source of educational aims. He cut to the very heart of Snedden's "sociological analysis" with the observation, "the notion that ideals can be evoked from a process of environmental fact-finding is just another of the many delusions to which our sinful flesh is heir." He said it was this "fallacious notion" upon which Snedden's 1924 volume, *The Sociological Determination of Objectives in Education,* was based. [46]

Like Dewey, Bode was an an educational philosopher who found Snedden's proposals narrow, limiting, and often undemocratic. From the mid-twenties to the early thirties their mutual antagonism rose and from time to time overflowed. Bode was especially critical of Snedden's attempt to employ "scientific fact-finding" to the identification of educational objectives. He insisted such identification was primarily a problem for philosophy in which science had no place. In his opinion, science was "Dr. Snedden's whole religion" and accordingly a chapter in his *Modern Educational Theories* was devoted to refuting Snedden's sociological determination of objectives. To Bode the separation of vocation from culture was the fundamental issue, and if Snedden's plan were followed it would lead to the development of an aristocracy.

The exchange between Bode and Snedden, very likely promoted by Payne to increase the circulation of his fledgling journal, gave Snedden opportunity to state his case quite pointedly. Snedden's "democratic aspiration" was for all men to have "much culture," "much social sympathy," "much liberalism of political outlook," but all irrespective of vocation. Presumably, one's vocation would be based upon circumstance, and Snedden said "men of powers" could read with delight from Browning, though they be "shoe repairers, dentists, or college professors." Carrying the controversy to the pages of the *Teachers College Record*, he dismissed as impossible any hope that either sociology or philosophy would ever identify the "ultimate values of education"; but as for proximate values, the task had just begun and educational values were no less real than were food values in dietetic science. When "all the children of all the people come to high school," he warned, they will not tolerate "the salt pork and rye bread of algebra, essay writing . . . dry-as-dust ancient history, . . . good as these are for intellectual stomachs." His hope rested with inventive teachers who would develop "current literature," "current world events," and "current social science thinking." [47]

In discussing this same question with the New York high school teachers a few years later, he predicted that "good, broad, general reading" would replace classical literature in the high schools, because the latter was too difficult to interest any but a very few. "The rank and file," he said, "still wisely prefer the *Saturday Evening Post* to Homer and Chaucer." [48]

When Snedden was thus quoted in the *New York Times*, his colleague from the Columbia faculty, Allen Abbott, came to a somewhat tempered defense of the classics. He believed some were likely to be too difficult for the kind of student coming to the high schools, as compared to the students of the nineties. But the classics had great value as works the race had seen fit to save "from the wreckage of time." He felt there were less difficult classics these pupils could handle, like *Mother Goose*, *The Arabian Nights* and *Huckleberry Finn*. The value of all classical literature lay in the "striking and vital form" it gave to concepts of human life and character, comedy and tragedy. He called the classics the means by which the race explained itself and kept itself going. While not an enthusiastic defense, to be sure, it was one that distinguished Snedden's values from his own. To Snedden the classics were of little use because only exceptional teachers could make them interesting, while to Abbott they had an intrinsic worth in themselves.

The book Snedden like to think of as his "big book," *Toward Better Educations*, was published in 1931. It was addressed to legislators, lay leaders, administrators, and "above all mature and far-sighted teachers" and all who as "the projectors of the ampler and more socially efficient education of the future" might be in a position to reshape the curricula. As for the present, he said, "America now fairly seethes with aspirations for better educations." [49]

Toward Better Educations developed quite naturally from the distinction he liked to make between his own educational differentiation, based upon aims varied according to probable destination, and that of other educators, based upon varied ability. As he saw the problem of the schools, it was not a question of "method," that is, of how to teach people of varied ability, but one of "aim," the question of what shall be taught people of varied destinations. First the sociologist would have to decide what the student would later do with his learning before the psychologist could be concerned with how well the student learns. He believed the sociologist was uniquely qualified to identify the aims of education because he was in a position to base them upon valid social and eudemic values, while the philosopher was not and usually had to resort to "faith aims." Snedden believed in "concrete aims" based upon "concrete analysis."

The year before, 1930, Snedden had prepared a single volume relating the science of "eudemics" to the formulation of educational aims. Educational values, purposes, or objectives, he said, must find their foundations in social values. "Educations of all kinds are *means* not *ends*," and only "optimum social (eudemic) values" could provide these ends. In successive chapters he went on to expand upon growths of individuals to optimum eudemic competency, which was synonymous with social efficiency, the sources of eudemic well-being, and the kinds of eudemic well-being, which were four in number — vocational, physical, social, and cultural. Snedden may have considered himself a pioneer, but his reviewers sometimes saw him otherwise. Instead of seeing Snedden's program as a new education to meet the new needs of society, James Skipper of Ohio State University found in it only "complacency and satisfaction with things as they are." [50] He believed the logical conclusion to be drawn from the book was that the sociological approach to objectives resulted in a total disregard for "the factor of rapid change." He said sociological investigation of the Snedden variety was capable only of yielding information concerning the status quo and made no attempt to provide the social theory needed to give direction to educational effort.

In *Toward Better Educations*, Snedden reiterated all the more forcefully his position that in a society such as ours it seemed "absurd" not to have developed "specific sciences" of "school arts," "neighborhood morality," and "recreative and other values." He asked, "Can educators . . . develop a great science of education paralleling in scope and importance [the] splendid sciences of preventive medicine, fruit growing, bridge-building, copper mining . . . and the like?" He believed they could. The way to "better educations" was a now familiar one; the "knowledge of most worth" should be selected for its usefulness to various case groups, and organized into lotments of work as "alpha" and "beta" subjects, education for "team societies" as opposed to "herd societies." [51]

Snedden's detractors had criticized his specific education as "undemocratic." In *Toward Better Education,* he replied that America had nearly a thousand expensive schools for the professional vocations, but almost none to provide school vocational training for the sub-professional vocations. This state of affairs, he reasoned, only gave special opportunity to those already endowed with wealth and position, while providing nothing for those with less ability and of meager economic circumstance.

Considering the question on a broader plane, Snedden thought "oligarchy" a useful antithesis of "democracy." He did not believe oligarchies were necessarily bad, for he said that on innumerable occasions they had saved human societies from ruin or brought them to higher states of efficiency. He acknowledged, " 'Democracy' as a symbol embraces clearly a very different embodiment of ideals and practices than those embraced under such other omnibus terms as 'social efficiency' " [52] He said one of the important responsibilities of the educator lay in keeping the democratic ideal in view while "maintaining the efficiency of the social group as a means to the well-being of all its members." In part this required the educator to assist the "weak" to self-fulfillment while protecting the interest of the strong. Resorting again to his favorite foil, Snedden made reference to Boyd Bode's *Fundamentals of Education* to illustrate his own position. Bode offered the ideal of "social democracy" as a more encompassing term than "political democracy." In reply Snedden posited, "the eternal question remains, 'How much can social efficiency stand of these several democracies?' "

In 1932, speaking to the school superintendents during the depression, Snedden took the stance of one bearing a message of hope, if not of the final solution to America's socioeconomic problems. He proposed to quiet their fears with the assurance that social change was not new in

world history and that present concerns had been undoubtedly intensi-
fied by a variety of "heavily emotionalized," exaggerated pronouncements from men and women otherwise possessed of good mental powers.
He pegged it a "new type of herd-mindedness" or "herd panic" resembling the incantations directed to pagan deities in other eras of history.
In contrast to Dewey's adaptive role for the school, as delineated in
School and Society, Snedden urged schoolmen to first conduct a dis-
criminating study of any proposed change and to rely only upon "the
really sane and competent evaluators of such change." As against the
Count's approach, that the school might be the engine of social change,
Snedden said the school was primarily an agency for the diffusion of
knowledge. The responsibility for selection of content belonged to the
administrators, and he warned them not to rely solely upon their own
judgment in this matter, but to defer instead to "centrally placed specialists," especially those in the "increasingly critical areas of social and
eudemic evolutions." [53]

Seemingly, from the foregoing, Snedden did not blush to suggest that
the efficient education of tomorrow must depend upon his field of specialization, and administrators must look there for the solution of
their problems. This time he offered not experiment and innovation,
but guiding purposes in a vocabulary rich in such phrases as "proven
social values," "concrete objectives," "tangible things of worth," and
"proven concrete social utilities." He illustrated his point with an example from the field of preventive medicine. Medical science had
discovered how to prevent cholera, yellow fever, diphtheria, and this
"socially useful knowledge" taught to a new generation had brought
about the virtual disappearance of these diseases. Even more urgent, he
believed, was the definition of similarly useful educational objectives in
the field of political citizenship. Only lacking, he said, was the "single,
simple focusing center for civil education" such as the "patriotically
well-oriented people of France, Japan, Italy, and Russia" possessed.

In 1931 David Snedden turned seer long enough to produce a short
popularly written book, *American High Schools and Vocational Schools
in 1960*. In it he intended to show what education directly related to
objectives derived by his system of sociological analysis would be like.
The tone of this book was so positive, so different from other of his
more polemic works, that William McAndrew, co-editor of *Educational
Review* after a stormy career as superintendent of schools in Chicago,

was moved to rejoice: "Lo, our David hath put aside his sling. He taketh up his harp and chanteth the glories of what shall be."[54]

Snedden chose for his format a supposed visit of Chinese educators to the United States thirty years hence in search of a system of education to serve as a model for their own country. He pictured China as independent, self-supporting, its conservation problem under control, its agricultural production in tune with the nation's needs, and ready to install a "modern" system of education. The situation was created to show the fruition of all Snedden demanded and prognosticated for American education. Ironically it resembled in assumption and detail the proposals later put forward by the life-adjustment movement which fell into disfavor in the middle of the 1950's and were all but forgotten by 1960.

One reviewer asserted that in his book David had found relief from his frustration in the fulfillment of his "Sneddenized" system of education, so consistently urged and so generally rejected. The world of 1960, as David created it, was a thoroughly "Sneddenized" world too. Mechanization would make unnecessary more than thirty hours of work per week. Family size would be restrained by law to three or four children, five to ten for families of "very superior stock and prosperity," and all incompetent persons would be sterilized. A National Production Apportionment Board would so regulate the labor supply that every worker might be employed and no field become overcrowded. School would be in session eight to ten hours each day, six days a week, and fifty weeks a year for all children of ages ten to eighteen. It would take a number of different forms: camping, workshop, sports activities, dramatics, experiences of nature exploration. During the planting and harvest seasons, when farms required additional labor, urban children would be taken to the country to do physical work. All would have a minimum of ten weeks of vocational education between the ages of eighteen and twenty-two and twenty-four weeks between the ages of twenty-two and twenty-five. The educational opportunities afforded in the superior homes of 1960, he believed, would make formal schooling unnecessary before the age of ten.[55]

Snedden said that by 1960 the subjects of the secondary school curriculum would also have undergone a substantial reorganization. They would no longer be organized according to the old abstract divisions of biology, government, mathematics, and English, but would yield to more functional organization. Thus, English in 1960 would be identified under such very descriptive and "concrete" titles as: Friendly Letter Writing, Business Letter Writing, Editorial Writing (an appreciational and amateur course), Platform Speaking, Debating, Reading to Audience, and English Technical Grammar (open only to superior minds). For science he suggested courses in The Stars, Tropical Life, and The Wonders of Synthetic Chemistry; in social studies he proposed Sources of Poverty, Best Methods of Testing the Efficiencies of the Several Government Agents, and a course in Correlations of Production and Consumption. Amateur Concert Singing, Camp Cooking, Social Values of the Photo-drama, Social Manners, Current Reading Interests, Harmonies within Family Life, and Wholesome Sexual Relations were other examples of functional subject organization suggested by Snedden. Of course, they were all to be organized into "lotments" of work and designated as "appreciational," "projective," or "developmental" studies.

The functional organization of the studies was to make the two-thirds less capable part of the population more socially efficient; he might have said to provide "life adjustment," but he did not use the term.

Snedden expressed the belief, "Too much democracy means general loss of efficiency, whilst too much efficiency . . . corrodes and destroys democracy"; but he thought both could be served within the school by providing for "equality of privilege and opportunity." To Snedden this meant no one should be required to take school work for which he had no proven need, or permitted to take "work or play for which he had not suitable ability and readiness or application." The sports program, he thought, best illustrated his intent. Only the most qualified were allowed to play on the best teams; there were inferior teams for the less qualified, and all that was needed to complete a program for all was a regimen of required, systematic, body-building activities for those "below par." He looked for much segregation of this kind, "in the interests of maximum functional efficiencies." Ideally, people would come to look upon their abilities and disabilities quite objectively.

In his review William McAndrew considered it Snedden "at his best." He said the "dreadfully serious little book [was] a warning, a hope, and a confidence." [56]

Snedden frequently referred to Ward's "telic" evolution, as opposed to natural evolution as a means of explaining his concept of progress. In a valedictory essay for the *Teachers College Record*, he said it was his "profound sociological faith" that progress would long continue, in spite of "devious turnings and dead ends." Who but a practicing educational sociologist was in a better position to cause "purposive evolution" was the clear implication of his message. Political government, he said, was perpetually fated to navigate the stormy currents of the "rock-bound straits which lie between two headlands"; the one was individualism, the other was identified with the necessities of large group social efficiency. Snedden acknowledged these as two chronically antagonistic forces. "High stages of social efficiency" in the past had been maintained for the purpose of contributing to one set of human values, he observed, "only at terrible costs to other values." [57]

His solution to this dilemma lay in correcting the "educational environment" which in the past had not effectively shaped people capable of administering "the greatest good of the greatest numbers" over the long term. The Soviet Union, Japan, Italy, and Germany, he noted, were presently showing how social control could serve as an important factor in national policy, and he promised Britain, Brazil, China, and the United States would soon effect similar control.

His great concern was the development of the human stock through education, which he said would arrest the "dry-rot of dysgenic fecundity." Snedden disavowed the theories of race superiority that had formed a part of Ross's teachings as prejudicial in an area where social scientists knew little and need "tread softly." Consistent with the eudemic approach to telic evolution, he proposed that the means to reversal of dysgenic evolution lay in "the self-education activities of large proportions of abler adults." He said "the *best* sixty per cent of American families are the best the world has even seen." With self-education he believed the 40 per cent could be improved. Was it not possible, he asked, that in future generations as many as 80 per cent of the people between the ages of twenty-five and seventy would be inspired to carry forward comparatively efficient self-education? He looked for the day when "scientific controls for *social health*" would be as efficient as "controls for physical health."

Snedden's final statement on his eudemic approach to telic evolution was also his most extreme. It came in his second to last year of active professorship and seemed shorn of any concern for the individual prerogative before the pressing demands of social efficiency. Describing a "case situation" some fifty years in the future, Snedden said, "In the poorer quarters of all large cities the department of domestic police requires those parents who, for whatever reason, can provide only defective and unwholesome environments — household and neighborhood environments — to send their children two to eight years of age to special nursery or kindergarten schools." Parents in more prosperous neighborhoods would not be permitted to send their children to school until after age eight. He looked for a prescribed program of play, sleep, and exercise for all between the ages of nine and eighteen with vocational education required until "licensed as competent." His forecast this time was for the year 1980.[58]

As time for retirement drew near, Snedden wrote appropriately of "Education for Leisure." Leisure had to be analyzed, he thought, because much of it was being used in harmful, wasteful, or inefficient ways. One needed to investigate the means and methods of diversion that most judges of good conduct pronounced harmful or beneficial, or, as another approach, self-examination might reveal to the individual how he could have put his leisure to better use in the past. Leisure time needed to be used in the service of one's separate "life strands" and to fulfill "social needs," rather than merely for personal pleasure.[59]

This observation brought Snedden to the final mutation in the development of his own school objectives. The life strands, he said, were really life careers, and eight or ten of these tangible sets of activities might be identified. He settled for eight: the vocational (or economic-service-producing career), the family-rearing career, the religion-sharing career, the politics-sharing or civic career, the health-conserving career, the culture-elevating career, the recreation or vigor-storing career, and the pleasure-seeking career. Some men and women had built their lives upon "one or a few of these careers" with "sad" consequences. Leisure time properly employed, he counseled, should achieve a balance among the several careers, each receiving its due. To effect this desirable state of affairs leisure must be "deliberately allocated" to each "career area." [60]

In 1935 David Snedden retired from his chair at Columbia and returned to Palo Alto and the redwood house he had left behind in 1905. David and Genevra traveled by way of Panama even as his parents had gone to California over three-quarters of a century before. Both felt most at home near the scenes of their youth and David's first professorship. Soon a new and modern house was erected on the site of the old one, adjoining the Stanford campus. There he lived an active retirement for sixteen years, gardening, writing, and visiting with others of his generation in the Stanford community, though probably not "deliberately allocating" time for each activity. Twice each year, until he was well into his eighties, he returned to the range for the semi-annual cattle drives, proud to be once again driving cattle as he had fifty years before, proud to be doing useful work.

Chapter VII

SNEDDEN'S ROLE

IN AMERICAN EDUCATION

In later years Snedden's pronouncements on education came to be criticized because he seemed to be concerned only with maintenance of the status quo. He seems to have had a limited view of the amount of future upward social mobility possible for the individual, except within certain carefully prescribed bounds. The rigid structuring of society he predicted, first by 1960, then by 1980, was not the main feature of his program for the schools, though it was a probable consequence. But his sociological determination of objectives with little allowance for changing circumstances and the introduction of new knowledge was another matter. The importance of this contribution may be readily verified from latter-day assumptions about education for life adjustment, and some current educational proposals for the "inner city."

In a paper given in 1922 before his state's academy of science, G. L. Cave, a New Hampshire school trustee, leveled an attack against what he believed to be the assumptions of the modern school. He said the end result was only "education for the life of today." He called the movement "Sneddenism" after its most "ardent proponent" and charged it was reducing the school program to "thin, denatured, intellectual food." He especially attacked Snedden's distinction between hard, systematic, chemistry and informational chemistry or informational courses in general science. "Unskilled minds," he said, were being "crammed with knowledge of facts and processes" when "trained brains" were needed, and they alone would find a useful place in society.[1]

"Sneddenism" as a viewpoint in education was a far more comprehensive system than that identified by Cave in his moment of truculence or frustration. It may never have been practiced as such, but there is little doubt that a specific and perhaps unique point of view may be readily identified with David Snedden. "Sneddenism," as a scheme of education was based upon "differentiation" of program according to the probable destination of the pupil and "flexibility" of course offering to meet differentiated needs. For Snedden, individualization of the program meant placing the student into a "case group" of like destination. Membership in a given case group depended upon three variables — environmental background, ability, and economic station with its concomitant probability of opportunity. He argued that only those students with optimum amounts of all three variables should be given education for those callings requiring a long and expensive period of schooling.

Educational arrangements for the optimum group little concerned Snedden, except as they provided a backdrop for the reorganization he sought to effect. When pressed, he conceded these were the students for whom the traditional studies had proved useful as prevocational studies; and he pointed to the professional schools of law, medicine, and engineering, as examples of "real vocational education" provided to serve this group. He argued that for the others, for the "rank and file," similar specialized schooling should be made available to prepare them in vocations appropriate to their own place in society.

Snedden considered the impecunious though intellectually able person as part of the rank and file because it did not seem likely he would have opportunity for upward mobility except in some vocation that required only a short period of training. He expressed a sincere concern that this individual be adequately trained in a marketable, useful skill, so as to provide him with a measure of independence and security in a competitive market, and be given adequate cultural and social resources to make of him a good citizen, happy in his station. He believed schooling in college preparatory courses was useless to this person because he had no immediate prospect of financing a college education. When he left school, Snedden argued, he would be as unprepared to earn a living as the intellectually uninterested pupil who was "driven out" of school by the same content.

Snedden was especially dubious that the largest segment of society, a group he sometimes estimated at 80 per cent of the population, could find any intrinsic value in the traditionally organized studies. He doubted their ability to acquire abstract knowledge and to impose it on them was only to hasten their departure from the schools. To hold them, he proposed a program of practical studies for which they could find direct and immediate value. To do this he would reorganize the studies and, where necessary, the educational arrangements themselves. In working his reorganization, Snedden tried to relate the education of each "case group" to specific aims determined by working back from what "good judges" considered to be the desirable practice of above-average members of the group in society. Once the specific and concrete objectives had been identified, he proposed to draw such elements out of the established subjects as could be considered useful for the specific purpose in view. In this way he hoped to produce, in the next generation of workmen and citizens, the best of those skills, traits, abilities, and beliefs necessary to success. It was this that G. L. Cave identified with "Sneddenism" in his opposition to education based upon "life for today."

Aims based upon life activities were not the unique contribution of David Snedden. Spencer had stated them in 1859. Others had come to find them useful, too, most notably Clarence D. Kingsley in the Cardinal Principles Report of his Commission on the Reorganization of Secondary Education and Franklin Bobbitt in his own work in curriculum planning. Snedden disagreed with both of these men in so far as they had not made provision for differentiation according to class or group, but this was not the issue that concerned Cave. It is more likely the New Hampshire trustee was merely reacting to the steady stream of publicity that flowed from Snedden's pen, or perhaps he recalled seeing Snedden's four kinds of education in the book, *Administration of Public Education*, which continued to enjoy a wide distribution.

Often regarded primarily as a vocational educator, Snedden considered that area only part of the larger field of educational sociology. Vocational education was interesting to him primarily as it contributed to total social efficiency. In this larger, and for Snedden "eudemic" approach, he liked to compare the teaching profession to the medical profession. With this understanding, schooling would have to be prescriptive in order to correct a fault or failing or to give a necessary skill or appreciation. Even when he spoke of opportunity for the individual, it was in terms of prescription to fit a case group or to fit a predetermined standard of civic behavior or physical efficiency.

Snedden's own educational background, under Ross and Devine, was concerned with the "social economy" as the context within which to view the problems related to the improvement of society. The use of this term was roughly parallel that of "political economy" as the frame of reference for economic problems; the latter was the field of specialization from which Ross, Patten, and Devine first came to consider those social implications of the economic system that became the "social economy." Snedden came to call this the approach of "applied sociology," an applied science drawing its content from many sources as did the applied sciences of medicine, engineering, and agriculture. Finally he settled upon the term "educational sociology" and was among the first to use it. His understanding of the field, however, remained that of one concerned with prescribing to ameliorate the ills of the social economy and in this it bore a direct relationship to his earlier study of the education provided by the juvenile reform school.

During most of his career in education Snedden identified four social utilities with the needs of the social economy; these utilities were synonymous with his four kinds of education — physical, vocational, social-civic-moral, and cultural. Unlike the seven aims of the Cardinal Principles Report, the utilities were not aims in themselves, but areas from which specific aims might be developed. Put into practice, the multitude of specific aims would be expected to create the socially efficient individual, a person possessed of vocational efficiency, physical efficiency, efficiency in his civic responsibility and social relations, and in the kind of personal culture appropriate to him.

In the details of organized schooling for social efficiency, Snedden relied heavily upon the idea of a six-year high school as the agency to provide a differentiated program of general education necessary to produce physical, cultural, and social "utilities." Children under the age of twelve were expected to receive education in the common learnings, and he was little concerned with schooling for them. He believed the basic skills were always best taught in the home, if it was an "advantaged" home, as he must have considered the home from which he had come and the home he was providing for his own children. Beginning with the junior high school years, however, the school was expected to provide "general education" for "good civism," "personal culture," and "health conservation," according to the particular needs of the pupil's particular case group. Vocational education, he insisted, must be left until after the student terminated his general education, either by graduation or by dropping out of the school of general education.[2]

Snedden could not consider the "dropout" with alarm when viewed within the framework of his "case groups." He considered the termination of formal education at an earlier date natural for some case groups. Differentiation would have provided these pupils with meaningful general education. Once "real" vocational education was begun, after the student left the school of general education — whether at age sixteen to enter a vocational school or later to enter a university school of medicine or engineering — Snedden's other three utilities must yield to the vocational and thereafter be relegated to after-hours pursuits. "Real vocational education," as he conceived it, was expected to be a full-time occupation approximating the hours and conditions of the working day and leading to the production of the marketable product. To Snedden, social efficiency meant fitting the individual for all areas of life as his place in society might decree.

In attempting to provide differentiation of course offerings for each case group, Snedden hit upon a style and vocabulary of his own but in practice he borrowed from vocational job analysis. His reorganization of studies was in "lotments" of work devoted to preparation for particular kinds of efficiency expressed in terms of "clock-hours" rather than semester credits. The individual elements of learning that went into any "lotment" of work were designated as "peths," and the lotments themselves were to be organized into "strands" of life activities roughly parallel to the "utilities." In description, the lotments related school work to the life of the present. Snedden suggested lotments in Friendly Letter Writing, Bedmaking, Stenographers' Spelling, and Make-up Penmanship, reminiscent of the courses in Blueprint Reading for Plumbers and Applied Design for Granite Workers suggested by Prosser for the vocational schools of Massachusetts a decade before.

In deciding upon the methods of teaching and the level of achievement required, Snedden's program divided the studies into "consumer" and "producer" subjects, designations probably borrowed from the report of the Douglas Commission of 1906. As he used these terms, the producer subjects were intended to be hard work while consumer subjects were supposed to teach attitudes or "appreciations" and would be self-defeating unless taught as "high-grade play." When Snedden argued for a longer period of compulsory education it was to extend this period of differentiated general education, especially to provide more training for efficient citizenship and the efficient use of leisure time. His concern was with the use of school time for preparation in total social efficiency rather than with the mere extension of schooling in itself.

As Snedden grew closer to retirement, in the early thirties, he became even more prescriptive in his demand for an educational program to produce social efficiency. It was at this time he offered as his ideal planned society the mythical Province of Zond, a place where each person was specifically trained for his particular niche in life and found satisfaction and security there. In moving America toward this ideal he envisioned a department of domestic police having as its function to force people to the kind of education predetermined for their special needs.

Confronted with the difficulties involved in relating his doctrines of social efficiency to the democratic ideal, Snedden found helpful an argument based upon an analogy to an athletic team. His society would be "team-like," with each member trained for the place he fit best. Every team, he reasoned, has its leaders and its followers. It was as important to the success of the team that the followers be trained in their roles as it was for the leaders to be trained to carry out theirs. He contrasted this with "herd-like" practices, which he said resulted when all were given the same education and expected to assume the same degree of responsibility in society. He contended this latter procedure was far more undemocratic because it denied opportunity to those for whom the single kind of education was not well suited. They were the "rank and file," the largest percentage of society.

Snedden seems always to have refused to consider the opportunity for social mobility afforded by the principle of free election and wide opportunity for choice. When he was forced to react to this possibility, early in his career, he expressed doubt that students, parents, or teachers could render a wise choice. Instead, much of what he came to consider the science of education, or more precisely educational sociology, was concerned with making these kinds of decisions for groups of people.

When pressed to make a choice between social efficiency and democracy, Snedden maintained efficiency must prevail. This position was quite consistent with other of his views, that the schools, as the only institution of society in the control of the government, should be consciously used for purposes of social control and should represent the majority view in society. This total devotion to the ideals of "efficiency" proved a source of alienation from others who also related their own aims to life activities, even from other educational sociologists. It was this distinction that set Snedden apart from the members of the Commission on the Reorganization of Secondary Education. In the implementation of his four kinds of education, as he sought to draw from them more specific aims applicable only to certain of his differentiated case groups, Snedden drew apart from Kingsley and the commission.

His program of schooling for children over twelve years of age became so differentiated that it could be criticized for setting apart students from various areas of society and fostering class education. The comprehensive high school was an important feature of the commission's program because it would ameliorate just this problem where already found; but the comprehensive high school was anathema to Snedden who especially singled out the industrial arts departments of these schools for derision as dispensing "denatured" vocational education. He felt justified in this criticism because their graduates were not prepared to take up the work of a journeyman in any given trade and thus he considered them a fraud perpetrated upon both student and taxpayer. While Snedden based his argument on the tenets of efficiency, Kingsley was concerned with the democratic values inherent in a learning environment where students from all walks of life might mingle.

Similar concerns alienated Snedden from the vocational education movement in the mid-twenties. In 1914, when Frank Leavitt made his preliminary report for the CRSE Committee on Vocational Education, he basically proposed Snedden's brand of specific vocational education. However, either because of general acceptance of the comprehensive high school or possibly because of a gradual recognition of the impractical nature of Snedden's extreme form of specific vocational education, the ardor of his colleagues cooled toward this aspect of "Sneddenism" in the years that followed. By 1925 they paid little attention to what he had to say on the subject. Snedden, nonetheless, held firmly to his original position, perhaps because it was an important part of his larger total program. By 1930 he had adjusted his views only in that he believed general education would soon be continued until the pupil reached the age of seventeen or eighteen and in "perhaps fifty per cent" of the cases it would be continued to age twenty; after that the student would look to his kind of full-time vocational school. In his own words, "the vocations of men may not be beautiful," but they carry "the superstructure of society."[3]

John Dewey was among the first to see the conclusion to which Snedden was pushing himself, that democracy must ultimately yield to efficiency. Dewey came to this conclusion twenty years before Snedden came to acknowledge the full extent of it himself. In 1914, reacting to Snedden's separate system of administration for vocational schools, Dewey had warned that setting them apart from schools of general education would only foster class education. Ultimately Snedden came to acknowledge Dewey's efforts to unify cultural and manual arts as an important contribution to more liberal schooling but quite outside of what he considered appropriate preparation for vocational education.

Snedden's differences with Dewey and other of the "progressives" of the twenties were of the same fundamental kind and continued through the years of his professional career. Most of the time he wrote off the contributions of this group as being romantic, idealistic or utopian. In another form of defense he categorized Dewey as an authority on method "with the understanding he was almost constantly writing about children four to nine years of age."[4] This argument seemed calculated to dismiss the significance of primary education and might explain, in part, his apparent inconsistency in urging delayed admission to school while emphasizing the importance of the school as an agency of social control. According to his "eudemic" approach, only a small percentage of children four to six years of age required schooling to supplant inferior homes. Children from fairly wholesome and normal homes, especially those "of superior intellectual heredity," would be withheld from school attendance altogether until the age of nine or ten. He claimed that for at least 60 per cent of American children, early schooling represented only over-stimulation and unnecessary regimentation. This gave him the opportunity to charge that "progressive" educators lacked the necessary confidence in the "growth-fostering powers" of various types of home.[5]

Boyd Bode and Gordon Hullfish both attacked the dualism Snedden had created in identifying producer and consumer education. Hullfish's criticism was very much like Dewey's argument. He said Snedden missed the real significance of the meaning of democracy and of democratic education by failing to see that the mind is a unity. By example, the blacksmith who had also enjoyed a cultural education would come to understand "the full social context of his work," while he believed Snedden's blacksmith would merely be efficient, or as Hullfish said, "skilled." Bode criticized Snedden at the same time for the "notion" that ideals could be "evoked from a process of environmental fact-finding." He concluded Snedden expected "sociology to work miracles" and he questioned the scientific quality of such procedures.[6]

Criticism of Snedden's doctrines from within the ranks of the educational sociologists was directed both against his theory of educational sociology as an "empirical science" — his preoccupation with life activities objectives — and against the class distinctions his objectives seemed likely to produce. But perhaps more than anything else he was engaged in a kind of inquiry that claimed little of their time and interest. His efforts in reply were couched in terms of "telic" evolution, but the inconsistency of planning improvement based upon mere maintenance of present status never seems to have troubled him.

Addressing the related question of the school's role in social change, not unlike that concerned with the teaching of the social studies which had precipitated his argument with Percy Davidson, Snedden presented the school as an institution of the majority, obligated to reinforce majority views. He conceded the school might cause its graduates to become aware of problems and provide them with an attitude receptive to change, but he never explained how he intended to accomplish this with an educational program based upon maintenance of the status quo. He made quite clear, however, that it was not the business of the schools to bring about social change.[7]

Ross Finney, like Snedden a pioneer educational sociologist, shared many of Snedden's views — the social control function of the school, the desirability of universal, public-supported vocational education, teaching directed to the inculcation of attitudes as opposed to teaching for independent powers of mind, to cite but a few. He differed from Snedden mainly on one point, what Finney chose to call "the viability of democratic ideals." In 1917 Finney professed to believe the high school had been "providentially raised up" to mitigate the social injustices of the day as he saw them from his professorship at the Valley City, North Dakota, normal school. In the details of organization for this goal, to achieve "a cultural democracy," he, too, differed from Snedden in the separation of vocational education from general education. To do this, he argued, would exclude a class or group from the "cultural benefits of civilization" and would subordinate that class to industry itself.[8]

In reviewing two of Snedden's books, *Cultural Educations and Common Sense* and *Toward Better Educations*, Finney considered the specialized vocational schools touted there "debatable to say the least" and turned his attention, instead, to literary criticism of the books. He complained of "redundant pages" and "obvious illustrations" and of Snedden's attempt to "ape the physical scientists" — criticism he would have been less likely to make had he been in full agreement with the author.[9]

Sociologist Charles Ellwood found Snedden's approach to the sociological determination of educational objectives narrowly confined to "practical educational problems." He interpreted this as the domination of the "educationist" in the developing field of educational sociology which he thought was best placed in the hands of the "sociologist." He concluded that Snedden's *Educational Sociology*, published in 1922, lacked "adequate sociological background." However, it was on the familiar ground of social values that he leveled his most direct attack. Snedden failed to grasp the "intimate relations between the educational process and the social process," he said, and he suggested Snedden look to Dewey's *Democracy and Education* "for a science of educational sociology." Snedden had been told by an educational sociologist, another pioneer in this new field of social science, that he was neither scientist enough nor sociologist enough.[10]

Nonetheless, in other quarters Snedden was listened to, respected, and numbered among the giants of American education in the period immediately following World War I and into the early twenties. He was described as "a clear thinker" who "courageously defies traditional superstitions" in the *Journal of Education*'s "Who's Who" account of the Atlantic City meeting of the Department of the Superintendence in 1921. The same year John H. Cook said in *Educational Review* Snedden's *Vocational Education* was so far ahead of practice as to cause "forward-looking conscientious schoolmen" to become discouraged by their own inadequacy. The American Chemical Society that year expected Snedden's differentiation of high school chemistry into "two radically unlike types of courses" to bring "new vitality" to the subject. When the teachers of Berkeley, California, set about the preparation of a new course of study in 1922, their several committees related the total program of the schools to Snedden's four kinds of efficiency. They deviated only in the separation of moral efficiency from civic efficiency and in identifying the "right use of leisure time" — Snedden's "personal culture" — as "avocational efficiency."[11]

Early in 1923 Snedden accepted the invitation of schoolmen from North Central Kentucky to join the former United States Commissioner of Education Philander P. Claxton, Charles McMurry, and A. E. Winship on a "Crusade" of twelve cities in the Bluegrass. The quartet was highly acclaimed. That year Northwestern University's John Clement considered Snedden's sociologically determined aims among the most prominent of recent times. He gave them equal billing with the Cardinal Principles Report, the objectives of the North Central Association's Unit Curriculum Committee, and Bobbitt's nine aims. No less flattering was Leslie Zeleny's use of Snedden's theories of liberal education, in company with the views of Matthew Arnold, Aldous Huxley, and John Dewey. However, the St. Cloud Normal School professor found them all wanting in their definition of liberal education and accepted as the only complete statement the one found in the Cardinal Principles Report. Though Zeleny may have been representative of a gradually changing point of view, as late as 1930 Charles C. Peters prepared a "Blueprint of an Optimum Citizen" in the best tradition of social efficiency. He gratefully acknowledged Snedden's influence in his preparation of the plan.[12]

By 1929, however, the educational world by and large seemed no longer to be paying attention to Snedden as it once had. Charges that he proposed an impractical, unconventional program were often hurled at him. In an earlier day his "extensive vocabulary, highly pedagogical vernacular, and his passion for minute and exhaustive analysis" were regarded with awe by some and said to "place his work almost beyond the reach of ordinary minds"; now the reviewers complained he was far too verbose and used an older, non-scientific approach. A study published by the NEA in 1923 listed three of Snedden's books among those found most useful by sixteen curriculum specialists and nine city superintendents polled; six years later a similar poll completely ignored all of his extensive publication.[13] To be sure he was growing older and there were other "new men" now to be heard from, Rugg, Counts, and French among them. Already past sixty years of age, he continued writing prolifically, and the year 1931 saw two of his most significant books come from the presses, *Toward Better Educations*, and *The American High School and Vocational School in 1960*. It would seem that though Snedden's position on schooling for social efficiency was not of itself repudiated, his program was no longer regarded with the same respect.

In the face of critical reviews and of even more fundamental criticism of his basic position, Snedden did nothing to change course or to compromise; he simply tried to interpret opposing arguments in his own terms. We may well inquire why he did not act to ease his lot by adjusting some of his thinking to shifting opinion and perhaps by writing less and weighing his words more carefully. It would seem that he found security in his program and was determined to carve out a body of dogma uniquely his own, as Ross had done and Spencer before him. Insecurity of position within the profession seems to have been ever present in the educational world where Snedden made his career. Two fateful events, the illness of an upper-grade teacher and the decision of the high school principal to continue his education in the East, projected Snedden initially into positions of importance within the Santa Paula school system in a remarkably short time. His inquiry into theories of economic reform was misinterpreted by the community and may have cost him his position almost overnight. Not until he was close to retirement did he again permit himself the luxury of such speculation. Upon leaving Stanford he faced financial insecurity in his first position growing out of a situation of deteriorating enrollment. It was a personal experience he may have long remembered, as in subsequent years he urged a reorganization of the studies as a necessary condition to keep the young adolescent in school. Snedden's departure from Stanford, his move to Massachusetts, his return to Columbia and a chair in educational sociology, while all opportunities for improvement, nonetheless were initiated by others in situations where he could do little but agree.

In his student days he had seen Ross make a whole new field for himself in sociology through his new doctrine of "social control." Using Spencer as his point of departure and drawing generously from his mentors, Devine, Dutton, and especially Ross, Snedden must have believed he too had carved for himself a similar niche with the new field called educational sociology, at least so he confided to his wife in 1908, in words remarkably like those Ross had written Richard T. Ely a decade earlier.[14] At that time, Snedden was already teaching a course heavy with content of educational sociology and he was contemplating a book on the subject when he was suddenly uprooted by the Massachusetts offer. From that time on, it appeared educational sociology was his means to status, his chance for independence in a new field, and a measure of security. He took comfort in the example of Pasteur, and it is certainly not without significance that he chose the analogy of that scientist's relationship to medicine to show the relationship of educational sociology to education. With this frame of mind, for him to compromise any part of his program would have been to surrender all.

Any consideration of Snedden's proposals must inquire to what extent he anticipated the initial statements of the life adjustment ideology of the mid-forties and early fifties. The life adjustment movement originated at a meeting of the Consulting Committee on Vocational Education in the Years Ahead held in the nation's capital in 1945. Charles Prosser, who was Snedden's first deputy commissioner for vocational education in Massachusetts and who subsequently gave a lifetime to that movement as director of Dunwoody Industrial Institute in Minneapolis, submitted the resolution in summation of the committee's findings. It said in part that some form of "life adjustment training" was a necessity for an estimated 60 per cent of American youth who were neither served well by the vocational school nor were likely material for college admission. The committee requested the United States Commissioner of Education to hold a conference of a series of regional conferences to consider the problem.

In compliance with this request, Commissioner John Studebaker took the first of the two options and called a select panel of outstanding persons from the field of secondary education to a two-day meeting in New York City in the spring of 1946. This conference called attention to "a perpetual and growing class of illiterate citizens" and to the "increased delinquency among youth," arguments no different from those used at the beginning of the century in support of vocational education. It indicted the "general high schools" for failing to serve all youth, even as Snedden had in his earliest arguments for a more socially efficient curriculum. The conference gave the Prosser Resolution the necessary stamp of approval to project it onto the national scene.

Like Snedden's education for social efficiency, education for life adjustment attempted to prescribe a relatively equitable distribution of learning activities important to various areas of life. Life adjustment education was interpreted by some as "concentration upon the needs of life with much less attention to subject matter and subjects." It called for "an increased emphasis upon education for home living, functional citizenship, . . . physical and mental health, . . . functional preparation for leisure . . . [and] greatly increased provision for work experience," all to be achieved through "greatly increased freedom from subject matter boundaries and from subject matter organization." Like

Snedden, the proponents of education for life adjustment ridiculed the "logical structure of the subject" on the grounds that it was "ordinarily useful to the specialist rather than the learner" and called for organization around problems, topics, and needs.[15] One cannot help speculating that the high priests of life adjustment found themselves caught with little more than a slogan phrase and simply appropriated much of what Snedden had been urging for so long.

The similarity of Snedden's program and life adjustment education tends to become blurred in two details. Snedden had proposed specific vocational education for everyone, as something of a capstone of the educational process, while Prosser, seemingly disenchanted with the sweeping claims made for the movement in its earlier years, initially had proposed that technical vocational education be provided for only 20 per cent of the school population. He assumed 60 per cent were unsuited for specific vocational education, though later, at the New York conference, he came around to the rather vague and reluctantly made concession that the vocational education forces of the country could contribute a potential service in the adjustment of these youth.

The other point of difference centers upon Snedden's own frequent use of the 60 per cent figure to represent the segment of society for whom he deemed "mass production methods in education" well suited. He generally regarded this 60 per cent in a favorable light, and it was the children from these homes Snedden believed need not attend kindergarten or nursery schools. Another time, while commenting upon "telic evolution," Snedden said, "the *best* sixty per cent of American families are the best the world has ever seen.[16] In connection with his own reorganization of studies he had identified the 60 per cent with the common people, neither "gifted" nor "unable minded," whom he intended to reach with his program. Considering the secondary schools historically, he criticized them for offerings that had always been "primarily for the intellectually and circumstantially most gifted," and in this he was one with the views of the Life Adjustment Conference sponsored by the United States Office of Education in the spring of 1946.

Proposing to speak in behalf of "the learned world," in the early and middle fifties, Arthur Bestor, Jr., probably became the foremost opponent of life adjustment education. In a broadside for the *New Republic*, he identified as anti-intellectualism in the schools those statements of educational policy that assumed it to be the "job of the schools . . . to meet the common and specific needs of youth." Like Snedden, he believed other agencies of society were not meeting the same responsibility to serve some of these needs, but unlike Snedden, he denied the schools' responsibility to accept them as residual burdens. "The idea that the school must undertake to meet every need that some other agency is failing to meet" he branded "a preposterous delusion." He, too, identified roughly the same four areas of education Snedden had found useful in his own educational proposals.[17]

As one manifestation of anti-intellectualism in the schools, Bestor singled out the efforts of the Illinois Curriculum Program to reorganize the curriculum in terms of contemporary needs and problems. Their program was based upon a body of "common learnings" drawn from the content of science, literature, history, mathematics, and other areas of the curriculum. Snedden's program, especially as found in his *American High Schools and Vocational Schools in 1960*, also called for a reorganization of subject matter in terms of needs and problems in place of the traditional logical organization of the studies. In spite of inconsistencies of detail, Snedden had conceded certain common learnings should be possessed by all, or at least by all members of certain "case groups."

Snedden's place within the anti-intellectual tradition may be seen from better perspective with the insight provided by Merle Curti's *The American Paradox*. Curti presents the dualism of the intellectual who lives the life of the mind and the man who works with his hands and perhaps glories in that work. He showed a blurring of the line between the two kinds of men under frontier conditions when intellectuals like William Byrd II, Benjamin Franklin, and Jared Eliot put their scholarly interests to work to improve man's well-being in a practical world. Curti found ample evidence of Americans looking to the scholar and the specialist in the years that followed for the knowledge that would improve life and provide the solution of important political problems, but paradoxically all the while viewing the scholar with suspicion.[18]

From this viewpoint David Snedden himself was a part of the American paradox. He was born and reared on the frontier where practical skills were of primary usefulness, often the means of survival. The emphasis he placed on "work" in his own life and the lives of others, even his use of the word itself as an ennobling term, helps to place him within this anti-intellectual tradition. Throughout his life Snedden valued knowledge for its usefulness, never for its own sake, and assumed the schools should never make cultural growth the sole or even an important educational purpose. His distinction between consumer and producer education — the first liberal and easy, the second practical and hard work — and the small place given "personal culture" in his total school program provides evidence of the anti-intellectual slant.

Snedden divided society into the few theorists and the "rank and file" who could not be expected to learn more than the practical and concrete applications of certain kinds of knowledge. As a consequence of this distinction he provided for the differentiation of civic education into the training of leaders and of followers. In vocational education he distinguished many case groups within the broader categories of the professionally trained, the skilled, and the semi-skilled.

When Snedden tried to relate himself to this dualism, however, he appears ambivalent. He always conducted himself as one of the intellectual elite, though on the basis of his own criteria for differentiation, the circumstance of his early environment — the one-room adobe ranch house — would place his "case group" well within the "rank and file." On the other hand, his frequent reference to his chair in educational sociology and vocational education as "David's work" reflects a value judgment that identifies him with the prevailing bias of the frontier. His efforts to give his son the "benefits" of agrarian experience and manual training are in line with this idea. It is likely he enjoyed the peculiar satisfaction that comes to a man who is cognizant he has moved to a more respected status in life.

When Snedden took his first academic work in education at Stanford, one of the pioneer schools to have a department of education, that subject was in an embryonic state. Even his first experience in sociology, under Ross and Powers, was in the department of political economy, as sociology had not yet fully evolved from the parent field. He hurried through much of what he got and never really developed an abiding interest in any established subject area.

Without a strong commitment of any kind, save perhaps to the ideas of Herbert Spencer and Edward Ross, Snedden drew initially from the burgeoning manual training movement and the social reform movements of the first decade of the twentieth century. As vocational education gained in popularity, he renounced his earlier allegiance to manual training and took up the new cause as a refinement of the old. The professional climate from which he rose to maturity in his career was one determined to heal the ills of society by means that were direct, immediate, prescriptive, and practical. "Efficiency" was the ideal of this age in business, in government, and in the orderly function of society itself.

Purposeful, intent to find a place of prominence in a new field he had helped to define, Snedden became the spokesman of the most thorough-going form of social efficiency. It was a reasonable consequence of the environment from which he rose, the intellectual content he found stimulating, and the major social reform movement where he had found a comfortable berth. Is it any wonder the young schoolman could so zealously espouse and, as he grew older, so tenaciously hold to the ideals of social efficiency? His proposals, put forward as "concrete" solutions likely to withstand the tests of time or as projections of what the future must surely hold in store, had the added appeal of offering surety in an area where it was not commonly found. However, it is possible his own story of upward social mobility, based upon hard work and keen intellect in the best tradition of the "American dream," is more eloquent in its message than his own proposals of education for social efficiency.

Reference Matter

NOTES

INTRODUCTION

1 David Snedden, "History as an Instrument in the Social Education of Children," *J. Pedagogy*, XIX (June, 1906), 259.
2 David Snedden, *American High Schools and Vocational Schools in 1960* (New York, 1931), p. 43.
3 William Bagley, *The Educative Process* (New York, 1905), p. 60.
4 "Trustees I Have Met," *J. Ed.*, July 15, 1915, p. 36.

CHAPTER I

1 Unless otherwise documented, the biographical material throughout is drawn from the following sources: David Snedden, *Recollections of Over Half a Century Spent in Educational Work* (Palo Alto, Calif., 1949); Genevra Snedden, *Mountain Cattle and Frontier People, Stories of the Snedden Family, 1867–1947* (Palo Alto, Calif., 1947); and "Picture History and Genealogy," a photo album compiled by Genevra Snedden. These materials were made available to the author by David Snedden's youngest daughter, Mrs. Nathan Finch of Palo Alto, Calif.
2 "Report of Official Visits of the School Superintendent of Ventura County, 1885," a handwritten daily journal found in the county schools office, Ventura, Calif.
3 This information on St. Vincent's is taken from: William E. North, "Catholic Education in Southern California," unpublished doctoral dissertation, Catholic University of America, 1936, pp. 117–20; Rockwell D. Hunt, *The First Half-Century* (Los Angeles, 1930), p. 91; James M. Guinn, *A History of California and an Extended History of its Southern Coast Counties* (Los Angeles, 1907), I, 362; William A. Spaulding, *History and Reminiscences, Los Angeles City and County* (Los Angeles, 1930), I, 133. Spaulding sets the date for the original founding of St. Vincent's College at 1855 and gives 1865 as the date for its second beginning when it was located in the adobe house of Don Vincente Lugo on the Plaza of the Old Pueblo. North shows evidence the school was in operation in 1860 and 1862 and suggests no cessation of operation.
4 Philip Conneally, S.J., "St. Vincent's College, History and Tribute," unpublished manuscript, Loyola High School, Los Angeles, 1961, p. 6. Isadore B. Dochweiler, a distinguished Los Angeles lawyer, received the first A.B. degree in 1887. In his *Recollections*, Snedden gave the year of his graduation as 1889. However, following his own account of his subsequent career — one year in the Fairview district, one year at Fillmore, and three at Santa Paula — one year remains unaccounted for prior to

his registration as a full-time student at Stanford in the fall of 1895. The "Minutes of the Ventura County Teachers Institutes" for 1891 through 1895 quite definitely place Snedden first at Fillmore, then at Santa Paula. The *Stanford Quad* of 1897, in which Snedden appears as a graduating senior, lists his previous degrees as an A.B. from St. Vincent's in 1890 and an A.M. in 1892. In his six-page sketch Fr. Philip Conneally, using local sources, also lists Snedden as having received St. Vincent's A.B. degree in 1890 and the A.M. degree in 1892.

5 Material in the chapter relevant to the work of the Ventura County Board of Education, unless otherwise noted, is from the "Minutes of the Board of Education of Ventura County, California," in the county schools office, Ventura, California.

6 Little is known of what went into the master's program or how it was conducted. After Snedden earned his second A.B. degree at Stanford, he no longer used the St. Vincent's degrees.

7 Gerald T. White, *Formative Years in the Far West: A History of Standard Oil Company of California and Predecessors Through 1919* (New York, 1962), p. 127.

8 On Nov. 3, 1899, the paper gave a glowing account of local growth. This was four years after Snedden left Santa Paula.

9 Information in this chapter concerning the constituency of Snedden's classes, unless otherwise identified, is from "List of Promotions, Ventura County Schools, Santa Paula District," bound volumes for 1893 and 1894 in the attendance office of the county schools office at Ventura, California.

10 Ventura *Free Press*, July 20, 1894, and Aug. 23, 1895. In his *Recollections*, Snedden stated that he became principal of the high school after one full year as principal of the grammar school and was high school principal there for two years. However, other evidence indicates he was principal of the high school for only one year. The *Free Press* of July 20, 1894, in its weekly "Santa Paula Sundries" column, states, "The high school term begins the first of August. Professor Snedden, ex-principal of the grammar school and Miss Younglove are the teachers employed." The minutes of the annual teachers institute for the 1893–94 school year show Snedden in attendance as principal of the grammar school and Watson Nicholson as principal of the high school. It is possible, of course, that Snedden could have substituted for Nicholson during the second semester, but if so it is nowhere noted.

11 Robert M. Clarke, *Narrative of a Native* (Los Angeles, 1936), p. 58.

12 The Santa Paula High School was of average size for its day. Of the 105 high schools in the state, 64 had fewer than 3 teachers and only 22 had more than 4. See May L. Cheney, "Education Department," *Overland Monthly*, Oct., 1896, education supplement, pp. 22–24.

13 E. M. Cox, "The County Institute," *West. J. Ed.*, X (Mar., 1905), 192; also see "Recent Official Opinions of Superintendent T. J. Kirk," *West. J. Ed.*, VIII (Dec., 1903), 817. It seems the taking of attendance was always something of a problem.

14 The material concerning the activities of the Ventura County Teachers Institute, unless otherwise cited, is from "Minutes of the Ventura County Teachers Institute" for the years 1891 through 1895, individual handwritten volumes deposited in the county schools office, Ventura, Calif.

15 When Amos G. Throop, Chicago businessman and politician, retired to southern California in the eighties he founded Throop University — later Throop Institute — at Pasadena as a philanthropic venture. It was incorporated on Sept. 23, 1891, as an institution for "liberal and practical" education and offered a traditional course of academic studies. After the first year, coincident with the appointment of President Keyes, the school turned to the "new education" in order to give "opportunity for practical training" in "manipulative skills." Polytechnic Hall was constructed to house the new departments of forge shop, machine shop, pattern shop, molding shop, woodworking, cooking, architectural drawing, and clay modeling. Mr. W. H. Parker was brought from Washington University of St. Louis to take charge of the "industrial lines." See Jeanne C. Carr, "Throop University, Pasadena," *Calif. Illus.*, II (Sept., 1892), 565, and Charles H. Keyes, "Manual Training in Secondary Schools," *Calif. Teach. Assn. Proc.*, 1893, pp. 92–109.

16 Keyes, *Calif. Teach. Assn. Proc.*, 1893, pp. 92–93.

17 Herbert Spencer, *Education, Intellectual, Moral and Physical* (New York, n.d.), pp. 9, 11, 16, 18.

18 Ventura *Free Press*, May 3, 1895.

19 "Straws in the Wind," *Overland Monthly*, Oct., 1896, education supplement, p. 32.

CHAPTER II

1 Unless otherwise noted, description of Stanford University in this chapter is drawn from Edith Mirrielees, *Stanford, The Story of a University* (New York, 1959), and Jesse B. Sears and Adin D. Henderson, *Cubberley of Stanford, and His Contribution to American Education* (Stanford, Calif., 1957).

2 "Minutes of the Ventura County Teachers Institute, 1892," in the county schools office, Ventura, Calif. According to the entry for Sept. 22, 1892, Superintendent Black made a motion "as a tribute to Leland Stanford Junior University . . . that the graduates . . . be placed on the same footing as regards certificates as the graduates of the State University." Also, see *Calif. Teach. Assn. Proc.* (San Francisco, 1893), p. 107, where Stanford University is listed with Harvard, Yale, Cornell, Michigan, Wisconsin, and California as among the top universities in the nation.

3 Edward A. Ross, *Seventy Years of It, An Autobiography* (New York, 1936), p. 54. Genevra Snedden recalled that when David later joined the Stanford faculty, in 1901, its average age was only five years older than that of the students. She reflected that it was often difficult to tell them apart. Frequently on a Sunday evening some of the students would come in to hear David read aloud beside his fireplace.

4 David Starr Jordan, *Evolution of the College Curriculum*, as quoted in Orrin Leslie Elliott, *Stanford University, The First Twenty-five Years* (Stanford, Calif., 1937), p. 70.

5 Elliott, *Stanford University*, pp. 72–73.

6 *Stanford Quad*, 1897, pp. 81, 239.

7 "Editorial Comment," *West. J. Ed.*, II (Aug., 1896), 2.

8 Interview with Dr. Harvey Hall, Registrar of Stanford University, on Aug. 29, 1962. In his *Recollections* Snedden recalled with pleasure a course on ethics with Griggs and one on evolution with Jordan, neither of which Dr. Hall could find on his record. It is possible, of course, that both courses were taken as "audits" or that they were given on a non-credit basis. Stanford's summer sessions, at this time, were conducted as an informal enterprise of the faculty. If either of the courses were taken under these auspices, they would have quite legitimately been omitted from his transcript. It will be recalled that Snedden became acquainted with Thoburn, a professor of biology, during one of these sessions, and Thoburn shared responsibility with Jordan for teaching Bionomics, the academic package for the evolution content. See the *Stanford Register*, 1894–95 and 1895–96, for course descriptions.

9 "Paso Robles People," San Luis Obispo *Breeze*, Feb. 1, 1900.

10 Ross, *Seventy Years of It*, p. 99.

11 This sequence is explained in a letter to his foster mother, Mrs. Mary Beach of Marion, Ia., Apr. 2, 1896, in Box 2, Edward A. Ross Papers, State Historical Society of Wisconsin.

12 Edward A. Ross, "Social Control," *Am. J. Sociol.*, I (Mar., 1896), 518.

13 Ross to his foster mother, Apr. 2, 1896, in Box 2, Edward A. Ross Papers, State Historical Society of Wisconsin.

14 Ross, "Social Control," pp. 518, 534.

15 *Ibid.*, pp. 519–20.

16 Edward A. Ross to Richard T. Ely, Aug. 6, 1900, in Box 2, Ross Papers, State Historical Society of Wisconsin.

17 Edith Monica Jordan, "The University and I were Young Together," in *Stanford Mosaic*, ed. Edith R. Mirrielees (Stanford, Calif., 1962), p. 8.

18 R. M. Shackelford to Samuel T. Black, Jan. 10, 1895, in "A Letter from a School Trustee That Has a Familiar Ring To It," *Pacific Educational Journal*, XI (Mar., 1895), 126–27.

19 *Ibid.* Also see "Political Interference with the Schools," *Calif. Teach. Assn. Proc.*, 1899, p. 123.

20 Details about school arrangements at Paso Robles, unless otherwise noted, are from the "Minute Book of the Board of Control of the Paso Robles High School, 1893–1909," and the "Minute Book, Board of Trustees of the Grammar School, 1895–1900," both in the high school office, Paso Robles, Calif.

21 San Luis Obispo *Tribune*, June 24, 1898.

22 See the San Luis Obispo *Breeze*, Feb. 1, 15, Apr. 5, 12, May 3, 1900, for the activities of the society.

23 Genevra Sisson, "The Teaching of Local History to Young Children," *West. J. Ed.*, II (Sept., 1897), 8. For her study of children's games and play activities demonstrating a "love of action," see Genevra Sisson, "Children's Plays," *Pacific Educational Journal*, X (June, 1894), 262–63.

24 *Docas* was published in 1898 by D. C. Heath and Co. and is still in print.

25 As chairman of the Committee on Student Affairs, Thoburn had become the arbiter of student discipline about the time Snedden graduated from Stanford. In appointing him to this position, President Jordan commissioned him to eliminate "unworthy persons from the rolls of the university classes." His authority was to be exercised against "not only those found guilty of specific acts of immorality or dishonesty, but on any whose personal influence is objectionable. Those who are dissipated, profligate, tricky, or foul of tongue should be removed though no specific act of wrong doing may be charged against them." It appears that while Ross was expounding his theories of social control from the podium, Jordan expected Thoburn to make a practical application of the doctrine, though probably not consciously intending to do so. His new responsibilities were described in a news item, *West. J. Ed.*, II (Sept., 1897), 7.

26 "How Shall an Institute be Conducted?" *West. J. Ed.*, II (Aug., 1897), 2. Unless otherwise noted, all the material concerning the San Luis Obispo County Teachers Institute is drawn from the local newspapers, the San Luis Obispo *Tribune* and *Breeze* for Oct. 3 and 10–15, 1897, Oct. 13–15, 1898, and Apr. 17–20, 1900, and from a scrapbook compiled by County Superintendent Mrs. A. C. Spafford Woods found in the county school office, San Luis Obispo, Calif.

27 "Minutes of the Board of Supervisors, San Luis Obispo County," Vol. H, entry for June 5, 1899, in the County Clerk's Office, San Luis Obispo, Calif. Snedden's name was first put forward in the fall of 1898 when board member Adelaide Spafford was elected county superintendent. Filed on Dec. 1, 1898, the petition touted Snedden as "one of the best educators of this county" and urged his appointment in order to bring representation to the territory east of the St. Lucia Mountains and to the high schools of the county. The document appeared to have originated in the office of R. M. Schackelford, whose name headed the list of twenty-one, followed by that of his office manager. Only the year before, a similar petition in large type on legal stationary with a blue backing — far more formal than anything else found in the file — was submitted in behalf of Miss Spafford's candidacy.

Though Snedden failed in his first attempt to win appointment to the Board of Education, he was more successful the following June. In the regular rotation of members, two of the six stood for re-election each year. Accordingly, in June, 1899, Snedden unseated C. H. Woods, principal of the Nipomo School and publisher of a local professional journal, the *Public School Reporter*. His petition of thirty-one names was far short of the hundred and fifty in support of Wood's candidacy, and the petitions of the other four candidates were almost as long. Unlike the others, however, his petition carried a personal covering letter to County Clerk Whicher. On the canary-yellow stationary of the Salinas Valley Lumber Company Shackelford wrote, "If you can do anything for Mr. Snedden I will esteem it a great favor. I hardly think that the Board will ignore our petition this time as there is no high school teacher on the Board of Education and surely we should have one. . . ." Snedden was appointed for a three-year term beginning July 1, 1899. The petitions and covering letter are in File 43–2, "Applications and Resignations, County Board of Education," in the County Clerk's Office, San Luis Obispo, Calif.

28 Unless otherwise noted, the work of the Board of Education is drawn from "Proceedings, San Luis Obispo County Board of Education," Vol. A, found in the office of the County Board of Education, San Luis Obispo, Calif.

29 San Luis Obispo *Breeze*, Jan. 19, 1900.

30 New York, 1886, pp. 97 and 124.

31 San Luis Obispo *Tribune*, Jan. 16, 1900. These are three representative questions of ten asked in the examination on the content of White's *Elements of Pedagogy*. It may be of interest to note that White's method in reading involved learning words as "wholes," drawn from the child's spoken vocabulary, using blackboard and charts in preference to a primer.

32 For various accounts of the club's activities see: Paso Robles *Record*, Oct. 7 and 21, 1900; San Luis Obispo *Breeze*, Jan. 25, Feb. 1 and Mar. 8, 1900. Subsequent accounts of community affairs are from the local newspapers or from the family biography.

33 Ward, *Dynamic Sociology* (New York, 1883), II, 552.

34 *Ibid.*, 486. Also see pp. 487, 537–38, 568.

35 *Principles of Sociology* (New York, 1896), p. 9.

36 Edward Ross to his foster mother, Mrs. Mary Beach, Oct. 7, 1894, Box 2, Ross Papers, State Historical Society of Wisconsin. In this letter Ross asked Mrs. Beach to send on to Stanford his file of back issues of the *Review of Reviews*. It may be recalled that at just this time he was working on his theory of social control.

37 Pp. 417–32.

38 *NEA Proc.*, 1899, pp. 182–85.

39 *Stanford Alumnus*, I (June, 1900), 185–98.

40 See Edward A. Ross, "The Educational Function of the Church," *Outlook*, Aug. 28, 1897, pp. 1036–40. It was written at the request of Fairchild in support of his "Educational Church." In the article Ross says, "To the sociologist, what keeps the church most alive is its power to fit human beings for harmonious social life. . . . It is in the last analysis, the repository of certain related ideas, convictions, ideals, symbols, and appeals which are admitted to have more efficacy in socializing the human heart than any other group of influences known to western civilization" (p. 1037).

CHAPTER III

1 A typescript of the courses taken by David Snedden while at Teachers College was supplied the author by Kenneth H. Beesley, Assistant Provost and Registrar of Teachers College, Columbia University.

2 Samuel T. Dutton, *School Management* (New York, 1903), Preface and p. 198.

3 Edward A. Krug, *The Shaping of the American High School* (New York, 1964), p. 249.

4 Material about Dutton, unless otherwise documented, is from Charles H. Levermore, *Samuel Train Dutton, A Biography* (New York, 1922), pp. 1–4, 21, 23, 29–36.

5 Samuel T. Dutton, "The Correlation of Educational Forces in the Community," *Ed. R.*, Apr., 1897, pp. 341, 343–44.

6 *Ibid.*, pp. 336–39; also see Dutton, *Social Phases of Education in the School and Home* (New York, 1899), Preface.

7 Samuel T. Dutton, "The Place and Function of the High School," *Ed.*, June, 1898, pp. 587–88.

8 "The Correlation of Educational Forces in the Community," *Ed. R.*, Apr., 1897, p. 347.

9 "Remarks," *Sixth N.Y. State Conf. Proc.*, 1905, p. 197.

10 See *School Review*, V (Dec., 1897), 672–75; and *Ed. R.*, Nov., 1896, pp. 335–47.

11 *Social Phases*, p. vii, and *Sch. R.*, V, 674.

12 "The Place and Function of the High School," *Ed.*, June, 1898, p. 591.

13 "The Relation of Education to Vocation," *Ed. R.*, Nov., 1896, pp. 335–45.

14 *School Management*, pp. 9–10.

15 Snedden's master's essay is in the library of Teachers College, Columbia University. Subsequent quotations in the next several paragraphs are from this source.

16 Charles W. Eliot, "Shortening and Enriching the Grammar School Course," *NEA Proc.*, 1892, p. 622, in Edward A. Krug, *Charles W. Eliot and Popular Education* (New York, 1961), p. 5.

17 *School Management*, p. 117.

18 Frank McMurry, "Concentration," *Ed. R.*, Jan., 1895, pp. 32, 36.

19 When Olaf reached high school age he chose the more Celtic name Donald. It was as Donald Scott Snedden that he took his doctorate in educational psychology at Columbia and served on the faculties of Harvard and New York universities. He died in a tragic yachting accident on Long Island Sound in the spring of 1931.

20 This and subsequent material about Cubberley, unless otherwise documented, is from Jesse B. Sears and Adin D. Henderson, *Cubberley of Stanford, and His Contribution to American Education* (Stanford, Calif., 1957).

21 *West. J. Ed.*, VIII (May, 1903), 380–81.

22 *Stanford Register*, Apr., 1902, p. 24. Subsequent material concerning course description and department responsibility, unless otherwise documented, is from this source.

23 See Irene Josephine Lawrence, "A History of Educational Sociology in the United States," unpublished doctoral dissertation, Stanford University, 1951, p. 24. Also see Edith R. Mirrielees, *Stanford, the Story of a University* (New York, 1959), pp. 101–2.

24 "Teachers Bureau," *Stanford Alumnus*, Apr., 1903, p. 117.

25 Frederic Burk, "Review of the Year," *West. J. Ed.*, VIII (Jan., 1903), 34–35. The following quotations are from this source.

26 "California Schoolmaster's Club," *West. J. Ed.*, VIII (Jan., 1903), 36.

27 Burk, *West. J. Ed.*, VIII, 30, 35.

28 Roy W. Cloud, *Education in California, Leaders, Organizations, and Accomplishments of the First Hundred Years* (Stanford, Calif., 1952), p. 117.

29 "The California Scholia Club," *West. J. Ed.*, VIII (Oct., 1903), 686.

30 "On Formal Discipline," *West. J. Ed.*, VIII (May, 1903), 299–300, 303–4, 307.

31 "The Value of Mathematics," *West. J. Ed.*, VIII (May, 1903), 310.

32 *West. J. Ed.*, VIII (Dec., 1903), 784, 786–89, 792–93, 798. The material of the next three paragraphs is also from this source.

33 *West. J. Ed.*, X (Mar., 1905), 261–65.

34 "The Teaching of History in Rural Schools," *West. J. Ed.*, IX (Sept., 1904), 616–18, 622.

35 Quotations and content are from statements attributed to Snedden in the San Diego *Sun*, Mar. 28, 1904 and Mar. 29, 1904; the Santa Barbara *Weekly Press*, Oct. 8, 1903; and the Redding *Courier-Free Press*, Nov. 10, 1903.

36 VIII (Nov., 1903), 719–22. Harr Wagner, the editor, was also one of the most popular of institute lecturers. His usual companion on speaking tours that ranged from Washington to southern California was Joaquin Miller, "The Poet of the Sierras." Also see "Solano County," *West. J. Ed.*, VIII (Nov., 1903), 767–68, for a request that the state use the $200,000 expended each year for the institutes to subsidize attendance at summer sessions instead.

37 "Educational Progress in San Francisco," *West. J. Ed.*, X (July, 1905), 556.

38 "Santa Clara Institute," *West. J. Ed.*, VIII (1903), 419, 507, and 763.

39 Irwin was president of the Irwin Wholesale Paper Company, the Quincy Compressor Company, and the Cabinet Manufacturing Company and for a time operated Overland, Maxwell, and Marmon automobile agencies. Upon arrival in Quincy as a young man he had taken a position as assistant teacher of mathematics at the Chaddock School for Boys, having had some teaching experience in his native Missouri. He became an admirer of Wisconsin's Michael Vincent O'Shea, and O'Shea reciprocated with the dedication of his book *Education as Adjustment* to Irwin in 1904.

Irwin bought O'Shea's books for distribution to his employees and to the teachers of Quincy.

Snedden and Irwin remained lifelong friends. Anna Grubb, Irwin's biographer and personal secretary for forty years, attributed to him a statement that would suggest some of the viewpoints both of Snedden and O'Shea: "The rank and file is slowly awakening to the fact that the school of life, in most cases, is superior to the study of books; that the few gifted should be highly trained and the mass should be given tools for their proper adjustment. . . . Isn't the prime consideration to be able to successfully adjust ourselves to our fellow men? . . ." See Anna B. Grubb, *Adventure in Enterprise, The Story of Leaton Irwin and the Company He Founded* (Quincy, Ill., 1947). Also see Irwin to O'Shea, Jan. 9, 1904; Irwin to Longman's Green and Co., Jan. 11, 1904; Irwin to *The Twentieth Century Home,* Jan. 7, 1904; in the O'Shea Papers, State Historical Society of Wisconsin.

40 The Quincy *Daily Journal* gave Snedden's week of lectures extensive coverage. All of the quotations are from this newspaper for the dates May 14, June 14 and 20–24, 1904.

41 He may have felt an absence of recreational activity in his own life. He wrote in 1949, "David had never had a real hobby. It has often been said of him that he never really learned to play. He has never enjoyed the lighter social conversations and meetings of congenial people" (*Recollections,* p. 53).

42 *Placer County Republican,* Auburn, Calif., Oct. 13, 1904.

43 San Luis Obispo *Weekly Tribune,* Apr. 4, 1902.

44 Santa Barbara *Weekly Press,* Oct. 8, 1903.

45 San Diego *Sun,* Mar. 28, 1904.

46 *West. J. Ed.,* X (Feb., 1905), 83–98; "To What Extent May the Training Given in Our California State Normal School Prepare for Secondary School Teaching," *West. J. Ed.,* X (May, 1905), 464.

47 *West. J. Ed.,* X (Mar., 1905), 187–88. Compare this presentation with her milder report of 1903, in which she bases her argument on reading for personal improvement and rich cultural experience. See Kate Ames, "Teachers Reading Course," *West. J. Ed.,* IX (Feb., 1904), 101–4.

48 David Snedden, "Conditions of Developing Special Teachers of Drawing and Manual Training in Every School," *West. J. Ed.,* X (Mar., 1905), 274.

49 "The Lectures of Jacob Riis," *West. J. Ed.,* X (Mar., 1905), 301–5.

50 Kenneth H. Beesley, Registrar, Teachers College, Columbia University, to Walter H. Drost, Oct. 20, 1962.

51 Shaw, *Review of Reviews,* XXI, 418. The quotations in the next three paragraphs are from this source.

CHAPTER IV

1 "The Other Side of the Compulsory Education Problem," XIX (Jan., 1907), 347–51.

2 P. 404. Subsequent quotations, in the next two paragraphs, are from pp. 419–23.

3 David Snedden, "History Study as an Instrument in the Social Education of Children," *J. Pedagogy*, XIX (June, 1907), 259–68.

4 This quotation and the material of the next two paragraphs is from David Snedden to David Eugene Smith, May 10, 1907, D. E. Smith Papers, in the Special Collections Room of the Butler Library, Columbia University.

5 Unless otherwise noted, material concerning Allen's activities is pieced together from the newspaper clippings, memorabilia, and correspondence in the IPS-Allen Papers in the State Historical Society of Wisconsin.

6 "Health is First," *Sch. J.*, LXXV (Feb., 1908), 607; "A Statement of the New York Association for Improving the Condition of the Poor, 1843–1905 — for School Children," a broadside in the IPS-Allen Papers; New York *Evening Post*, June 29, 1906.

7 *Proc., Thirty-third Annual Sessions* (Philadelphia, 1906), pp. 422–23. Devine was forced to miss these sessions in order to carry out his duties as Relief Director in the aftermath of the San Francisco earthquake and fire.

8 William H. Allen, "The Longer or Shorter School Day," *Charities*, XIV (May 5, 1905), 761–63. Raymond Callahan recognized Allen as one who with Harrington Emerson and James P. Munroe did much to "prod" educators to "achieve efficiency." Callahan, however, is especially concerned with administrative efficiency, the more economical operation of the schools. See *Education and the Cult of Efficiency* (Chicago, 1962), p. 63. This kind of efficiency, as an aspect of economical government operation, was indeed part of Allen's thinking, but he was also capable of being interested in social efficiency — the use of the curriculum to produce the more efficient member of society. See Allen, *Health and Civics* (Boston, 1909).

9 *School Reports*, p. 141.

10 Elmer E. Brown to David Snedden, Apr. 20, 1908, in IPS-Allen Papers, State Historical Society of Wisconsin.

11 "A Shifting of Ideals Respecting the Efficiency of Formal Cultural Studies for all Pupils," *NEA Proc.*, 1908, p. 589. For Snedden's reply see p. 590.

12 "Differences Among Varying Groups of Children Should be Recognized," *NEA Proc.*, 1908, pp. 755–56.

13 Discussion, *NEA Proc.*, 1908, p. 615.

14 "The Combination of Liberal and Vocational Education," *Ed. R.*, Mar., 1909, p. 241. Also see *NEA Proc.*, 1908, p. 757.

15 For the history of this field, see the unpublished doctoral dissertation of Irene Josephine Lawrence, "A History of Educational Sociology in the United States," Stanford University, 1951.

16 David Snedden, "Should There Be a Difference in the High School Training of Boys and Girls?" *Yearbook of the High School Teachers Association of New York City, 1908–1909* (New York, 1909), pp. 34–35; and David

Snedden in *Ed. R.*, Mar., 1909, pp. 239–41, for the material of this and the next two paragraphs.

17 David Snedden, "Pedagogical Departments in Colleges and Universities," *NEA Proc.*, 1908, p. 695; David Snedden, "Review of Seeley's Elementary Pedagogy," *Ed. R.*, Nov., 1908, p. 415.

18 David Snedden, "Should There Be a Difference in the High School Training of Boys and Girls?" *Yearbook of the High School Teachers Association of New York City, 1908–1909*, pp. 33–38, for the remaining discussion of Snedden's address before the association in the next several paragraphs.

19 David Snedden, "Educational Tendencies in America," *Ed. R.*, Jan., 1910, pp. 16–31. The material for the remaining discussion of this section is from this source.

20 *Report of the Massachusetts Commission on Industrial and Technical Education* (Boston, 1906), p. 1.

21 Winship had been on the scene in Massachusetts since the late sixties, initially as a teacher in the Bridgewater Normal School. He was a member of the Board of Education at the time of its consolidation with the Commission on Industrial Education. His observations may be considered unusually knowledgeable, though slanted to the same viewpoint as Snedden. See "The Massachusetts Legislature, Review of the Work of the Session of 1909," *J. Ed.*, June 23, 1909, p. 39.

22 Jesse W. Burks to William H. Allen, Oct. 24, 1909, in IPS-Allen Papers, in the State Historical Society of Wisconsin.

23 *NEA Proc.*, 1909, pp. 523–26.

24 "Teachers College, Columbia University," *J. Ed.*, Apr. 21, 1910, pp. 425–27.

25 "Snedden the Man, as Told by Friend," *Boston Herald*, Nov. 22, 1909. The clipping is in the IPS-Allen Papers, State Historical Society of Wisconsin. Miss Irene Lawrence, in her dissertation on the history of educational sociology (Stanford, 1951) found the first course given at Teachers College under the title Educational Sociology appeared in the catalog for 1910. She indicates Henry Suzzallo gave the course at that time.

26 "Snedden in Massachusetts," *J. Ed.*, Nov. 25, 1909, pp. 547–48.

CHAPTER V

1 Interview with Mrs. Nathan Finch, Dec. 26, 1961.

2 Diary of Ernest Carroll Moore, Jan., 1913, Microfilm Reel 1, in the Special Collections, University of California at Los Angeles.

3 David Snedden to William Orr, Feb. 15, 1910, in Box 1, The William Orr Papers, Library of Congress; *Union* (Springfield, Mass.), Feb. 13, 1910. Also of interest is a testimonial letter from Bertha McConkey, secretary of the Springfield school committee, to Orr, Apr. 29, 1910, Box 1, Orr Papers.

4 See Joseph B. Groce, manager of the Groce Education Bureau, to William

Orr, Feb. 12, 1910; John Riley, City Superintendent of Holyoke, Mass., to Orr, Feb. 12, 1910; Franklin E. Heald to Orr, Feb. 20, 1910; Frederick W. Atkinson to Orr, Feb. 16, 1910; all in Box 1, Orr Papers, Library of Congress.

5 IX (Apr., 1909), 353.

6 *Union* (Springfield, Mass.), Feb. 13, 1910, clipping in Box 1, Orr Papers, Library of Congress.

7 David Snedden to William Orr, Feb. 24, 1910, Box 1, Orr Papers, Library of Congress.

8 Unless otherwise identified, the material of the next several paragraphs is from the *Seventy-Fourth Annual Report of the Board of Education* (Boston, 1911), pp. 9, 16–37.

9 May, 1910, pp. 537–49.

10 "The Vocational and Industrial School," *NEA Proc.*, 1910, pp. 367–68.

11 *Seventy-Fifth Annual Report* (Boston, 1912), pp. 32–34.

12 "Educational Intelligence," *J. Ed.*, Feb. 1, 1912, p. 136.

13 "What They Say," *J. Ed.*, Jan. 11, 1912, p. 31.

14 Pp. 60–64.

15 David Snedden, "Differentiated Programs of Study for Older Children In Elementary Schools," *Ed. R.*, Sept., 1912, pp. 131–35, 138.

16 David Snedden, "Intermediate Industrial Schools," *NEA Proc.*, 1910, pp. 782–83.

17 Ellwood Cubberley, "Does the Present Trend Toward Vocational Education Threaten Liberal Culture," *Sch. R.*, XIX (Sept., 1911), 463. For Snedden's reply see pp. 487–88.

18 *Sch. R.*, XIX (Sept., 1911), 481–82.

19 *Ibid.*, 488.

20 David Snedden, "Practical Arts in Liberal Education," *Ed. R.*, Apr., 1912, pp. 378–80, 384; discussion, *NEA Proc.*, 1910, pp. 1113–14. Also see Snedden, "Need for Better School Reports and Publicity," *J. Ed.*, July 14, 1910, pp. 34–35.

21 David Snedden, "Certification in History," *History Teachers Magazine* III (May, 1912), 100–105.

22 Clarence D. Kingsley, "University High Schools," *New York City High School Teachers Assn. Bul.*, No. 2 (1907–8), 40–42.

23 Clarence D. Kingsley, "The Need of High School Accommodations in Brooklyn," *New York City High School Teachers Assn. Bul.*, No. 2 (1907–8), 35–39. The map was prepared in the living room of the Seelman home at 410 Fourth St., Brooklyn. The Seelman residence was just four doors from the Manual Training High School and neighbor to the home where Kingsley found his boarding place. Miss Seelman was a teacher in the Girls High School of Brooklyn. Their marriage was performed in the same living room some years later with Dr. Henry Neumann of the Brooklyn Ethical Culture Society and the CRSE officiating. For additional information on Kingsley, see Walter Drost, "Clarence Kingsley, the New York Years," *History of Education Quarterly*, Fall, 1966, pp. 18–34.

24 Clarence D. Kingsley, "Report of the Committee on Increase of High School Accommodations," *New York City High School Teachers Assn. Bul.*, No. 4 (1909–10), 17–18.

25 Walter H. Eddy, "Final Report of the Committee on Revision of the High School Course," *New York City High School Teachers Assn. Bul.*, No. 5 (1910–11), 26–27.

26 Clarence D. Kingsley, "Second Report of the Sub-Committee on Girls Preparatory Courses for Training School," *New York City High School Teachers Assn. Bul.*, No. 4 (1909–10), 61–67.

27 In "Report of the Committee on Conferences with the Colleges," *New York City High School Teachers Assn. Bul.*, No. 4 (1909–10), 19–21.

28 "Committee on High School and College Articulation," *NEA Proc.*, 1911, pp. 561–63.

29 U.S. Bureau of Education Bulletin 7 (Wash., D.C., 1913). See also "Evolution of Entrance Requirements," *J. Ed.*, Mar. 27, 1913, p. 345.

30 "American Institute of Instruction," *J. Ed.*, July 18, 1912, pp. 89–90.

31 Kingsley, *New York City High School Teachers Assn. Bul.*, No. 5 (1910–11), 13; "Report of the Committee on Articulation of High School and College," *NEA Proc.*, 1912, pp. 667–68.

32 *Ibid.*, p. 673.

33 *Seventy-Fifth Annual Report*, p. 38.

34 *Seventy-Sixth Annual Report*, pp. 24–26.

35 *Seventy-Fifth Annual Report*, p. 38; also see the *Seventy-Sixth Annual Report*, pp. 65–66, 69; *Seventy-Seventh Annual Report*, p. 37.

36 Kingsley prepared a syllabus for such a course in community civics for the New York schools and it appears to have been introduced experimentally there. Also see Clarence D. Kingsley, "How Can We Best Secure A Working Agreement Between Colleges and High Schools," *Proc. Assn. Middle States and Maryland*, 1913, pp. 62–63.

37 Clarence D. Kingsley, "The Reorganization of Secondary Education," *J. Ed.*, May 15, 1913, p. 543.

38 Diary of Ernest Carroll Moore, entries for Feb. 2 and 28, 1913, Microfilm Reel 1, in the Special Collections, University of California at Los Angeles.

39 *Seventy-Sixth Annual Report*, pp. 18–20, 29–30, 110, 116–20. The discussion of the next two paragraphs is from this source.

40 *Seventy-Seventh Annual Report*, pp. 26–33, 40, 106, 121–26. The discussion of the next several paragraphs is from this source.

41 Kingsley, *J. Ed.*, May 15, 1913, p. 544, and Nov. 26, 1914, p. 514.

42 *Seventy-Seventh Annual Report*, pp. 127, 130, 133–34.

43 Kingsley, *Proc. Assn. Middle States and Maryland*, 1913, pp. 61–62, 66–67.

44 Material concerning this meeting is from "Educational News," *J. Ed.*, May 14, 1914, p. 554; David Snedden, "Teaching History in Secondary Schools," *History Teachers Magazine*, V (Nov., 1914), 277–82; George L. Burr, "What History Shall We Teach?" *History Teachers Magazine*, V (Nov., 1914), 283–86.

45 This discussion and that of the Snedden-Bagley controversy is from David Snedden, "Practical Arts in Liberal Education," *Ed. R.*, Apr., 1912, pp. 379, 380, 384; James Van Sickle, "Review of 'Problems of Educational Readjustment' by David Snedden," *Ed. Adm. and Sup.*, I (Feb., 1915), 222–23; "Editorial," *School Review*, XXII (Apr., 1914), 262; William Bagley, "Fundamental Distinctions Between Vocational and Liberal Education," *J. Ed.*, Mar. 29, 1914, pp. 339–43; "Snedden-Bagley," *J. Ed.*, Mar. 12, 1914, p. 285.

46 John Dewey, "Industrial Education – A Wrong Kind," *New Republic*, II (Feb. 20, 1915), 71–73; also see "Policy of Industrial Education," *New Republic*, I (Dec. 19, 1914), 11–12. For Snedden's reply see "Vocational Education," *New Republic*, III (May 15, 1915), 40–42.

47 Samuel T. Dutton to David Snedden, March 19, 1914, in Charles H. Levermore, *Samuel Train Dutton, a Biography* (New York, 1922), pp. 147–50.

48 *Seventy-Eighth Annual Report*, pp. 22–23, 32–39, 60–62.

49 See David Snedden, "Problems of Art Education," *Sch. and Soc.*, III (May 13, 1916), 396–97.

50 The material for the discussion of this report in the next several paragraphs is from pages 23–27, 39, 102–6, 115–16, 146–47.

51 P. 25. See *Seventy-Seventh Annual Report*, p. 24.

52 Diary of Ernest Carroll Moore, Jan. 23, 1916, Microfilm Reel 1, in the Special Collections, University of California at Los Angeles.

53 Material of this and the next two paragraphs is from David Snedden, "Principles of Aim, Organization and Method in General Science Teaching," *Sch. and Soc.*, I (Mar. 27, 1915), 438–39; E. A. Strong, "General Science Teaching," *Sch. and Soc.*, I (Apr. 17, 1915), 562–63; David Snedden, "General Science Teaching," *Sch. and Soc.*, I (May 8, 1915), 675.

54 "Bagley-Snedden," *J. Ed.*, Mar. 9, 1916, pp. 256–57; David Snedden, "Our National Shortcomings in Education," *Sch. and Soc.*, III (June 3, 1916), 817; George A. Brown, "Snedden's Un-American Theories of School Administration," in "Educational Survey," *School and Home Education*, XXXV (Apr., 1916), 245–47.

55 XIX (Feb., 1916), 332–36. For Snedden's reply see "Mr. Snedden's Reply as to Un-American Theories of School Administration," in "Educational Survey," *School and Home Education*, XXXV (May, 1916), 283–84.

56 "Twenty-Five years at Teachers College," *J. Ed.*, Mar. 19, 1914, p. 322.

57 "Snedden to Columbia," *J. Ed.*, Jan. 27, 1916, p. 99; "Professor Snedden," *J. Ed.*, Feb. 17, 1916, p. 183; David Snedden, "An Educational Quest," *Sch. and Soc.*, III (June 10, 1916), 843; "Dr. Snedden Returns to T.C.," *Teachers College Record*, XVII (Mar., 1916), 208.

58 "The Snedden Banquet," *J. Ed.*, May 25, 1916, p. 576. Also see Boston *Transcript*, May 20, 1916, "Farewell to Snedden."

59 Snedden, *Sch. and Soc.*, III (June 10, 1916), 833–35, 840–43.

60 David Snedden to William Orr, July 14, 1916, Box 1, Orr Papers, Library of Congress; "William Orr's Change," *J. Ed.*, June 15, 1916, p. 659.

CHAPTER VI

1 Genevra Snedden, "The Early Married Life of David and Genevra Snedden," pp. 44–45.
2 "College and Department News," *Teachers College Record*, XXVIII (Mar., 1922), 178. The meetings were those of the Association of Academic Principals of New York State, the Philadelphia Forum, the New York Modern Language Association, the Brooklyn YMCA, the Camp Directors Association, the Home Economics Division of the Connecticut State Teachers Association, the Vocational Club of Albany, and the Rural and Secondary School Teachers Section of the Alumni Conference of Teachers College.
    Accounts of the alumni meetings are from the *Teachers College Record*, XVII (Nov., 1916), 489–90; XVIII (Mar., 1917), 197, (May, 1917), 305, (Sept., 1917), 408. According to one account Dean Russell returned Snedden to Teachers College especially for his ability to move among people and stimulate discussion. Personal interview with Thomas Briggs, Jan. 24, 1962.
3 Charles Judd to the membership, Mar. 14, 1917 and Jan. 14, 1918, Elliott Papers, Memorial Library, Purdue University.
4 The material for this discussion is drawn from Cassius J. Keyser, "Scientific Books, Recent Books in Mathematics," *Science*, July 7, 1916, pp. 27–28; David Snedden, "Compulsory Mathematics, an Explanation," *Science*, Aug. 11, 1916, pp. 204–5; "The Status of Mathematics in Secondary Schools," *Sch. and Soc.*, VI (Nov. 17, 1917), 576–77; David Snedden, "Discussion and Correspondence," *Sch. and Soc.*, VI (Dec. 1, 1917), 651–52; Charles N. Moore, "Mathematics in Secondary Schools," *Sch. and Soc*, VII (Jan. 7, 1918), 54–55.
5 XXVI (1918), 578, 582, 589, 592. The argument continues in Charles N. Moore, "Discussion and Correspondence," *Sch. and Soc.*, VIII (Nov. 23, 1918), 622–23, and David Snedden, "Discussion and Correspondence," *Sch. and Soc.*, VIII (Dec. 14, 1918), 714.
6 "The High School of Tomorrow," *Sch. R.*, XXXV (Jan., 1917), 3–12.
7 See Clarence D. Kingsley, "The Study of Nations: Its Possibilities as a Social Study in High School," *Sch. and Soc.*, III (Jan. 8, 1916), 37–41.
8 David Snedden, "Current Problems of Air in Physics Teaching," *Sch. and Soc.*, VIII (Nov. 30, 1918), 631–35.
9 E. Milton Fairchild to Edward A. Ross, Mar. 17, 1896, Edward A. Ross Papers, State Historical Society of Wisconsin.
10 Description of the Fairchild program, unless otherwise noted, is from Walter Hines Page, "Teaching Morals by Photography," *World's Work*, XIX (Mar., 1910), 12721–24; and Wyllys Rede, "A New Method of Making Character," *Independent*, Oct. 26, 1911, p. 917.

11 E. Milton Fairchild, "Society's Need of Effective Ethical Instruction in School and Church, and the Suggestion of an Available Method," *Am. J. Sociol.*, IV (Jan., 1899), 441–42.

12 Twenty-five hundred copies of the Hutchins Code were distributed in schools of Pittsburgh, Pa. See *NEA Proc.*, 1918, pp. 20–22, and *Sch. and Soc.*, XIV (Aug. 20, 1921), 94–95.

13 Milton Fairchild, "Character Education Methods Competition," *NEA Proc.*, 1917, pp. 763–64.

14 Snedden, "Teaching Morality," *Ed. R.*, Oct., 1926, pp. 160–62.

15 Milton Fairchild, "Character Education Methods Competition," *NEA Proc.*, 1918, p. 121; David Snedden, "Improvement of Character Education," *J. Ed.*, Aug. 8, 1918, pp. 144–45. The contest was won by Professor Edwin Starbuck of the State University of Iowa who had served on the Stanford faculty with Snedden in 1901. He used the twenty thousand dollar award to found the Institute for Character Research at Iowa in 1927.

16 Milton Fairchild, "A High School Course in Personal Rights and Obligations," *Sch. and Soc.*, XXI (June 27, 1925), 785–86.

17 Henry Neumann, *Moral Values in Secondary Education, A Report of the Commission on the Reorganization of Secondary Education* (U.S. Bureau of Education Bulletin 51 [Wash., D.C., 1917]), pp. 5, 8–10, 23–27.

18 David Snedden, "The Cardinal Principles of Secondary Education," *Sch. and Soc.*, IX (May 3, 1919), 518–19.

19 Elsewhere Neuman reacted against the scientific determination of moral and ethical values. The function of science, he said, was in finding ways by which ideals might be effectively served.

20 This is evident from the William Orr diary, entries for Feb. 22–26, 1915, in the Orr Papers, Library of Congress, and from the William H. Kilpatrick diary, entry for Feb. 25, 1917.

21 Snedden, *Recollections*, p. 40.

22 Snedden, "The High School Principal's Place in Reorganizing Objectives of High School Education," *First Yearbook, National Association of Secondary School Principals* (Chicago, 1917), pp. 32–36.

23 The material for this discussion is from David Snedden, "The Cardinal Principles of Secondary Education," *Sch. and Soc.*, IX (May 3, 1919), 520–27; "Vocational Education in Massachusetts: Some Achievements and Some Prospects," *Manual Training Magazine*, XVIII (Sept., 1916), 1–4; "Promoting Industrial Education," *J. Ed.*, Feb. 10, 1916, p. 145; "Educational Sociology: Its Possibilities," *Am. J. Sociol.*, XXV (Sept., 1919), 146; and Clarence Kingsley, in "Discussion and Correspondence," *Sch. and Soc.*, X (July 5, 1919), 18–20.

24 Snedden, "High School Reorganization – Some Practical Next Steps," *Ed. Adm. and Sup.*, VIII (Feb., 1922), 83, 87, 90, 97–98. The paper was delivered Dec. 30, 1921.

25 Frank Leavitt, "Reorganization of Manual Arts, Report to be Presented by the Manual Arts Committee of the NEA, Commission on the Re-

organization of Secondary Education," *Industrial Arts Magazine*, II (July, 1914), 4–5.

26 William T. Bawden, *Leaders in Industrial Education* (Milwaukee, 1950), p. 174.

27 P. P. Claxton to E. A. Ott, May 14, 1918, and Claxton, "Education for the Establishment of Democracy in the World," July 2, 1919, reprint of an address before the NEA. Claxton Papers, Special Collections, University of Tennessee.

28 P. P. Claxton to C. A. Bennett, Nov. 20, 1919; and *Middle-West Vocational Education Assn. Bul.*, Oct. 1919, both in the Commissioner's Papers, Record Group 12, National Archives.

29 The material for the discussion that follows is from Snedden's several editorial contributions to *Vocational Education Magazine* successively: I (Nov., 1922), 167–68; (Oct., 1922), 81–82; (Dec., 1922), 251–52; II (Sept., 1923), 1–2; (Oct., 1923), 91; (Dec., 1923), 261–62; (May, 1924), 709–10; (Sept., 1923), 1; (Oct., 1924), 961; (Dec., 1924), 1097–98; also see "The Vocational Education Convention at Detroit," *Industrial Arts Magazine*, XII (Jan., 1923), 34.

30 Bawden, *Leaders in Industrial Education*, p. 174.

31 Snedden, "Educational Sociology; The Possibilities," *Am. J. Sociol.*, XXV (Sept., 1919), 130–34.

32 Snedden, *Ed. Adm. and Sup.*, VIII, 83–98.

33 The material of this and the next three paragraphs is from David Snedden, "Liberty of Teaching in the Social Science," *Sch. and Soc.*, XIII (Feb. 12, 1921), 185–86, 190; "Discussion and Correspondence," *Sch. and Soc.*, XIII (May 5, 1921), 295–96.

34 Snedden, "National Society for Educational Sociology," *Sch. and Soc.*, XVII (Mar. 24, 1923), 327; "Case Group Methods of Determining Flexibility of General Curricula in High Schools," *Sch. and Soc.*, XVII (Mar. 17, 1923), 288–92; "Proposed Revision of Secondary School Subjects Looking to More Effective Education in Personal Culture and Good Citizenship," *Sch. and Soc.*, IX (Feb. 8, 1919), 159–64. See also Ellsworth Faris, "Reviews and Book Notes," *Sch. R.*, XXX (Nov., 1922), 708.

35 Snedden, "Educational Sociology; Its Possibilities," *Am. J. Sociol.*, XXV (Sept., 1919), 148–49. The books were *A Digest of Educational Sociology* (New York, 1920); *Vocational Education* (New York, 1920); *Educational Sociology* (New York, 1922); *Civic Education* (White Plains, N.J., 1922).

36 This discussion is drawn from David Snedden, "What's Wrong with the Schools?" *Ed. Adm. and Sup.*, VIII (May, 1922), 276–85, and "Can Sociology Produce a New Synthesis of Educational Theory?" *Ed. Adm. and Sup.*, X (Mar., 1924), 175.

37 Snedden, "Bobbitt's Curriculum-Making in Los Angeles," *Sch. R.*, XXXI (Feb., 1923), 104–8.

38 The discussion of this and the next five paragraphs is from these sources by David Snedden: "Education for a World of Team-Players and Team-Workers," *Sch. and Soc.*, XX (Nov. 1, 1924), 554–56; "The Real Emotional

Determinism," *Sch. and Soc.*, XVII (June 30, 1923), 703–5; "An Uncon-
sidered Source of Criteria of Educational Values," *Teachers College Record*, XXVII (Mar., 1926), 596–98; *What's Wrong with American Education* (New York, 1927), pp. 22–23.

39 *Sch. and Soc.*, XVIII (Aug. 25, 1923), 211, 214–215.

40 Snedden, *Sch. and Soc.*, XX, 556.

41 The discussion of these divisions as well as material concerning "lotments,"
"strands," and "peths," is from David Snedden: "Junior High School Offerings." *Sch. and Soc.*, XX (Dec. 13, 1924), 741–43; "Planning Curriculum Research," *Sch. and Soc.*, XXII (Aug. 29, 1925), 262–64, and
Sch. and Soc., XXII (Sept. 5, 1925), 287–93; "New Aims in Education," *Teachers College Record*, XXIX (Feb., 1928), 398; "Planning
the Curriculum," *Sch. and Soc.*, XXII (Sept. 12, 1925), 320–26.

42 The discussion that follows is from David Snedden: "Sociological Analysis
as Basic to Educational Sociology," *J. Ed. Sociol.*, I (Jan., 1928), 264;
"The Socially Efficient Community," *J. Ed. Sociol.*, II (Apr., 1929),
465–70. The 2 per cent figure is from "Progress Towards Sociologically
Based Civic Education," *J. Ed. Sociol.*, III (Apr., 1930), 493–95. See also
"Sociology Applied to Curriculum Making," *J. Ed. Sociol.*, III (Sept.,
1929), 23.

43 Snedden, *J. Ed. Sociol.*, III, 496; *Sch. and Soc.*, XXII, 328.

44 Snedden, "A Source of Educational Sciences," *Sch. and Soc.*, XXIII (June
19, 1926), 762–63.

45 I (Feb., 1928), 363; II (Mar., 1929), 442–43.

46 Boyd H. Bode, "Why Educational Objectives," *Sch. and Soc.*, XIX (May
10, 1924), 531–39; David Snedden, "Don't Overload Curriculum-
Makers!" *Ed. Adm. and Sup.*, XII (May, 1926), 299–303; H. Gordon Hullfish, "Looking Backward with David Snedden," *Ed. R.*, Feb., 1924, pp.
61–69; Boyd H. Bode, "Reply to Editorial," *J. Ed. Sociol.*, I (Feb.,
1928), 308–11; Bode, *Modern Educational Theories* (New York, 1927).

47 Snedden, "Educational Philosophy Versus Educational Sociology," *J. Ed.
Sociol.*, I (Mar., 1928), 375; "Next Steps for Curriculum Makers," *Teachers
College Record*, XXX (Dec., 1928), 208–9.

48 Snedden, "New Aims in Education," *Teachers College Record*, XXIX
(Feb., 1928), 401; "Professor Snedden Attacks the Classics; Professor Abbott Defends Them," *Teachers College Record*, XXXII (Jan., 1931),
386–88.

49 New York, pp. iv, 6.

50 *School Educations; Sociological Sources of Value* (New York, 1930), p.
14. For Skipper's review see *Ed. Adm. and Sup.*, XVIII (Oct., 1932), 559.

51 Pp. 12, 15, 53, 324, 338.

52 *Toward Better Educations*, p. 324.

53 Snedden, "Education for a Changing Social World," *NEA Proc.*, 1932,
pp. 641–45.

54 "Snedden as Prophet," *Sch. and Soc.*, XXXIII (May 2, 1931), 612. While
not signed by McAndrew, the style of the article was clearly his own and

in marked contrast with that found previous to his affiliation with the magazine. McAndrew joined the *Educational Review* in 1924 about the time he became school superintendent for the city of Chicago. With the Nov. 3, 1928, issue of *School and Society, Educational Review* was merged into that magazine and continued as a separate section under the editorship of William McAndrew. It was usually devoted to book reviews.

55 The discussion is from pages 8–11, 15, 43, 116, 119. The review was by P. W. L. Cox in *J. Ed. Sociol.*, V (Jan., 1932), 315.

56 "Snedden as Prophet," *Sch. and Soc.*, XXXIII, 612.

57 "Rough Going Ahead: Some Social Faiths and Doubts," XXXV (Mar., 1934), 671–84.

58 Snedden, "Distributions of Expensive Learnings," *Teachers College Record*, XXXV (Nov., 1933), 139–40.

59 *Teachers College Record*, XXXV (Feb., 1934), 390–95.

60 *Ibid.*, 393–94.

CHAPTER VII

1 "Education for the Life of Today," *Sch. and Soc.*, XVI (Sept. 9, 1922), 282–84, 288.

2 Snedden, "The Relationship of Vocational and General Education," *NEA Proc.*, 1924, p. 1004.

3 Snedden, "Vocational Education's Modern Trend," *Wis. J. Ed.*, LXIII (Nov., 1930), 127–29.

4 *Toward Better Educations*, p. 19.

5 David Snedden, "The Culture of John Doe," *Teachers College Record*, XXXII (Apr., 1931), 619–27; "Objectives in Education — How to Distinguish," *Ed. R.*, May, 1924, pp. 239–46; "Shall We Keep the Children Out of School?" *New Republic*, Dec. 4, 1929, pp. 40–41.

6 Gordon Hullfish, "Looking Backward with David Snedden," *Ed. R.*, Feb., 1924, pp. 61–69; Boyd H. Bode, "Why Educational Objectives?" *Sch. and Soc.*, XIX (May 10, 1924), 531–39.

7 Snedden, "Education and Social Change," *Sch. and Soc.*, XL (Sept. 8, 1934), 311–14.

8 Ross Finney, "Social Studies in the Junior High School," *J. Ed.*, Dec. 20, 1917, pp. 633–34; *A Social Philosophy of Education* (New York, 1928), pp. 245–46.

9 *Am. J. Sociol.*, XXXVIII (Sept., 1932), 302–3.

10 See his review, *Am. J. Sociol.*, XXVIII (Mar., 1923), 609–10.

11 Mar. 17, 1921, p. 286; Cook, Sept., 1921, pp. 177–78; "Educational News and Comment," *Sch. R.*, XXIX (Nov., 1921), 646–48; H. B. Wilson, "Preparation of the Course of Study," *NEA Journal*, XI (June, 1922), 223–24.

12 "A Kentucky Crusade," *J. Ed.*, Jan. 25, 1923, p. 87; John Addison Clement, *Curriculum Making in Secondary Schools* (New York, 1923), pp. 30–35; Leslie D. Zeleny, "A Conception of a Liberal Education in American High

Schools," *Ed.*, LIV (Sept., 1923), 15–44; C. C. Peters, *Objectives and Procedures in Civic Education, An Intensive Study in Curriculum Construction* (New York, 1930), pp. vi, 55.

13 See book reviews by P. W. L. Cox, *J. Ed. Soc.*, V (Jan., 1932), 315; E. E. Hill, *Chicago Schools Journal*, VI (Oct., 1923), 74–75; E. George Payne, *J. Ed. Sociol.*, II (Mar., 1929), 442–43. The NEA studies are "Vote of Expert Opinion on Most Helpful Books Dealing with High School Curriculum Problems," *NEA Res. Bul.*, I, No. 5 (1923), 234–58; "Helpful Books Dealing with High School Curriculum Problems," *NEA Res. Bul.*, VII, No. 4 (Sept., 1929), 234–58.

14 Ross said of his book *Social Control*, "I cut the headwaters of scores of burning questions. . . . My book will monopolize its field for perhaps twenty years." Ross to Ely, Aug. 6, 1900, Box 2, Ross Papers in the State Historical Society of Wisconsin.

15 Maris M. Profitt, "Secondary School Life Adjustment Training for Sixty Per Cent of Our Youth," *Sch. Life*, XXVIII (July, 1946), 6–7; Harl R. Douglass, *Education for Life Adjustment* (New York, 1950), pp. 42–43.

16 Snedden, "Ameliorating Mass Production Methods in Educations," *Teachers College Record*, XXXII (Jan., 1931), 341; "Shall We Keep the Children Out of School?" *New Republic*, Dec. 4, 1929, p. 41; "Rough Going Ahead: Some Social Faiths and Doubts," *Teachers College Record*, XXXV (Mar., 1934), 679; "What Next in Developing Individual Powers?" *J. Ed.*, June 8, 1931, p. 608.

17 Arthur E. Bestor, Jr., "Anti-Intellectualism in the Schools," *New Republic*, Jan. 19, 1953, pp. 11–13. Bestor's moral, vocational, and physical educations were based upon understandings not unlike Snedden's. This similarity is especially evident with respect to physical education in which he placed heavy emphasis upon the knowledge of physiology and development of physical fitness while tending to discount the importance of athletics. He expected vocational education to result in vocational competence, as did Snedden, but for him the role played by the school was the antithesis of Snedden's. He urged the school be made to provide theoretical training and practical work, where necessary, be placed under other auspices.

18 Merle Curti, *American Paradox: The Conflict of Thought and Action* (New Brunswick, N.J., 1956), pp. 11–13, 95.

BIBLIOGRAPHICAL NOTE

The most important source of information on the lives of David and Genevra Snedden is their own autobiographical writing. Mrs. Snedden possessed a keen sense of history which she may have shared with her husband in their later years. Her typescript, "The Early Married Life of David and Genevra Snedden," covering the period from 1897 to 1917, has a charm all its own and deserves publication. Her *Mountain Cattle and Frontier People* (Palo Alto, Calif., 1947) published for family and friends, is in the nature of a family history. It shows the development of the Snedden Land and Cattle Company from Samuel Snedden's original herd and consequently is in part concerned with David's boyhood home and early life on the cattle range. Mrs. Snedden's sense of history is especially evident in her organization of a family album as the "Picture History and Genealogy" of the Snedden and Sisson families. Snedden's own *Recollections of Over Half a Century Spent in Educational Work* (Palo Alto, Calif., 1949), published when he was past eighty, is remarkably accurate in reporting events that transpired at the turn of the century. All of these materials are in the possession of Mrs. Nathan Finch, of Palo Alto, California, Professor Snedden's youngest daughter, who generously made them available. *Mountain Cattle and Frontier People* is also in the Library of Congress. Mrs. Finch placed a copy of the *Recollections of Over Half a Century Spent in Educational Work* in the Memorial Library of the University of Wisconsin; other copies may be seen at Stanford and at Columbia University.

Little archival material remains from the long history of St. Vincent's College prior to its acquisition by the Society of Jesus in 1911. Father Philip Conneally, S.J., librarian of Loyola High School in Los Angeles, where the cornerstone of the main building still bears the inscription "St. Vincent's College," has been its most faithful historian. From time to time he has published what he has been able to piece together of its early history, mainly for the local Jesuit community. Additional perspective concerning the founding of St. Vincent's, its curriculum, and changing leadership may be gained from "Catholic Education in Southern California," a 1936 doctoral dissertation at Catholic University of America by William E. North. A vivid picture of the Los Angeles David Snedden knew as a student at St. Vincent's College is found in *Sixty Years in Southern California, 1853–1913: Containing Reminiscences of Harris Newmark* (Boston, 1930), edited by Maurice H. and Marco R. Newmark. The book contains two references to David's uncle, Peter Wilson, and some interesting material about Throop University. An article by Jeanne C. Carr, "Throop University, Pasadena," in *California Illustrated* for September, 1892, presents a contemporary account of that institution by a member of the board of trustees. *History and Reminiscences, Los Angeles*

City and County (Los Angeles, 1930), by William A. Spaulding, was found to be a useful local history for this period and its describes some of the business activities of David's uncle, Peter Wilson.

There is a considerable amount of archival material relating to David Snedden's career as a schoool master in Paso Robles, Ventura, and San Luis Obispo, California. The attendance office for the Ventura County schools has a separate volume entitled "Lists of Promotions" for each of the years he served the Santa Paula schools. In each is a page assigned to him on which test grades are recorded and the final disposition of each pupil in his classes noted. The Ventura County school superintendent is also in possession of the "Minutes of the Board of Education of Ventura County" for each of those years. The county superintendent served as board secretary, and this source provides an intimate picture of Snedden's responsibilities as a board member. "Minutes of the Ventura County Teachers Institute," a separate volume for each year, are at the same place. An ordinary classroom register was used for the handwritten entries with a record of attendance always on the first page or inside the cover. In most instances the newspaper reports of the sessions appear to have been copied directly from the minutes. A volume entitled "Ventura County School Trustees" contains a brief account of the activities of each local school board from 1891 to 1893. Here too, in a plain notebook, will be found the "Report of Official Acts" of Superintendent C. T. Meredith during the 1884–85 school year when the school district was created in the Lockwood Valley. In another notebook, "Report of Official Visits of the School Superintendent of Ventura County," kept for the year 1885, Superintendent Meredith reported his visit to the Lockwood School and gave his evaluation of the teacher, Mr. Aram.

The "Minute Book of the Board of Control" of the high school and a similar volume kept by the Board of Trustees of the grammar school were found in the principal's office of the Paso Robles High School. The entries for the years of Snedden's tenure there are set down in his own flowing hand. In the same place may be found the only surviving class register of one of his teachers, that of Miss Sara Cory who taught German, Latin, and English in the high school during the 1899–1900 school year. The class register was an official record book prepared by the State Board of Education in which attendance, promotions, test grades, and visitors to the classroom were to be noted and provides some insight to the school program.

The petitions for appointment to the County Board of Education in behalf of David Snedden and others may be found in File 43–2, Applications and Registrations, County Board of Education, in the offices of the county clerk of San Luis Obispo County. The action taken on the applications is recorded in Volume H, "Minutes of the Board of Supervisors," at the same location. The "Record of Proceedings of the Board of Education" are kept in similar large, leather-bound volumes. Volume A, for the years 1897 to 1900, when Snedden served on this board, is in the San Luis Obispo county schools office. When Mrs. A. C. Spafford Woods became county superintendent in 1898 she undertook to compile a scrapbook of "Programs, Directories, Orders, Notices,

Manuals, Official Bulletins," of her administration. This valuable volume is also in the county schools office at San Luis Obispo.

Regrettably the local Santa Paula newspapers were lost in a fire some years ago. Only a few issues of the Santa Paula *Chronicle* could be found. These were from the year 1899 and are part of the holdings of the Los Angeles Public Library. The December 1, 1899, edition was a special issue intended to promote the community's commercial activity, and since it was published only four years after Snedden's departure, it was useful to this study. The Ventura County Free Library has a good file of the Ventura *Free Press*. This newspaper published reports of the annual teachers institutes and also carried a weekly column, "Santa Paula Sundries," which appeared to be material clipped from local Santa Paula papers.

The Paso Robles Public Library has an extensive file of the local paper, the *Record*. The San Luis Obispo newspapers, the *Breeze* and the *Tribune*, both gave school news extensive coverage. In addition, the *Tribune* carried a weekly "clip-sheet" column, "Paso Robles People," which appeared to carry contributions from three different Paso Robles newspapers. The files of both papers are maintained in good condition in the San Luis Obispo County Free Library.

Newspapers in the extensive files of the California State Library in Sacramento are an important source of material concerning the various local teachers institutes. Useful reports of Snedden's addresses before these groups in California may be found in the *Marin County Tocsin*, San Rafael; *San Benito Advance*, Hollister; *Yreka Journal*, Yreka City; *Weekly Trinity Journal*, Weaverville; *Weekly Press*, Santa Barbara; *Courier–Free Press*, Redding; *Placer County Republican*, Auburn; *Stanislaus County Weekly News*, Modesto; *Woodland Daily Democrat*; and the San Diego *Sun*. Probably the most complete coverage of any teachers institute was that reported in the Quincy *Daily Journal* for the week of institute work conducted by Snedden in the Illinois river town in 1904.

The activities of the California Teachers Association, the California Council of Education, the Scholia Club, and the educational scene generally in the Golden State during the years from 1896 to 1906 are best reported in Harr Wagner's *Western Journal of Education*. Though the *Overland Monthly*, via an educational supplement, was the official organ of the California Teachers Association during part of this period, the *Journal* carried all of the reports, proceedings, and activities of both the association and the Council of Education, frequently giving them more complete coverage. The *Pacific Educational Journal* was the official educational organ of the state until 1897. "California and Her Schools," an article in the July 3, 1890, issue of the *Journal of Education*, and *Education in California* (Stanford, Calif., 1952), by Roy W. Cloud, provide detailed information concerning local educational arrangements in the state.

Robert M. Clarke's *Narrative of a Native*, published in Los Angeles in 1936, contains an interesting account of David Snedden as a classroom teacher in Santa Paula by a former student. A picture of Snedden with his pupils in front of the little brick building which had once been the Santa Paula Academy adds much to the charm of the book. Gerald T. White's *Formative Years in the Far West: A History of Standard Oil Company of California and Predecessors Through 1919* (New York, 1962), and *Black Bonanza* (New York, 1950), the story of the Union Oil Company by Frank J. Taylor and Earl M. Welty, both contribute useful information about the commercial development in the Santa Paula region. Several multivolume local histories were useful for their descriptions of school facilities and identification of community figures: James M. Guinn, *A History of California and an Extended History of its Southern Coast Counties* (Los Angeles, 1907); John S. McGoarty, *California of the South* (Los Angeles, 1935); Anna L. Morrison and John H. Haydon, *History of the San Luis Obispo County and Environs* (Los Angeles, 1917); Sol N. Sheridan, *History of Ventura County* (Chicago, 1926); and Yda Addis Storke, *A Memorial and Biographical History of the Counties of Santa Barbara, San Luis Obispo, and Ventura, California* (Chicago, 1891).

The David Starr Jordan Papers in the Stanford Collection of the Stanford University Library provided additional insight about the professional arrangements of the small, intimate university of the turn of the century supplementing the excellent material found in *Cubberley of Stanford, and His Contribution to American Education* (Stanford, Calif., 1957) by Jesse B. Sears and Adin D. Henderson, *Stanford Mosaic* (Stanford, Calif., 1962) and *Stanford, the Story of a University* (New York, 1959) by Edith Mirrielees, and *Stanford University, The First Twenty-Five Years* (Stanford, Calif., 1937) by Orrin Elliott. The Stanford Collection also has a bibliography of David Snedden's professional publication during the period of his professorship there and the script of a radio speech made shortly after his retirement in 1935. His first published article appeared in the Stanford *Sequoia*, the student literary magazine, in January, 1896. Files of this magazine, the *Stanford Alumnus*, the *Stanford Register*, and the *Stanford Quad*, the student yearbook, are in the Timothy Hopkins Room of the Stanford Library. His address, "Education for the Rank and File," appearing in the first volume of the *Alumnus* (June, 1900) is particularly interesting as an early statement of his position on educational aims.

David Snedden's master's essay, "Flexibility in the Course of Study," is in the library of Teachers College, Columbia University, and may be obtained on microfilm. Snedden's doctoral dissertation, *Administration and Educational Work of American Juvenile Reform Schools* (New York, 1907) was published as a Teachers College Contribution to Education.

Regrettably, no separate file of Snedden papers is known to exist, probably a consequence of his moves from California to New York, to Massachusetts, back to New York, and again to California. However, the manuscript collections of various of his contemporaries contain material useful to the study.

The Albion Small Papers and correspondence with George Vincent in the President's Papers in the Special Collections Room of the Library of the University of Chicago provided useful information on the developing field of educational sociology. "A History of Educational Sociology in the United

States," by Miss Irene J. Lawrence, an unpublished doctoral dissertation at Stanford University, provides a detailed account of the development of this field. She credits Snedden with being its most prolific writer during the period of the twenties. The Edward A. Ross Papers in the State Historical Society of Wisconsin contain useful background material for the development of Ross's doctrine of social control while at Stanford. His letters to Mrs. Mary Beach of Marion, Iowa, his foster mother, are especially appealing and candid. They acquire additional significance when used in conjunction with his autobiography, *Seventy Years of It, An Autobiography* (New York, 1936). The *American Journal of Sociology* carried a good many of Ross's articles and in particular was responsible for having projected his doctrine of social control upon the national scene.

The Charles McCarthy Papers and the Michael Vincent O'Shea Papers, also in the State Historical Society of Wisconsin, are especially useful for the wide cross-section of educational reform movements they contain. The McCarthy Papers have much material relating to vocational education, including correspondence with Frank Leavitt which indicates that at one time Snedden offered Leavitt the post of deputy commissioner for vocational education. The O'Shea Papers are rich in material of the child study movement as well as an interesting correspondence with Leaton Irwin of Quincy, Illinois.

The David Eugene Smith Papers in the manuscript room of the Butler Library at Columbia University include the lengthy and revealing letter of 1907 from Snedden to Smith cited in the text. The William Orr Papers in the Library of Congress for the most part deal with Orr's work with the YMCA, but there are several interesting newspaper clippings relating to his earlier career as a schoolman in Massachusetts. There are also several letters of congratulation upon his appointment as Snedden's deputy commissioner for general education, and some brief diaries of his trips to conventions of the NEA and the Department of the Superintendence.

The papers of William H. Allen's Institute for Public Service in the State Historical Society of Wisconsin give some indication of the many facets of the efficiency movement in which Allen took an interest. For this study, the material of his Committee on the Physical Welfare of School Children was particularly useful. Although much of this content remained in the files of the New York City Bureau of Municipal Research and subsequent moves by Allen resulted in a further culling of the papers, the collection contains much material from all phases of his colorful career.

The Ernest Carroll Moore diary, detailed, refreshingly frank, with an occasional touch of irony, is available on microfilm in the Special Collections of the University of California at Los Angeles. Regrettably, all too often when this old friend from California went to Brookline from New Haven or Cambridge to visit Snedden the latter was away, presumably on the "banquet circuit."

The E. Milton Fairchild Papers in the manuscript department of Duke University are only a small collection, and unfortunately the files of the

National Institution for Moral Instruction could not be found. The collection contains some correspondence of his wife, Salome Cutler Fairchild, and communications between Fairchild and the Baltimore office of the institute. Other material concerning the activities of the institute may be found in the following sources: *The Present Status of the Teaching of Morals in the Public Schools* (Nashville, 1926), a doctoral dissertation of Thomas J. Golightly published as a George Peabody Contribution to Education; *A Brief History of Character Education* (April, 1932), an Extension Bulletin of the University of Iowa by Howard V. Meredith and James C. Maury; "Teaching Morals by Photographs," by Walter Hines Page, in the March, 1910, number of *World's Work*; and "A New Method of Making Character," by Wyllys Rede, in the October 26, 1911, issue of *Independent. Character Education Methods, The Iowa Plan* (Wash., D.C., 1922), published by the institute, contains some historical overview of the movement which received contemporary notice in *School and Society* and the *Journal of Education* via Milton Fairchild's letters to the editor.

The files of the United States Commissioner of Education, in Record Group 12 of the National Archives, contain much of Fairchild's movement — the Educational Church, the Moral Education Board, the National Institute for Moral Instruction, and finally the Character Education Institute — as he worked to gain the support of the Bureau in the capacity of "special agent." These files are also rich in material concerning the NEA Commission on the Reorganization of Secondary Education and the several reports of the commission published as bulletins of the Bureau. Here, especially, is to be found evidence of Clarence D. Kingsley's important role in this work.

The Philander P. Claxton Papers in the Special Collections of the University of Tennessee at Knoxville reflect his strong interest in southern educational projects; however, they also provide good evidence of his demanding travel schedule and the apparent limitation placed upon his active participation in any of the several projects of the Bureau or even so important a work as that of the CRSE. His letters to his wife, frequently on the embossed stationary of the Overland Limited, the Sunset, or the Century, are appealing bits of Americana describing the country through the eyes of a man who made his home in a Pullman lower berth.

A few items in the Jane Addams Papers in the Friends Library at Swarthmore College give evidence of Edward T. Devine's central position in the social settlement movement. *The Charity Organization Society of the City of New York, 1882–1907* by Lilian Brandt, published as the twenty-fifth annual report of the society, is a useful source for the activities of Devine's organization which may be augmented by numerous articles in the *Proceedings of the National Conference of Charities and Corrections*, published annually, and Devine's own *Charities and the Commons*, which later became *Survey* magazine.

The Charles H. Judd Papers in the Special Collections of the University of Chicago provide information about the Cleveland Conference. Additional material may be found in the papers of his close friend, Edward Elliott, at the Memorial Library of Purdue University. The material of both collections are from office files and relatively incomplete.

Perhaps the single most pleasant experience gained from this study was derived from visits and correspondence with persons who at sometime or other were contemporaries of David Snedden or Clarence Kingsley. The late William H. Kilpatrick, who knew David Snedden as a colleague on the faculty of Teachers College and Kingsley as a member of the Reviewing Committee of the CRSE, generously permitted the writer an unhurried perusal of his extensive diaries. Professor Thomas Briggs, colleague and next-door neighbor to David Snedden while the latter was at Columbia, provided both authoritative observation and anecdote in an extended interview and several letters. He too was a member of the Reviewing Committee of the CRSE and remembers some of the deliberations and the contributions of various members. Briggs, especially, credited Kingsley with the major contribution to its success. Professor John Childs, a colleague of Snedden in the thirties, was in a position to evaluate his faculty role at that date. Professor John Guy Foulkes shared with the writer his memories as a student under Snedden in the early twenties. Professor Jesse Sears provided insights rendered even more valuable through his close family association.

Miss Florence Seelman of Brooklyn, New York, provided valuable information about her late brother-in-law, Clarence D. Kingsley, in several interesting and lengthy letters. The Seelman family home was adjacent to Mr. Kingsley's boarding place and only a few doors from the Boys' Manual Training High School where he taught. Some of the committee projects of the New York High School Teachers Association, under his direction, were carried forward in the Seelman living room. Her observations were especially helpful in providing leads about Kingsley's New York years and an appraisal of his personality. Dr. Henry Neumann, leader of Brooklyn's Ethical Culture Society when Kingsley was one of the trustees and also a member of the Reviewing Committee and author of its report on Moral Education, shared his memories of Kingsley's work on the CRSE. Mr. Israel Thurman of New York was a close personal friend of Kingsley and provided many valuable insights.

The sole biographical sketch of Kingsley is to be found in the *National Cyclopedia of American Biography*, based upon material supplied by Mrs. Kingsley shortly after his death. The Colgate University Archives contain a letter from Mrs. Elizabeth Seelman Kingsley to the Alumni Secretary dated January 12, 1927, in which she provides additional information concerning her husband's career and some quotations from letters to his mother. His many contributions to the work of the New York High School Teachers Association are reported in the bulletins of the association — sometimes called yearbooks — and published during the year following that of their date. Beginning with the 1906-7 school year, they provide a published source of papers and committee reports presented before the association.

The annual reports of the Massachusetts State Board of Education under Snedden's administration as commissioner contain detailed reports on various phases of education in the state. Some of these articles were prepared by Kingsley, Charles Prosser, and other members of the board's staff as well as by the commissioner.

It is unlikely a complete bibliography of David Snedden's extensive publication will ever be brought together. He was an unbelievably prolific writer. His earliest articles, with the exception of one in the 1896 issue of *The Sequoia*, appeared in the *Public School Reporter* published by C. H. Woods of Nipomo, Templeton, and Santa Maria, California. "Professor" Woods is well remembered in San Luis Obispo County even today and known to have published such a journal; like so many other of these small local educational publications of the day, all issues seem to have disappeared.

Most of his professional contributions while a member of the Stanford faculty, including some committee reports for the California Teachers Association, appeared in the *Western Journal of Education*; an article based upon the work of his master's essay appeared in the *Educational Review* for December, 1903, under the title "The Six-Year High School." For the period of his first professorship at Teachers College, the *Kindergarten Magazine and Pedagogical Digest* and the *Educational Review* are most helpful. His first contribution before the NEA appears in the *Journal of Proceedings* of the association in 1908. During this time two of his articles were published in Edward T. Devine's *Charities and the Commons*, and a paper delivered before the National Conference of Charities and Corrections in May, 1906, at the conclusion of his doctoral program, may be found in the *Proceedings* of the conference's annual session for that year. Single articles appeared in these years in the *Journal of Pedagogy* and *Education*.

For almost the entire period, Albert Winship's *New England Journal of Education*, later simply the *Journal of Education* — but always "Winship's Journal" among schoolmen — is the single most useful source. Winship wrote with appealing candor from personal association with most of the participants in educational dialogue. He was constantly on the move in search of educational news and recalled having first met Snedden at the time he was still a rural teacher in California, possibly at a teachers institute. His position may be described as generally favorable to the "new men" in education.

Probably no periodical surpassed *School and Society* in the total number of contributions from Snedden's pen. The first volume of this publication, January to June, 1915, carried five of his articles, and his contributions continued even after his retirement in 1935. The columns of discussion in this magazine are especially useful for the variety of controversial topics appearing there. Nicholas Murray Butler's *Educational Review* also carried a great many of Snedden's articles and addresses from 1903 well into the 1920's, after Frank Pierpont Graves assumed editorial responsibility. In 1924, about the time he became superintendent of schools for Chicago, William McAndrew joined *Educational Review* and remained as editor of the "School and Society" section following merger of the two magazines in November, 1928. He possessed an engaging writing style and seemed generally sympathetic to Snedden's point of view.

The *Teachers College Record* was most valuable for the period of Snedden's second professorship at Teachers College, both for its news items and for the several articles from Snedden appearing there. While he was commissioner of education in Massachusetts *The History Teacher* twice carried highly interesting accounts of his presentations before the New England History Teachers Association. *School Review* and after 1915 *Educational Administration and Supervision* published a good many of his papers. As editor of *Vocational Education Magazine* for most of its short life, Snedden was responsible for a regular monthly editorial. They were especially interesting for the wide range of topics considered. After its founding in 1927, the *Journal of Educational Sociology* accepted a number of articles from Snedden. The initial volumes of the *Journal of Educational Psychology*, 1910 to 1912, *The Nation's Schools*, 1928 to 1930, and the first yearbooks of the National Association of Secondary School Principals, 1917 through 1923, published many of his contributions, but in each case the relationship was broken off in later years. Occasional articles in *Atlantic Monthly, New Republic, Science, Manual Training Magazine, Annals of the American Academy of Political and Social Science*, and the *Journal of Rural Education*, testify to the scope of his audience and his breadth of publication.

The *High School Quarterly*, edited by Joseph Stewart, a member of the Reviewing Committee of the Commission on the Reorganization of Secondary Education carried frequent articles concerning the commission's work. *World's Work, Independent, Review of Reviews, Outlook*, and *Charities and the Commons* published articles about the schools from time to time which were usually presented from either the social service or the social settlement point of view.

In the concluding pages of his *Recollections*, Snedden provides the scholar with a resumé of his published works, twenty-four in all, in the fields of educational administration, educational sociology, and vocational education. Several were published as textbooks or course syllabi and developed quite naturally from material that appeared first in one of the professional journals. It would serve no useful purpose to repeat the list here. However, for the purpose of this study, five have particular significance. They include his dissertation, *Administration and Educational Work of the American Juvenile Reform Schools* (New York, 1907); *School Reports and School Efficiency* (New York, 1908), with William H. Allen; and *Administration of Public Education in the United States* (New York, 1908), with Samuel T. Dutton. All three may in one way or another be considered as adjuncts to his graduate work at Columbia. The last of these books represented a pioneer effort in the field of educational administration and enjoyed especially wide acceptance for the next twenty years, a circumstance which tended to identify Snedden with this field long after the main focus of his work had shifted to educational sociology. He considered *Toward Better Educations* (New York, 1931) his most important book, and so it is in the sense that it represents his most comprehensive statement of educational purpose, especially as it is addressed to counter the positions taken by John Dewey, William H. Kilpatrick, and Boyd Bode. His *American High Schools and Vocational Schools in 1960*, published at the same time, presents an illustration of how a system of education might operate following Snedden's proposals calculated to produce a socially efficient society.

Raymond E. Callahan's *Education and the Cult of Efficiency* (Chicago, 1962) aptly describes the zeal with which Americans at the beginning of the twentieth century embraced the ideals of efficiency and delineates a phase of the movement applied to educational administration which was collateral to but different from Snedden's education for social efficiency. *Efficiency and Uplift* (Chicago, 1964), by Samuel Haber, places the efficiency ideal within the framework of the social reform movement and identifies its broad application to social agencies other than the school. Edward Krug in *The Shaping of the American High School* (New York, 1964) traces the development of American secondary education in the important period from 1890 to 1920. He identifies the social service and the social control purposes in American education as two contributing antecedents of the social efficiency movement and calls attention to the importance of David Snedden in the development of this point of view.

INDEX

Abbott, Allen: defense of classics, 173

Academic subjects, 112, 113

Administration of Public Education in the United States, The, 82–83, 91

Age groups. *See* School population

AICP. *See* Association for Improving the Condition of the Poor

Aims in education: determine content, 63; for the rank and file, 92; sociologically determined, 135, 174; chosen by good judges, 149, 184

— faith aims: compared with specific, 138–39, 142–43

— four aims, Snedden's: in *Administration of Public Education*, 82; means to efficiency, 92

— practical: normal school's example, 133; in general education, 148; as anti-intellectualism, 196–97

— specific: to improve course of study, 64; subjects subordinate to, 83; determine method, 92; called for, 114–15; in history, 115, 128: based on social needs, 128; in art and English, 133; and faith aims, 138–39; for efficient teaching, 139; of Bobbitt, 165; drawn from social utilities, 148, 185; in moral education, 151; in non-vocational studies, 157; and reorganization of studies, 184. *See also* Life-activities aims

Alderman, Edwin, 79

Allen, Charles, 153–54

Allen, William Harvey: background, 85–86; conflict with William Maxwell, 86–87; and Snedden, 87–90; offered Massachusetts commissionership, 97–98; appraisal of, 99; interest in efficiency movement, 210n8; mentioned, 72, 120

Alpha subjects, 148–49

Anti-intellectualism, 195–96

Aram, William, 10

Arithmetic: aims determine content, 63; usefulness, 63, 133. *See also* Mathematics

Arsenal High School, 156

Aspirationist: defined, 165

Association for Improving the Condition of the Poor, 86–87

Atkinson, Frederick W.: appraisal of Massachusetts scene, 104; mentioned, 103

Ayres, Leonard, 145

Bagley, William: pioneer of social efficiency, 4; views on education, 130–31; mentioned, 129, 138

Bailey, Thomas, 25

Banner, John Casper, 25

Barnes, Earl, 25, 27

Bawden, William T., 161

Bestor, Arthur Jr.: compared with Snedden, 195–96, 220n17

Beta subjects, 148–49

Bishop, John Remson: criticism of academic program, 90

Black, Samuel T.: Ventura County superintendent, 15; Snedden's appraisal of, 17; institute activity, 18, 33; on child study, 23–24; mentioned, 70

Bobbitt, Franklin: compared with Snedden, 4, 165, 170

Bode, Boyd: criticism of Snedden, 172, 189–90

Boy Scout movement, 155, 164

Briggs, Thomas, 142

Brookline, Massachusetts: schools described, 47–48, 101

Brown, Elmer E.: praises Snedden's book, 89; mentioned, 33, 56, 85

Brown, George A.: opposed to specific aims, 138–39

231